International Library of Sociology

Founded by Karl Mannheim
Editor: John Rex, University of Aston in Birmingham

Arbor Scientiae
Arbor Vitae

A catalogue of the books available in the **International Library of Sociology**
and other series of Social Science books published by Routledge & Kegan Paul
will be found at the end of this volume.

Theory of liberty, legitimacy and power:

new directions in the intellectual and scientific legacy of Max Weber

Edited by
Vatro Murvar

Routledge & Kegan Paul
London, Boston, Melbourne and Henley

First published in 1985
by Routledge & Kegan Paul plc
14 Leicester Square, London WC2H 7PH, England
9 Park Street, Boston, Mass. 02108, USA
464 St Kilda Road, Melbourne,
Victoria 3004, Australia and
Broadway House, Newtown Road,
Henley on Thames, Oxon RG9 1EN, England

Set in Times, 10 on 11pt
by Input Typesetting Ltd, London
and printed in Great Britain
by St Edmundsbury Press,
Bury St Edmunds, Suffolk

Library of Congress Cataloging in Publication Data

Theory of liberty, legitimacy, and power.
(International library of sociology)
Bibliography: p.
Includes index.
1. Weber, Max, 1864–1920—Political science—Addresses, essays,
lectures. 2 Weber, Max, 1864–1920—Sociology—Addresses, essays,
lectures. 3. Liberty—Addresses, essays, lectures. 4. Legitimacy of
governments—Addresses, essays, lectures. 5. Power (Social
sciences)—Addresses, essays, lectures. 6. Political
sociology—Addresses, essays, lectures. I. Murvar, Vatro,
1920—   . II. Series
JC263.W42T47 1985   306'.2   84–22333

British Library CIP data also available

ISBN 0–7102–0355–1

To Bernadine

Contents

Part II   Historical-comparative case studies

Notes on contributors

Thomas Burger is Associate Professor of Sociology at Southern Illinois-Carbondale. His research interests and publications are in the areas of sociological theory and social stratification. He is currently working on a monograph on the nature of social prestige.

Susan K. Croutwater is a graduate student in history and sociology with an interest in interdisciplinary theoretical and historical comparative studies. Her specialty is in Islamic studies, particularly in the medieval movements of Muslim mysticism.

K. Peter Etzkorn is Professor of Sociology at the University of Missouri-St Louis where he also serves as Associate Dean of the Graduate School and Director of Research. In addition to membership in several professional societies he is also a member of the *Institute International de Sociologie* and the Society of Ethnomusicology for which he serves as Editor of the Journal of Ethnomusicology. He has conducted research on the sociology of music and sociological theory and published extensively. At present he is working on a study of the relations between music and politics.

Edith E. Graber is Professor of Sociology at Lindenwood College (Missouri). Her specialties and publications are in sociology of law and history of sociological theory. She has translated one of Weber's essays (1981) and conducted research on Weber at the University of Munich.

William W. Mayrl is Associate Professor of Sociology at the University of Wisconsin–Milwaukee. His teaching and writing interests are in the areas of contemporary social theory, the sociology of knowledge, and the philosophical foundations of social thought. His published works include critical analyses of phenomenological sociology, ethnomethodology, and structuralism. He has also written several interpretive essays on the sociology of Lucien Goldmann.

Vatro Murvar is Professor of Sociology and Coordinator of the Max Weber Colloquia and Symposia at the University of Wisconsin. He is a specialist in theory and political historical-comparative sociology and currently engaged in studying modern patrimonialist power structure and legitimacy. He is the author of several books and of numerous articles or chapters published in professional journals and symposia.

Patrick C. West is Associate Professor of Environmental Sociology at the University of Michigan, School of Natural Resources. His interests and publications are in the area of natural resource sociology in which he utilizes Weber's approach to human ecological analysis.

David C. Yu is Professor of Religion and Philosophy at the Maryville College (Tennessee). His specialty is in studying the impact of religion on China. At the present time his research is focusing on the ancient mythologies within Chinese culture.

Preface

Max Weber's opus is a source of an apparently unending intellectual excitement, argumentations, and conflicting interpretations from Japan to continental Europe, England, the United States, Canada, and slowly but surely to the developing world.

In the Weber Colloquia and Symposia at the University of Wisconsin-Milwaukee, and at the international/national and regional annual meetings of professional associations over a period of several years, over 140 lectures on various aspects of his legacy have amply witnessed these unusual phenomena. Will his legacy ever be liberated from all the misconceptions and misinterpretations commencing in his own time and rapidly accumulating after by his posterity?

In the promotion materials for this book we initiated the claim that this book has no competitors. Even the title may surprise some. The theory of liberty, inseparable from the other two, has not been associated with Weber's name as the theory of power has been, and to a somewhat lesser degree the theory of legitimacy. Isolated from each other, the various theoretical assumptions classified him quite inappropriately as legal positivist, legalist and a host of other labels.

The editor expresses his special gratitude to Peter Hopkins for his professional understanding of a particular situation, for his steady encouragement over a long period of time and for suggesting we cut the Gordian knot by sending him the manuscript instead of waiting for some slowly developing finalizations.

While individual authors have indicated their appreciation to those who helped them, the editor acknowledges here his indebtedness to colleagues whose skills and patience have improved the quality of those segments they read: Thomas Burger, Cornelius

Cotter, Charles Glock, Scott Greer, Harry Johnson, Guy Oakes and others. Thank you is due to the participants in the Max Weber Colloquia and Symposia from their inception in 1976; their questions and discussions have guided the authors toward a better final formulation. Their contributions at the Colloquia dealt with aspects of Weber's work outside the theme of this book and have been published elsewhere. None of them could be held responsible for ideas finalized here.

1 Introduction:

Theory of liberty, legitimacy, and power: new directions in the intellectual and scientific legacy of Max Weber

Vatro Murvar

The stature of Max Weber (1864–1920) as an interdisciplinary historical-comparative scientist has steadily grown in the last two or three decades. This is in part due to the impact of the recently translated segments of his unfinished opus, which are quite set apart from the traditional notions on Weber. His intellectual and scientific legacy is continuously being compared with the thought of Machiavelli, Hobbes, Rousseau, Tocqueville, Marx, Nietzsche, Burckhardt, Jellinek, Keynes, and others. Nowadays the automatic identification of his name with the image of a one-book author or 'The Weber Thesis' (which sadly enough reflected one of his least significant, highly tentative works) is almost gone from the academic and publishing world.

Some decades ago Giovanni Papini said that the fiercest penalty a creative, innovative and productive man must pay is the existence of so-called disciples who attempt to appropriate his 'doctrine' for their own individual, petty, and quasi-intellectual activities. In Weber's case it was not really disciples, which he did not wish to have, but posterity some decades after his death. Paradoxically, the controversies of Weber's lifetime, when he was always in favor of liberty against the political-industrial establishments of Germany, Austria, and Russia and their respective imperialisms that he hated so intensely, have been almost forgotten today. In contrast, Weber is now being made controversial post mortem by the living posterity now grown internationally. These alleged post-mortem Weber controversies are actually rooted in many fresh misconceptions and misinterpretations of his still incompletely translated opus.

Moreover, ritual genuflection before the legitimacy-bestowing authority replaces a genuine willingness to take the author seriously: there are plenty of books and articles in which references

1

to Weber amount to no more than lip service. While being often mentioned and seldom read is one of the tragic consequences of greatness, another is being the target for a flood of interpretations and reinterpretations. Though the line between legitimate and illegitimate variants is not always easy to draw, it can be fairly said that Weber has been misinterpreted with remarkable thoroughness and frequency. Some of the misinterpretations have enjoyed considerable longevity, so much so as to become orthodoxy. Misinterpretations of his original work can be found in all areas: from epistemology and sociology of knowledge and art, through political and economic sociology, to sociology of law, revolution, religion, and ideology. (For a list of some misconceptions within just one major area – which persist despite strong objections by the specialists, see this author's 1983:3–7.)

While it is well known that Weber's opus is a torso with several contemplated but not executed limbs (such as revolutions and usurpations, Talmudic Judaism, Islam before and after the tenth century, medieval Catholicism and others), it has not been specifically understood that there are several major theoretical and methodological gaps which he deliberately left open-ended because in his judgment there was insufficient evidence at the time to warrant a sound theoretical settlement.

If this is true, then Weber's intellectual and scientific legacy cannot and should not be accepted as a revered or fixed treasure, as has frequently been done by the worshipping posterity of some great masters. Since Weber has no dogmas to offer, no discipleship need apply. Instead, he genuinely worried whether or not posterity would take him seriously enough to criticize and reject any of his conceptual tools or theoretical propositions that could not be accepted or modified.

Over and over, Weber offered his rationale: research is by definition an unending process and data collected through it are constantly liable to even dramatic corrections. 'The stream of immeasurable events flows unendingly towards eternity'. And Weber continued (1949:84):

> The cultural problems which move men form themselves ever anew and in different colors, and the boundaries of that area in the infinite stream of concrete events which acquires meaning and significance for us, i.e., which becomes an 'historical individual,' are constantly subject to change.

Consequently, at times Weber on principle avoided extracting from insufficient data, especially historical-comparative data, formal conceptualizations and definitions to compete with all other existing ones, particularly when a definition or concept in his opinion would be premature or confined to limited data. Repeatedly, Weber expressed this position. It is, therefore, hard to understand why his programs and practices of self-limitation, chosen by design and purpose, not by neglect, were overlooked by those who criticize him precisely for this distinctive virtue as if it were a major failure.

System-building: Ideological or scientific?

Throughout his entire intellectual development Weber managed more or less successfully to resist the perennial temptation in Western thought to build a doctrinal, ideological and/or scientific system. This fundamental commitment was discovered relatively early, but its significance seems not to have reached the consciousness of many. Apparently (at least to this editor's knowledge), Loewenstein was the first to state very strongly that to Weber no ideologies are absolutes. 'All ideologies – whether conservatism or liberalism, capitalism or socialism – are to him only the history- and milieu-conditioned reflections of certain constellations of [material and non-material] interests.' In the context of the historical development of ideas, Loewenstein said that this stand of Weber represents one of his most significant achievements. Because of it, Weber became, in a proper sense of the word, the overcomer (*Überwinder*) of ideological contradictions and contrasts (1966b: 135).

Indeed, he very clearly recognized and feared the thin dividing line between ideological visions of a beautiful future and the scientific ordering of strictly empirical data – a line missed by many creative humanists and social scientists. Of course, some neglected their own originally conceived scientific propositions in favor of working on the blueprints for a perfect society: at some point in their lives they chose more exciting activism over slow, painstaking, often-inconclusive data gathering. Weber feared to cross that line and end up on the, for a scientist, wrong side. However, he was skeptical about the feasibility of a social-scientific system, at least in his time, and sharply criticized all the existing social-scientific systems.

Simey said that Weber, in contrast to other theorists, postulated that theory takes second place to empirical evidence drawn from patterning of the past (1967:94). Freund emphasized that Weber was a pure analyst solely concerned with gaining sound knowledge of historical data and interpreting it within verifiable limits – greatly helped by an encyclopedic knowledge which no other sociologist has since equaled. Indeed, what is striking in Weber's work is the total absence of preconceived notions or *a priori*

3

syntheses. Not Durkheim, but Weber, Freund concluded, was the first in practice to place sociology on a strictly scientific basis (1969:13). Rossides affirmed that Weber 'never became the fountainhead of a movement' and that 'this is due to the absence in his thought of the metaphysical synthesis (or goal) that permeates (and vitiated) the thought of most Western social theorists.' He added, 'Max Weber is the only non-metaphysical social scientist . . . the only one to develop a genuinely scientific social science' (1972:183).

In all this, Weber seemingly had only one predecessor, Montesquieu. In contrast to all the system-builders, ideological or social-scientific, neither Montesquieu nor Weber produced any piece of work that could even remotely be labeled as a blueprint for a perfect society. Even though an overwhelming lifelong passion for the growth of liberty consumed them, there is in their writings an unusual, almost peculiar absence of any ideologies, doctrines, or beliefs, especially the dogma of inevitable progress toward societal perfection. Instead of ideological digressions, Montesquieu and Weber proceeded from an apparent near-chaos of confusing phenomena toward the possibility of developing an intelligible conceptual whole with the purpose of making history at least understandable, if not explainable. The historical-comparative methodology emerged in the works of both, but there have been few actual takers. Social scientists who do not use historical-comparative materials in their theoretical quest will in all likelihood continue to produce abstract and non-evidenced 'social-scientific' systems.

Like any other intellectual challenge, the new trends in rediscovering Weber's intellectual and scientific legacy *as it is* may or may not encounter a degree of resistance, if not hostility, generated by the well-established schools. But these new trends seem substantive enough to suggest that no amount of pressure against them will be successful in the long run. To continue criticizing Weber for his allegedly 'non-theoretical' and 'excessively empirical' approach and for his subsequent failure to 'sufficiently' systematize his work is to contradict the very definition of science. If science is the creation of all scientists, past and present, then no definitive social-scientific system can be produced. This may appear trite, but it is not. Many scientists enjoy the fantasy that they or their masters have said the last word.

A consensus emerging?

From Montesquieu to Weber to the present, the most discerning observers of power structures with their respective legitimacies and of absence of liberty seem to agree on a very general, but seminal, notion of the misery and the poverty of human experience with the rulership, but to disagree on labels, terms, and conceptualizations. The earlier writers refer variously to oriental/ Asiatic despotism, the oriental/Asiatic mode of production, absolutism, 'enlightened' despotism, theological, metaphysical or metapolitical, or other exploitative stages or substages of mankind's development: the more recent ones refer to caesarism, caesaropapism, statism, totalism, totalitarianism, etc. Evidently, some were quite naturally committed to the beautiful dream of a perfect society which will someday, somehow, somewhere replace human helplessness against the unreachable and seemingly indestructible power unity/identity in the hands of the One Rulership.

Speaking of Auguste Comte and Karl Marx, Topitsch commented that, despite considerable differences in their blueprints for a perfect society, they 'were united in their conviction that the progress that was guaranteed by science would of necessity overcome these problems and bring about a reign of happiness on earth.' For Weber, 'on the contrary, the belief that a historical law – whether in linear or dialectical form – could guarantee the achievement of an objectively or absolutely valuable final position, did not belong fundamentally to the realm of what can be scientifically substantiated' (Topitsch, 1971:11).

This experience of a belated contact with Weber's legacy in that 'twilight atmosphere of furtive intellectual dishonesty' may approximate the same sense of direction as was discovered by the contributors to this volume independently of each other. Their contact with Weber's 'resurrected' legacy had, as it did for Topitsch, 'the effect of lightning: the blurred outlines suddenly stood out hard and clear, and whoever had once seen them now saw the world in an entirely different way.' They also agree that 'the most profoundly exciting aspect of his work' was his 'uncompromising quest for truth, with which the attack was here directed against all wishful thinking' (1971:8). The contributors to this volume are moving resolutely toward a more precise understanding, appreciation, criticism, and potential determination of not only Weber's 'handling' of, but also his own specific advancement within, the theory of liberty, legitimacy, and power, with special emphasis on how much of it has survived the test of time.

This volume consists of two parts: Part I Theoretical perspectives and Part II Historical-comparative case studies.

In Part I, Theoretical perspectives, the authors have selected five major (in their estimation) theoretical perspectives on liberty, legitimacy, and power within Weber's legacy; in their respective chapters they test Weber's propositions in the light of modern research and suggest some modifications and reconceptualizations when needed.

In Chapter 2 Burger presents Weber's analysis of the structure of social stratification in which differentials in wealth, political power, and social prestige are closely related to the distribution of power, especially in modern societies. He focuses on Weber's propositions on prestige, which raise a number of significant questions. The fact that some modern rulerships cleverly exploit the seemingly insatiable human hunger for prestige through the monopoly of a sophisticated differential system of rewards and penalties makes Burger's essay extremely valuable.

In Chapter 3 Murvar compares modern patrimonialism, which is today the globally dominant type of rulership, with traditionalist patrimonialism. Contrary to the hopeful anticipation of the still current modernization theories which Weber rejected eight decades ago, modern patrimonialism has successfully utilized all the new technological advancements to solidify its power and its legitimacy. A rationale and evidence for why it remains a global phenomenon are presented by following numerous substantive clues in his early writings, which are also supported by the most recent research.

Graber's conviction that the core of Weber's substantive sociology lies in his sociology of law, especially its multiple aspects of analysis of liberty versus power structure, is shared with some leading authorities in this area. Yet Weber's sociology of law is probably one of the most neglected segments of his opus. In Chapter 4, Graber explores the reasons for this neglect in contrast to the richness of the subject matter and the significance of Weber's sociology of law for modern scientific research.

In Chapter 5 Mayrl argues that Weber's personal commitment to human liberty presented a potential conflict with his equally strong commitment to social science. Weber overcame this conflict not only through his position on ethical neutrality but, more importantly, by developing an approach to scientific explanation that was similar in many respects to the 'causality of free acts' found in Kant's discussions of free will and moral action. Unlike Kant, however, Weber based his notion of causality not on metaphysical principles but on the concrete empirical realities of everyday life.

In Chapter 6 Etzkorn investigates Weber's discourse on rationalization and shows how, for Weber, the comparative study of art, alongside religion and ethics, provided significant access to the rational demystification of history toward greater freedom of artistic creativity as protected by basic human rights. He brings the concept of rationalization into the context of Weber's personal involvement with the aesthetic life of the German middle class in the nineteenth century. Weber's quest for scientific understanding in this area of social history is crucially related to his methodological treatment of the distinctions between 'sein' and 'Sollen' as well as between 'Nacherleben' and 'interpretieren'.

Part II, Historical-comparative case studies, starts with Chapter 7, in which Yu examines the applicability of Weber's conceptualizations in the Chinese cultural context and discovers a number of strong affinities between Maoism and Confucianism. While analyzing the differences between the two, he proposes that Maoism is perhaps more essentially religious than Confucianism. Yu also reflects on the Maoist deviation from original Marxism and the traditional roots of the 'originality' of Maoism. He offers a rationale that Weber's various propositions, especially within the sociology of religion and political sociology, will become increasingly appropriate analytical tools for the study of religious and political aspects of Maoist and post-Maoist China.

In Chapter 8 Croutwater criticizes the concept of sultanism as a subtype within Weber's typology of rulership and legitimacy as not being evidenced in Ottoman history. Although throughout Islamic history there are some instances that conform to Weber's subtype of sultanism as an arbitrary rule, she demonstrates that the Ottoman power structure and its legitimacy, with the sultan as a typical patrimonialist ruler, appears to be an excellent case study of historical support for Weber's patrimonialist rulership and legitimacy.

Chapter 9 thematically unifies the preceding chapters by Yu and Croutwater by documenting that the up-to-date research on Chinese and Islamic power structures and legitimacies supports most of the basic propositions formulated by Weber seventy to eighty years ago. Also, Murvar analyzes some striking, definitive similarities in China's past and present power structures as well as in her historical and modern legitimizing ideologies.

In Chapter 10, West suggests that Weber's historical-comparative studies contain an implicit but comprehensive human ecology of environmental influences on social structure. Thus, Weber's mainly historical-comparative opus represents major theoretical and empirical support for the position of human ecologists and environmental sociologists who stress today that societies and social change cannot be adequately understood in isolation from the broader environmental context.

Part I

Theoretical perspectives

2 Power and stratification: Max Weber and beyond

Thomas Burger

I

Max Weber's propositions on classes, estates (*Stände*), and parties,[1] as well as some of his more specific analyses, have placed him among the classic and continuingly relevant contributors to the study of what today is called 'social stratification'[2]. The 'three-dimensional' view of social inequality, usually taken to be the hallmark of his approach, has become rather influential in the literature on the topic, and his observations on social prestige are commonly credited with having established the social-structural significance of these phenomena in social life. Yet in spite of these assessments, and despite the vigor of Weber's intellectual and scientific legacy, the secondary literature does not contain a single account which brings into the open the analytic structure underlying Weber's statements, i.e., the systematic assumptions and conceptualizations embodied in them.[3] The present chapter takes some first steps toward filling this gap. In addition, on the basis of the interpretation offered, two more specific problems are discussed. One concerns the idea, which has some currency, that Weber provides the evidence and the arguments to show that the political sector of societies is sufficiently insulated or independent from other sectors to make the notion of an economically dominant 'ruling class' unrealistic. The other, which has not received any attention in the literature, concerns the insufficiency of Weber's conceptualization of the phenomena of 'social honor'. An attempt is made to repair this insufficiency in a way which is informed by Weber's general analytic schema. The results of this attempt, however, though within his legacy, definitely go beyond Weber's own ideas, since he is simply silent on certain matters.

11

II

An interpretation of Weber's ideas about 'social stratification'[4] may conveniently start with his (1968:927) statement that ' "classes," "status groups,"[5] and "parties" are phenomena of the distribution of power within a community'. It identifies three types of social formation which are related to power differentials.

It is a well-known premise of Weber's sociology that the emergence, continued existence, and change of social arrangements are to be considered as due to the structurally constrained activities of individuals in the pursuit of their subjective goals. As Parsons (1949) has amply documented, it is fruitful to ask a number of questions about these goals, concerning their origins, contents, relationships with each other, and the like. Unfortunately, except for Parsons (who was pursuing his own ideas), Weber's work has never been subjected to any systematic analysis of this kind. Consequently, certain features of his sociology have not attracted the attention which they deserve. Of these features, three are of special significance for the subject matter under consideration. First, the main 'goal'-category with which Weber operates throughout his sociological-historical analyses is that of 'interest'. This is a highly ambiguous concept, as he himself notes,[6] and it is never explicitly defined by him. Second, he conceptualizes at least a portion of individuals' activities as the pursuit of 'life or survival chances.' Again, no explicit definition is offered, and it is not quite clear what conduct does not qualify as such. There can be little doubt, however, that the improvement of their life chances is prominent among the contents of people's interests. Third, Weber assumes that people have more than one (type of) interest and keep others in mind even while pursuing a particular one.

As might be expected, the notion that individuals typically pursue their subjectively perceived interests is central to Weber's observations on social stratification. However, in the absence of any good analysis of the theoretical connotations and implications of 'interest' in his sociology, no attempt is made here to give a formal definition. What is offered instead is an indication of how he uses 'interest' (1968:939) *in the context of his pronouncements on stratification*. Here it is crucial to realize that a systematic underpinning of these statements is a distinction between three 'spheres', namely, what may be called the 'economic', the 'social', and the 'political'. Corresponding to these spheres are three types of distributable things (which may conveniently be called 'transferables') whose appropriation may become the goal of individuals' actions: utilities (*Nutzleistungen*) (1968:63, 68), social honor, and

12

political power.[7] Each sphere is constituted by the totality of the activities which, within an historically developed 'order' or structure,[8] are (primarily or partially) intended to influence the distribution of the corresponding transferables among the potential possessors. If a person's effort is to influence this distribution so as to effect the preservation or increase or least possible decrease of his or her share, then this person pursues his or her interest (as subjectively perceived), be it economic (material), 'social', or political. Inherent in this pursuit, however, is the tendency for the participating individuals to come into conflict with each other. The source of this in the economic sphere is the relative scarcity of goods and services with its implication that one person's or population segment's share can be increased only at another's expense. In the political and social spheres it is due to the hierarchical nature of political power and social honor.

'Conflict' (*Kampf:* struggle) is defined by Weber (1968:38, 636) as a social relationship in which participants' actions are guided by the intention to realize their own wills against the resistance of the other participant(s). To varying degrees, such conflict is a component of all but some of the most ephemeral relationships. The outcome of conflicts is, *ceteris paribus*, a function of the suitable resources or means that the participants can avail themselves of in their efforts to get what they want. These means or resources, which may be situationally rather specific and usually have varying applicability, form the 'bases'[9] of the (situationally more or less specific) 'power' of the conflicting parties. Thus, the power [*Macht*] of an individual, or of a number of individuals, is, very generally, 'the chance . . . to realize their own will in a social relationship [*Gemeinschaftshandeln*] even against others who are participating in the relationship'.[10]

Weber's characterization of classes, estates, and parties as phenomena of the distribution of power in a community, then, must be interpreted in the context of the ideas:

1 that individuals pursue structurally generated interests in the economic, social, and political spheres;
2 that in so doing they come into conflict with each other and
3 that some of them, due to their situationally superior resources, are more successful in getting what they want than others.[11]

The problem now is to specify exactly how these social formations (classes, estates, parties) fit into this framework. To this purpose it is useful to begin with a brief look at Weber's conception of 'class', since this presents the fewest difficulties.

There are two formal definitions of 'class', an earlier and a later one (1968:302 and 927ff). The latter describes 'class' as 'all persons in the same class situation', where 'class situation' is the typical chance of being provided with certain goods, of living in certain external circumstances (*äussere Lebensstellung*) and of going through certain experiences in life (*inneres Lebensschicksal*) (1964:223, 680). This chance is the consequence of a person's control over goods and skills and of the income-producing ways in which these can be used within a given economic order. The earlier account provides the supplementary statement 'that the decisive moment which represents the common determinant of the individual's fate, is the kind of chance [of deriving income through the offering of goods and services – TB] in the *market.*' Class situation is, in this sense, ultimately market situation.

These statements leave little doubt about the main sense in which Weber considers classes to be phenomena of the distribution of power: they are pluralities of individuals with approximately equivalent abilities to secure (labor or commodity) market-mediated life chances, which is to say that they are pluralities of individuals each of whom has roughly the same power in the market (i.e., power in economic exchange).[12] The important implication, of course, whose far-reaching character must be realized, is that where there is no market, there are no classes. Another significant implication is contained in Weber's (1968:635; 1964:489) conception of the market, constitutive of which is 'the competition [conflict – TB] – even though it may be a unilateral one – for chances of [formal free – TB] exchange among a plurality of individuals interested in exchanging'. What this entails is the idea that pluralities of individuals who are supplied with products and services by means other than their participation in such an exchange system, even where one exists, are not 'classes' in Weber's sense of the term, but 'estates'.[13] And from this, in turn, it follows that a society's class structure does not necessarily embrace its whole population.

A second sense in which classes might be characterized as 'phenomena of the distribution of power' is in the context of a distinction between a 'ruling' class and 'ruled' or 'exploited' classes. It is sensible, however, to delay the discussion of this possibility until Weber's statements on 'parties' have been considered. For the time being, therefore, it may be concluded that, for Weber, 'classes' are pluralities of individuals of similar market power (i.e., control over income-producing goods and skills) and therewith of similar life chances in all those respects which are related to such power.

III

While classes are constituted through the differential distribution of transferables (of the economic type) which results from the structurally conditioned unequal success of competing individuals, the constitution of political parties is quite different. Weber (1968:284; 1964:211) defines 'parties' as 'associative relationships [*Vergesellschaftungen*] based on [formally] free recruitment; their purpose is to secure power within an organization [*Verband:* corporate group] for their leaders and therewith to provide their active participants with (ideal or material) chances (for the realization of particular substantive goals [*sachliche Ziele*], for the attainment of personal advantages, or for both.)' What produces parties, therefore, are the *purposes* of individuals, not their (relative) successes in realizing these purposes. Accordingly parties cannot simply be considered as the direct parallel in the political sphere of what classes are in the economic sphere. With regard to the common interpretation of Weber, of course, this raises the question of whether there is any symmetry to the 'three-dimensional' conception with whose authorship he is usually credited. Clearly, if there is such a symmetry, it must be found elsewhere than at the level of 'party'. Presumably this is the consideration behind the frequent substitution in the literature of 'power' for 'party' in the presentation of Weber's views.[14] However, without a reasoned explanation of the relationship between 'party' and 'power', such a substitution is of little value.

In Weber's (1968:48, 53–4; 1964:34) scheme of things, it makes sense to speak of (political) parties only within an 'organization', which is defined as

> a social relationship in which participation is restrictively regulated or closed to outsiders, and the maintenance of whose order is guaranteed by specific individuals whose actions are directed specifically to ensure the implementation of this order; these individuals comprise a *leader* ([*Leiter:* someone who directs – TB] and, as the case may be, an *administrative staff* which usually also has delegated powers [*Vertretungsgewalt*].

The presence of a leader (and an administrative staff) in an organization means that the organization's members are subject, in various respects, to the leader's commands. Such an organization is thus always a 'ruling organization'. When Weber (1968:54, 901) talks of political parties, he usually refers to parties which operate in a ruling organization of a particular type, namely a 'political organization' (*politischer Verband*). The latter is a ruling organiz-

15

ation whose existence, and the enforcement of whose regulatory orders, within a specific territory is continuously guaranteed by the threat and application of physical force on the part of the administrative staff.

Parties are inseparable from ruling organizations whose leadership is contested since it is the *raison d'être* of parties to conquer or to gain influence over this leadership, especially to provide the leaders from their midst and to control the administrative staffs. The attempts to reach this aim involve them in struggles in the political sphere, that is, the sphere which is constituted by individuals' pursuit of their 'political' interests (and their institutional framework). Such interests are defined by Weber (1946:78; 1964:1043) as 'interests in the distribution, maintenance, or transfer of power,' and 'politics' for him is the 'striving for a share in the power or for influence on the distribution of power, either among states or among the groups within a state. . . . He who is active in politics, either as a means in the service of other aims – ideal or egoistic – or "for its own sake," that is, in order to enjoy the prestige which its possession yields.'

By taking account of Weber's (1968:946, 952; 1964:695, 701) statements about the internal structure of a typical ruling organization (*Herrschaftsverband*), it is easy to see that the social formations which, in the political sphere, are the equivalent of classes, are not 'parties' but 'rulers' (*Herren, Herrscher, Herrschende*) and 'ruled' (*Beherrschte*). Constitutive for these two population aggregates is the uneven distribution of (legitimate or usurped) powers of command (*Befehlsgewalten*), or powers of rule, whereby all those qualify as 'rulers' whose claimed and actually exercised powers of command do not derive through delegation from other power holders. The emergence, maintenance, or change of this distribution is the result of struggles or conflicts between individuals and groups of individuals, yet it is important to recognize a crucial respect in which these struggles differ from competition in the economic sphere. This difference lies in the fact that it is possible for people, at least in principle, not to participate in a market, simply by supplying their wants by means other than formally peaceful exchange. Accordingly, as already mentioned, a categorization of people by class does not necessarily include the whole population of the social unit under consideration. The categorization of a ruling organization's members in terms of 'rulers' and 'ruled' (or some more refined classification along these lines), in contrast, is exhaustive. The reason is that it is not possible to withdraw from the political struggle on this level. The decision not to 'participate' is not a decision not to be 'part' of it, i.e., to pursue political interests in an alternative way, but merely an acknowledgment of defeat without a fight. In this respect a ruling organization is like a race in which some who are entered decide not to leave their starting blocks. They are listed as losers even though they did not run.

The uneven distribution of the powers of command (that is, their concentration in one or a few persons or offices) within a ruling organization becomes ultimately institutionalized through legitimizing beliefs. The emergence and existence of the latter must not be taken to mean that the struggle over the distribution of the powers of command has come to an end in principle or in all respects, or that the political interests of the rulers and the ruled are no longer in conflict. Rather, on the part of the losers the development of such beliefs mostly signifies an accommodation to the fact that, for various reasons, they find themselves no longer able to fight effectively for some of their aims. Helped along and complemented in this by the generally observable need of any power and any advantage in life (*Lebenschance*) to justify itself, they represent a somewhat precarious adjustment which renders the situation psychologically more tolerable. As Weber (1968:953–4; 1964:701–2) said:

> If one takes any noticeable contrasts in the fates and situations of two people, perhaps concerning their health, or their economic or social success, or whatever, the most casual observation shows that, even when the purely 'accidental' cause of the difference is patently obvious, the better-off person feels the never-ceasing need for having the right to look upon his advantage as 'legitimate', to consider his position as 'merited' and that of the other as somehow self-inflicted and 'deserved'. This same need makes itself felt in the relation between positively and negatively privileged groups of people. . . . Every highly privileged group develops the myth of its natural superiority, especially that of its 'blood'. Under the conditions of a stable distribution of power and, accordingly, a social order composed of 'estates', . . . even the negatively privileged strata accept this myth. But in times in which pure class situation comes into the fore without disguise, unambiguously, and visible to all as the power which determines one's fate, that very myth of the highly privileged about everyone's being solely responsible for, and therefore deserving of, his lot often represents one of the factors which arouses the most passionate resentment of the negatively privileged strata.

The struggle over the pattern of distribution or concentration of the powers of command within a ruling organization is not the only struggle occurring in its political sphere. For a given distributive pattern does not necessarily come to an end with the deaths of its champions, or the 'fall' from power of its protagonists, but it may be transferred more or less intact to successors or replacements. The possibility, then, for new people to move, within a given power distribution, into established places of command opens a distinct area within which a particular type of political struggle may, and usually does, go on. This is the context in which 'parties' belong and this is where at least some individuals have the option to participate or not to participate. It is this struggle to which Weber refers when he speaks of some people being active in politics and of others as being the passive objects of politics; he is not referring to the struggle between rulers and ruled. It is imperative for any interpretation of Weber's statements on politics to keep these two areas of the political struggle distinct (which is not to say that there are no connections).

IV

It must now be asked in exactly what sense(s) Weber (1968:951) considers parties to be 'phenomena of the distribution of power'.[15] One quite obvious answer is that an uneven distribution of powers of command in a structure of domination, or the subjectively envisaged possibility of such a distribution, is a necessary precondition for the existence of parties. A second answer points to the fundamental purpose of parties, namely, their participation in the struggle for (legitimate or usurped) powers of command within a structure of domination. Finally, they may also be considered 'phenomena of the distribution of power' in the sense that their formation is a means with whose help individuals, who are rather powerless in isolation, attempt to compete successfully with their opponents.

At this point, now, it is convenient to mention a few considerations about the implications of Weber's framework for the notion of 'ruling class'. A fair proportion of the secondary literature appears to be pervaded by the idea that the three-dimensionality of Weber's model, or at least his separation of economic and political power, is somehow significantly at odds with, and superior to, a vaguely formulated 'crude' Marxist view (there never seem to be any sophisticated Marxists) concerning the role of the political apparatus in society. This is the view that societies are so constituted that the dominance of a class in the economic sector sets certain parameters to government action, constraining it in a fashion which ensures the perpetuation of the structural sources of this dominance. Marxist authors, of course, vary in their conceptualizations of this relation, but most seem to agree on the fundamental determination of the 'political' by the 'economic'. With this none-too-precise claim taken as a target, then, Weber's differentiation between economic and political power and his treatment, on the typological level, of political domination without systematically linking it to the structure of the economic sector may appear to entail the position that events in the political sector are rather autonomous and follow their own laws. While there is probably *some* truth to this, it is, however, necessary to be cautious about any such unqualified inference, especially in view of the fact that Weber himself operates with some notion of 'ruling class' (although in an undefined fashion) (Beetham 1974:178–9). What really is at stake here is Weber's conception of the overall integration of society. Weber does not elaborate such a conception, perhaps because it does not lend itself to an ideal-typical representation (Parsons 1949:607, 610). Yet this lack of an explicit elaboration should not simply be taken as a manifestation of innocence regarding the problem of social-structural interconnections. There is no good reason to dismiss the idea that implicitly Weber holds some definite views on these matters. Apart from Bendix's (1960:257ff) rather weak attempt, the literature contains no comprehensive effort at their explication; given the magnitude of the task, it cannot be tried here either. What can be accomplished, however, is a first exploration of the implications, for the issue at hand, of the distinction between power in the economic sphere and power in the political sphere.

The problem of a 'ruling class' conception within Weber's framework is the problem of the foundations or bases of power and of the implications which the particularities of these foundations have for its typical uses. At first sight, it seems that Weber (1968:53, 943) has very little of a systematic kind to say on this score. In the context of his general considerations on 'power', he mentions that concretely it may be based on a multitude of diverse things, and for the rest he declines to attempt their systematization or categorization. On further inspection, however, it turns out that his ideas are not quite as indefinite as may at first appear. To grasp what is involved it is necessary to know that Weber peculiarly connects the pursuit of certain types of substantive interests, i.e., participation in a particular sphere, to certain types of actions, i.e., to the utilization of certain types of resources. For instance, in relation to individuals' economic interests, Weber (1968:63, 68; 1964:43) presents two types of action: 'economically oriented' action and 'economic' action. The former is defined as conduct concerned with taking care of a want for utilities (*Nutzleistungen:* uses to which items may be put). The latter is a

19

special case of the former: ' "Economic action" [*Wirtschaften*] is a *peaceful* exercise of one's powers of disposal [*Verfugungsgewalt*] which is *primarily* . . . economically oriented.' 'Economically oriented' action thus is distinguished from 'economic' action either (a) by not being primarily oriented to the need for economic provision (*Vorsorge*), or (b) by being primarily so oriented but using non-peaceful means. Weber (1968:64) then concurs with Oppenheimer in the contrast of 'economic' and 'political' means. 'It is indeed appropriate to separate the latter from the "economy".' 'Economy' now is defined as 'an autocephalously . . . ordered *continuity* of economic action.'

The economic sphere, for Weber (1968:635), is constituted not by the totality of *economic* action, but rather by the totality of *economically oriented* action (and the structural conditions affecting it). The market, as a partial sector of the economic sphere, however, is characterized by economic action. 'Power' in the market is the ability to appropriate utilities against competition and it rests overwhelmingly on the control over 'economic' means, that is, items which have utility (goods and services). Now it might be asked just what it is that allows these 'economic' means to function as a 'basis' of power. This can be clarified with the help of the consideration that to each power must correspond a complementary weakness. If, simply speaking, power is the ability to have one's way, this implies some vulnerability of the party over whom power is exercised. It is in this context that an important distinction made by Weber (1968:943; 1964:692) becomes relevant.

> We will only call to mind that, in addition to numerous other possible types, there are two types of domination which are diametrically opposed to each other. On the one hand, there is domination by virtue of a *constellation of interests* (especially by virtue of a position of monopoly), and on the other hand there is domination by virtue of authority (power of command and duty to obey).

Domination by virtue of constellation of interests exploits the dominated parties' strivings to attain their personal aims. Hence it is the capacity for a successful pursuit of interests that is made possible by a situation in which the dominated, 'through their "formally" free actions, follow their own rational interests as the circumstances inescapably dictate them'. Domination by virtue of authority, in contrast, appeals not to (formally 'free' and rational) self-interest but to an absolute duty to obey, regardless of the obeying party's own motives and interests. What is exploited here is not the fact that people want certain things, but their belief that the dominant party has a right to command and to find compliance. Whenever Weber (1968:53; 1964:38) speaks of 'domination' (*Herrschaft*) without specifying its basis, he refers to domination by virtue of authority, which is defined as 'the chance to find, on the part of a specifiable set of persons, compliance with a command of specific content'.

For Weber, power in that sector of the economic sphere which he calls 'market' is power by virtue of a constellation of interests. Power in that part of the political sphere which, for lack of a special term, might be called the 'structure of rule', is power by virtue of authority. Thus the type of domination which defines a plurality of people as a dominant *class* is their ability to profit, through exchange, from the self-interested proclivities which induce individuals to participate in the market, while the domination of *rulers* is their ability to exploit the willingness of the members of the ruling organization (*Herrschaftsverband*) to comply with certain commands. With regard to the issue of 'ruling class' this might be taken to solidly establish the view that a dominant *class* cannot 'rule' because it is lacking in the specific resource on which political domination is based. However, such a conclusion should not be drawn too hastily. In one sense, of course, it is unobjectionable: in Weber's terminology it is nonsense to speak of the 'rule' of a class. 'To rule' for him has the technical meaning of 'to have powers of command', and the totality of individuals constituting a class do not have such powers. Yet this terminological usage must not detract from the substantive problem at stake. This is the problem of whose economic and ideological interests are disproportionately furthered as a result of action in the political sphere, or, expressed differently, for the advancement of whose interests the state apparatus is instrumental. In this regard, the implications of Weber's terminological distinctions are more complicated than frequently appears to be assumed.

In terms of Weber's framework, the problem of the 'ruling class' must be formulated as a problem of the connection between the economic and political spheres. Here, the basic mistake to be avoided is that of identifying the political sphere with 'political' action and the economic sphere with 'economic' action. Rather, these spheres must be viewed as consisting of 'politically oriented' action and 'economically oriented' action, respectively (plus the structural conditions influencing each). This is to say that political interests can be and are pursued not only by recourse to 'political' resources, but through the use of 'economic' and other types of means as well. Similarly, the attainment of economic goals may be, and often is, through 'political' means. The implication is that

21

individuals, or pluralities of individuals, may be powerful in a particular sphere in two ways, namely:
1 because of their control of sphere-specific resources, and
2 because of their control of other resources.
Expressions like 'economically powerful' or 'politically powerful' are non-specific with regard to the bases of power and must not tacitly be assumed to refer to sphere-specific resources only.

Weber, of course, nowhere comes even close to holding that power in a particular sphere is based only on sphere-specific resources. On the contrary, the major feature of all his non-typological studies is the tracing of between-sphere connections, conceptualized as the use of means 'belonging' to one sphere in the pursuit of things 'belonging' to another. The differentiation between domination based on authority and that based on constellation of interests thus does not *per se* declare the idea of 'ruling class' as mistaken. This becomes especially clear with the realization that the postulate of such a class is not the postulate of its ability to (formally) command, but that of the relative prevalence of its economic and ideological interests in the context of government action or inaction. In other words, what is asserted concerns the *content* of the rulers' commands and their effects, and not the commands' formal authorship. Weber's preoccupation with the elements, power resources, and structural features of political rule does not really address the question of the state's instrumental character as it is postulated by Marxists, but first of all must be understood as an attempt to understand the nature of the instrument. Presumably the assumption here is that the nature of the instrument places limits on what can be done with it. From this point of view, of course, there is some reason to believe that the distinction between the two types of domination is relevant to the issue of the content of commands. It points to the fact that the rulers have a power basis of their own which they may be able to use when their own interests are opposed to those of the economically dominant class. Whether, or in what sense, Marxists would deny this, and what exactly the general implications of this situation are, cannot be discussed within this chapter.

It is, however, necessary to mention some typically Weberian observations, namely, that rulers are above all interested in the maintenance of their rule, that this rule must be financed, that the support of specific population sectors is crucial for the maintenance of the rule, that the rulers themselves have certain material and ideological interests, and that the wishes of the bulk of the population are only intermittently given any weight, yet that their belief in the rule's legitimacy is of importance, etc. Clearly, except for excluding the extreme position – that the exercise of political power is entirely structured by its assumed instrumental function for the dominance in the market of a class – no quick and simple conclusion can be drawn from this, and nothing of the kind is attempted. A major precondition for any sensible assessment of the issue must be a precise conceptualization of 'ruling class'; this involves, at a minimum, decisions concerning the proper definition of 'class', the meaning of 'rule', the identification of 'class interests', and the specification of the standard used to measure the degree of success in the pursuit of interests. Since there is a good deal of disagreement on these things in the literature, it is neither necessary nor desirable to take a definite stand in the present essay. As a preliminary finding, however, it can be said that the distinction between domination based on authority and domination based on constellation of interests is a conceptual distinction which *per se* does not have any directly decisive implications for the problem of 'ruling class' since the issues surrounding the latter are issues which concern not so much the distinction, but the relationship, between these two types of domination (Miliband 1977:67ff). Regarding this relationship, Weber frequently points to instances where the economically dominant classes had their ways in the political arena. However, to what extent these remarks should be given systematic significance is a question which must await a more thorough analysis than could be attempted in the present context.

V

The preceding sections presented an attempt to understand classes and political parties as phenomena of the distribution of power by making explicit some of the guiding ideas which underlie Weber's statements on these subjects. Before turning to the analysis of estates, it seems useful to provide a brief summary of the main results obtained so far.

In Weber's view, social life can be conceptually decomposed into a number of spheres of activity. Each such sphere may be visualized as consisting of individual activities (as well as the structures in which they take place) to the extent to which they are specifically or partially oriented toward the attainment of a particular type of goal. Constitutive for the dynamics of a sphere, thus, is the structurally generated concern of individuals and groups of individuals with a particular type of goal, such as the acquisition of material goods, the exercise of authority over others, or the attainment of specific inner states. The spheres, their number, and the corresponding types of goals are never presented by Weber (1946:323ff) in any clear systematic form (the

Zwischenbetrachtung comes closest to it), nor is anything explicit said about the bases of their existence. Thus, there is nowhere a statement to the effect that, for instance, by virtue of their make-up and the conditions of social life, humans share a set of basic concerns in which they are involved, whether they like it or not. There is, of course, some reason to believe, as this author (1976:37–9, 79–80) suggested, that Weber quite clearly distinguishes an economic, a political, and a social sphere.

Corresponding to this obvious tripartition is another one which is rather implicit and not very well developed. This refers to the apparent assumption – manifesting itself in the labelling of certain types of action – that there is a kind of conduct which represents the point of crystallization of the particularity of each sphere. This kind of conduct is defined by the use of specific types of means and resources in the pursuit of sphere-specific goals. Thus, Weber's (1968:54–5; 1964:39) distinction between 'economically oriented' action and 'economic' action alludes not simply to a difference in the actor's major preoccupation but clearly also involves a distinction between 'properly' economic resources (goods, skills) and extra-economic ones (force), with the use of the former entailing a specific kind of conduct, namely (formally) peaceful exchange. Similarly, there is 'politically oriented' action and 'political' action. The former is action which 'aims at influencing a political organization's leadership [*Leitung*], especially the appropriation or expropriation or redistribution of allocation of powers of government'. Such action may rely on all sorts of means. 'Political' action, in contrast, is defined as a politically oriented undertaking which ultimately relies on a specific resource, namely force or violence.

For purposes of reference, the types of action characterized by the reliance on sphere-specific means in the pursuit of sphere-specific ends (e.g., typically 'economic' resources in the pursuit of typically 'economic' ends) may be called 'pure' types; all other types may be called 'hybrid'. In each sphere, the dealings of individuals with each other through actions approximating the pure type result in specific phenomena, viz. 'classes' in the economic sphere, and 'rulers' and 'ruled' in the political sphere. Parties, as based on voluntary membership, result from activities of a hybrid type. 'The essence of all politics is,' as Weber (1958a:335) said, '. . . *struggle* [*Kampf*], *solicitation* of allies and of a voluntary following', and this solicitation potentially involves the use of all kinds of means.

It is now time to direct our attention to Weber's statements on estates. As in the cases of 'class' and 'party,' the guiding question is that of the sense in which these social formations are 'phenomena of the distribution of power.' An answer to this question encounters considerable difficulties since Weber's thought on the matter is analytically not well developed. This is perhaps somewhat surprising considering the great importance of the concept of estate in his sociological-historical writings. Nevertheless, it must be noted that his remarks on the subject do not rest on a systematic set of concepts to the same extent as his remarks on class and party.

Estates, according to Weber, are social formations which must be located in the 'social' sphere of collective life, where 'social' is understood in the sense that it has, for instance, in the labeling of a ball or a wedding reception as 'social events' or 'social occasions'. In analogy to the procedure followed in the conceptualization of the economic and political spheres it might be reasonably assumed, then, that this sphere is defined by the totality of all 'socially oriented' actions and their structural circumstances, with 'social' action being the 'pure' type of the pursuit of sphere-specific goals through reliance on sphere-specific resources. Weber never introduces these or equivalent concepts, but, of course, the absence of a formal definition of 'socially oriented' action does not necessarily mean the absence of its idea. Indeed, what this idea is can be easily inferred from a number of Weber's (1968:305–6; 1964:226) statements regarding 'estate' (*Stand*): ' "Estate" is a plurality of persons who, within an organization [*Verband:* corporate group], successfully claim (a) a special social worth . . . and (b) special estate monopolies'. 'Estate situation' is, Weber (1968:932; 1964:683) said, 'every typical component of people's fates in their lives which is determined by a specific, positive or negative, social estimation of the *"honor"* which is tied to some attribute shared by a plurality of persons.' It is clear from this that what is at stake in the 'social' sphere is 'social honor', and that accordingly the actions which constitute this sphere are actions reflecting people's concern with the degree of honor which they think is or should be accorded to them or others.

The 'social' sphere, then, is the place where people attempt to acquire 'social honor'. The question which must be asked is whether Weber identifies any activities or resources as specific to the pursuit of this goal. The answer is provided by his (1968:305–6; 1964:226) statement that social worth is based on occupational prestige, lineage prestige, style of life and, hence, formal education. In addition, Weber (1968:932, 938) unambiguously declares that, in the long run, material wealth regularly has a decisive impact on people's positions in the 'social' sphere, and that power (of command) may have prestige attached to it. Now, if the previously introduced distinction between 'pure' and 'hybrid' types of action has any validity, it may be held that the wealth-

25

or power-(of command)-based pursuit of social honor qualifies as (hybrid) 'socially oriented' action, whereas 'pure' 'social' action is the attempt to acquire honor through a particular style of life or through one's descent. This inference finds some support in Weber's (1968:306) emphasis that material wealth *per se* is of no direct relevance to social honor, and that whoever claims a certain degree of social honor must *above all* display a specific style of life (Weber, 1968:932; 1958b:39).

'Estates' are the social formations which result from the differential success of individuals in their efforts to claim social honor. It appears reasonable to posit that everyone in a society is part of some estate since everyone has some style of life – assuming, of course, that there are no styles of life not subject to assessment in terms of social honor. Furthermore, the categorization of a person as belonging to some particular estate in society is independent of whether or not he or she cares about, or is concerned with, such things as social honor. In this respect the social and political spheres are similar: by very participation in an organization the individual is involved in a struggle in these spheres. 'Non-participation,' i.e., passivity, is not an escape from this struggle but merely the willingness to be satisfied with what is left after the winners have taken their shares.

The moment has now arrived for the consideration of the idea that estates are phenomena of the power distribution within a community. One interpretation is obvious and has already been mentioned. Social honor may be the result of political power and is, in the long run, connected to the material fortunes of individuals. These, of course, are not sphere-specific resources, and it is important to note in this context:

1 that powers of command do not necessarily entail great social honor, and
2 that honor normally also stands in sharp opposition to the pretensions of wealth as such (Weber, 1968:926, 932).

This immediately raises the question of the circumstances in which power and wealth *are* conducive to claims of a special honor, and the answer is presumably when they are complements or components of appropriate styles of life and/or descent, i.e., when they are connected with or transformed into a sphere-specific resource. In this respect, however, estates are phenomena of the distribution of power in the sense that some people are able to extract from others the admission of their 'social' superiority on the basis of their possession of life-style elements or lineage memberships which are considered to be honor-engendering. Thus, estates are social formations the conceptualization of whose emergence and persistence is formally completely analogous to that of classes and rulers/ruled. They are all manifestations of the differential ability of individuals to attain sphere-specific ends under competitive conditions; this differential ability is seen as a typical consequence of their differential control over appropriate resources (especially sphere-specific ones).

Weber's treatment of life style and lineage prestige as power resources specific to the 'social' sphere, while in line with the overall symmetry of his ideas on social stratification, introduces a substantive claim which must not go without some scrutiny. Two questions are especially relevant. The first concerns the explanation of how, in general, lineage prestige and life styles or life-style elements can be resources in the struggle for social honor. Why should people respond to the display of styles of life specifically by granting or withholding this particular transferable? The other concerns the explanation of the relationship between a specific style of life and/or descent and a specific amount of social honor. What is it that determines the rank order of life styles or lineages within a group? The remainder of this essay is devoted to answering these questions. In doing this it will be necessary to go beyond mere exegesis, especially with regard to the first question, which is ignored by Weber. For a start, however, it is useful to present some of Weber's main statements about estates.

An estate is a plurality of persons who can effectively lay claim to, or have effectively imposed upon them, a specific degree of 'social honor' in association with some feature that is common to them. Its members share feelings of affinity toward each other and on this amorphous basis act to maintain social distance from outsiders whose 'honor' is considered inferior. The extent to which this is carried through may vary and depends (among other things) on the stability of the distribution of power in the economic sphere under whose constraints estate formation takes place. The differentiation and structuration of a society into estates is thus a matter of degree; its beginnings are gradual and it may never become full-blown.

The shared feature which provides the point of reference for an estate's specific honor receives its practical significance through its association with a characteristic mode of life ideally common to all those who exhibit the feature. This feature may be a particular *amount* of material possessions, but it usually is not. As a matter of fact, the principle according to which honor is distributed is sharply opposed to the principle according to which the market operates (1968:936; 1964:687):

> The market and its economic processes know nothing . . . of 'personal distinction'; it is dominated by 'impersonal'

27

[*sachliche*] interests and knows nothing of 'honor'. The estate order [*ständische Ordnung*] signifies just the opposite, namely structuration according to 'honor' and estate-oriented mode of life. As such it would be threatened at its very root if mere economic acquisition and mere, naked, blatant economic power *per se,* its origin outside the estate order still openly visible, could bestow upon anyone who has won them the same or . . . in effect even greater honor than those with vested interests in the estate order could claim for themselves by virtue of their mode of life.

Accordingly, individuals with greatly varying amounts of material possessions may belong to the same estate, at least in principle. However, this is a rather precarious state of affairs, and it is normal for wealth over time to have significant influence on a person's ability to pretend that he belongs to a certain estate.

The formation of an estate begins when people who feel, on the basis of some shared feature, that there is an inner affinity between them, start to exert social pressure on each other in the direction of conformity with a specific mode of life. Those who do not conform are excluded 'socially', that is to say, interaction with them is restricted to utilitarian and task-oriented dealings, as in business, because they are not considered 'social' equals. The point of origin of an estate order, thus, is a usurpation (1968:933). A set of persons claims 'social' superiority through all sorts of exclusionary maneuvers, and to the degree to which they are successful in finding actual acceptance of this claim, an estate comes into being. The implication is that in a group characterized by a number of estates, all except the top and bottom ones are the result of a mixture of usurpation and imposition. Each estate has its inferiority in relation to those above it imposed on it, while it has usurped its own superiority *vis-à-vis* those below. This relative inferiority/superiority is at first purely conventional, i.e., neither institutionalized nor upheld by any stronger action than social approval or disapproval. Yet once it has shown itself to be a stable feature of everyday social life, it can easily find formal legal recognition. At the extreme point, this may be supplemented by distinctions and sanctions of a religious nature and thus take the form of a hierarchy of castes.

The statement that the formation of a hierarchy of estates rests essentially on usurpation provides a partial answer to the question of the relationship between a specific mode of life and a certain degree of social honor. Apparently this relationship is not intrinsic but is 'claimed,' that is to say, fictitious; its 'reality' is one of consensual attribution rather than of 'natural' connection. Thus, the ability to attain social honor seems to be a function not so much of the particular features of a certain mode of life as of people's ability to propagate successfully the excellence of any mode of life, regardless of its peculiar specificity. What this appears to mean, then, is that in the last analysis an estate's social honor is not really a matter of life style but of economic and political resources.

This is a conclusion which, it might seem, is also drawn by Weber in the guise of a number of more or less explicit remarks and assumptions concerning the extra-'social' preconditions of estate formations. Thus he states (1968:928; 1964:680) that 'a plurality of persons, such as slaves, whose fortunes [*Schicksal*] are not determined by the chance to participate on their own account with goods or services in the market, are technically not a "class" (but an "estate").' He (1946:83; 1964:1049) also calls 'estates' those pluralities of persons 'who in their own right possess the means for military undertakings, or the material equipment or personal powers of rulership which are important for the purposes of administration.' In these contexts, estates clearly are defined by reference to their members' individually appropriated economic or political resources rather than their life-style patterns. Yet the significance of these statements should not be overinterpreted, for what Weber does here (admittedly rather illegitimately) is to transform empirical connections into definitional equivalencies.[16] In other words the fact that estates usually occur on the basis of, or in association with, certain economic and political circumstances, causes Weber at times to use the latter as definitional criteria (1946:300; 1920:273–4):

> We understand by *estate* situation a chance of particular groups
> of persons to be accorded positive or negative social *honor,*
> *primarily* determined by differences in the character of their
> *mode of life* (hence, mostly their *education*). Secondarily,
> . . . it tends very often and typically to be connected with a
> monopoly, either of rights of rulership or of a specific type
> of income and acquisition chances which by law are guaranteed
> to this stratum. Thus, when all these characteristics are
> present (which of course is not always the case), an 'estate' is
> a group of persons who are associated . . . through the
> character of their mode of life, their specific conventional
> notions of honor, and their legal monopoly of economic
> chances. . . .

Weber's decision to emphasize life-style patterns in the constitution of estates at the expense of their economic and political foundations is, systematically, in line with the logic underlying

29

his tripartite schema and, substantively, based on the ideas that economic and political power on their own do not usually carry social honor and that the understanding of estates as the building blocks of a hierarchy of honor must therefore focus on their specifically honor-engendering elements. The position, however, that these are life-style elements rather than something else (such as wealth or powers of command) is simply put forward in a declaratory fashion as a matter of fact, not of argument. Yet even if the link between life style and social honor is the simple fact which Weber announces it to be, this does not absolve us from the necessity of understanding it. For, if the link between particularities of life style and levels of social honor is not one of intrinsic 'nature', that is, is not independent of human interference, then the problem arises of why humans universally attribute social honor to elements of life style rather than to other possible things. Or, to put it somewhat differently, the question which must be posed is that of the peculiar meaningful affinity between patterned-mode life and people's conception of social honor. This is a question which Weber does not address (although there are some suggestive remarks), and to which the last section of this essay will attempt to provide an answer.

VI

'Social honor' is not something which is by 'nature' and 'intrinsically' connected to certain things. Rather, it is something attributed to them by humans on the basis of a particular mode of thought. This is to say that certain items bring honor because people consensually think about them in terms of a framework which attaches an honorific significance to certain things, a despicable quality to others, and a relatively neutral condition to the rest. The understanding of honor-related phenomena therefore requires the identification of this underlying thought pattern. This task is attempted here with the help of the assumption that the relevance of a particular item to social 'honor', although fictitious and a matter of conventional imposition cannot be entirely without pattern but, in order to function as an organizing principle, must be meaningfully or symbolically adequate. In other words, it is assumed that the attribution of honor (or despicability) has a certain meaning to people, and that this meaning places limits on the circumstances under which things can be considered honorable (or despicable). the task which poses itself, consequently, is to understand exactly what is done when a person is honored and, on the basis of this, to identify the peculiar features with which honor (or despicability) is associated, and to make sense out of this association.

Social 'honor' is a term left undefined in Weber's writings, and this state of affairs also characterizes the more recent literature on social 'status' (unless one wants to take as theoretically serious its conceptualization as a 'reward' or a collective judgment of 'esteem' or 'prestige'). It is, however, commonly accepted that differences in social honor are, at least on the prescriptive level, associated with expressions of deference by the inferior party toward the superior one. Now, if Durkheim's analysis of the sacred is not entirely mistaken, a show of deference or respect entails the acknowledgment of a kind of moral inferiority on the part of the person who defers. Vice versa, that to which deference is expressed must be in a position of moral ascendancy. Thus, the basis of social honor, the resource by virtue of whose possession a certain honor can be effectively claimed, must be some quality which endows the owner with a sort of moral superiority.

If the considerations presented so far make any sense, then the identification, by Weber, of patterned mode of life, lineage charisma, and a number of other items as the bases of positive or negative social honor amounts to the claim that there is a moral dimension to them, or to their possession. Such moral significance naturally cannot be a matter of intrinsic properties but must be considered fictitious, imposed by consensual attribution and valid only as long as enough people agree on it. In other words, the concretely various bases of social honor are significant not by virtue of some shared 'intrinsic' or 'natural' feature but by virtue of a conventionally imposed one. The problem is to find out just exactly what this property is. Here Weber is of little help, yet fortunately the stratification literature contains some hints which, if assembled correctly, suggest an answer.

In every society, according to Dumont (1970), Leach (1964), and others, there are highly insulting ways of likening people to animals. The principles governing this type of communication are not yet entirely understood, but it is clear that the insulting quality of such comparisons is related to the lumping together of two kinds of things which are normally kept distinct, i.e., humans and animals. In other words, calling a person by a certain animal name is insulting because it amounts to the denial of this person's qualification as a human.

The concern with the maintenance of the distinction between man and animal betrays its precariousness, a precariousness which is recognized by the acknowledgment that humans can regress to a state of animality. At the bottom of this is the insight that humans and animals are not without a certain affinity. The form

31

in which this insight finds its expression is some version of an image of man as *homo duplex:* the idea that the human being is composed of two parts, an organic, animalistic, or 'natural' one, and a 'social', 'spiritual', or 'moral' one; that the former is unruly and impulsive and requires control by the latter; and that this control is not perfect but can break down.

Some distinctions are made in society (in the 'social consciousness') between people of relatively superior and relatively inferior 'humanity' (conceived as remoteness from or closeness to 'animality'), and the attribution of social honor or despicability is the manifest social expression of, and response to, this (ascribed) quality of individuals (or categories of individuals). What the upper strata really claim, therefore, when they demand high social honor as their due, is the superiority of their nature. The imposition of low social rank on population groups is, accordingly, a claim of the worthlessness of their nature, i.e., their near-animality and therewith their moral despicability. The belief, in the upper strata, in the readiness of lower-strata persons to give in to their organic impulses, and their consequent relegation to quasi-animal status, is only one manifestation of this thought pattern, although perhaps the most revealing one.

The proclamation, by a person or a category of persons, that there is a superior nature is obviously not a claim which only needs to be made to be granted. It must have some plausible back-up, some visible features by reference to which such a claim can be persuasively supported. Naturally, the foremost such feature is general success in the struggles of life, especially as documented by the possession of wealth and political power. It is hard for people not to acquiesce to the idea (if ever so reluctantly) that outward success is, in some way, a result of superior qualities, rather than of luck or circumstances, especially when they tend to ascribe their own successes to effort and skill rather than coincidence. The second such feature, and perhaps the one with the most irresistible impact, is charisma. This is defined by Weber (1968:241; 1964:179) as 'the consideration of a person's quality as extraordinary . . . due to which he is treated as endowed with supernatural, superhuman, or at least specifically extraordinary powers or properties which are not accessible to just anyone, or due to which he is treated as god-sent or exemplary and therefore as "leader".' The third feature, finally, is some display of cultural refinement. Thus, to assert one's humanity one must emphasize what is specifically human: the achievements of civilization. What counts here, however, are not simply the outward trappings but an 'inner' refinement and cultured 'being', i.e., the control of impulses in the form of disciplined and normatively shaped patterns of all life-expressions: thoughts, feelings, emotions, speech, actions.

Cultural refinement, charisma, and economic and political power are not on the same level, as far as their relations to social honor are concerned. Charisma is a quality of a person's 'being' or 'nature' and thus is the direct object of awe, deference, and respect. In contrast, there is nothing particularly honorable about general success in life (and especially the possession of economic and political power) *per se*. Whatever significance it has, it has as an *indicator* of the possessor's superior quality, and the same is true of features of cultural refinement. There is nothing intrinsically honorable to modes of speech, dress codes, or table manners. They are, however, clear indicators of a person's impulse control, of the subordination of the organic.

The special importance of cultural refinement becomes apparent when it is related to the facts of vertical social mobility. The estate structure is not an open system; especially in the upper strata there is a tendency to restrict claims of superiority not only to oneself, but to one's descendants as well. In other words, there are always efforts at work to make social rank *de facto* and perhaps even *de iure* inheritable. Naturally this goes hand in hand with a theory of the inheritability of inferior or superior humanity, i.e., a higher or lower quality of what is transmitted in the lineage. 'Every highly privileged group,' as Weber (1968:953; 1964:701) said, 'develops the myth of its natural superiority, especially that of its "blood",' its better 'stock', or superior 'breeding'. The logical implication of this is the rejection of the *parvenu*, the *nouveau riche*, whose recent success is too incongruous with the defects of his birth to be accepted as a genuine indicator of his worth without reservation. Yet all this must carry some plausibility, at least in the eyes of those who are secure in their superior position, if not of those who are rejected. In other words, the superiority of their own kind must be constantly visible to the strata who claim it (and to everyone else), and this is accomplished by the display of cultural refinement. For this refinement is a matter of long training which begins early. This education, i.e., the forming of an unshaped, inchoate human organism into a civilized being approximating a particular image of humanity, entails the imposition of patterns of acting and thinking, of modes of speaking and manipulating the body, of tastes and preferences, and of particular structurations of emotions and effects. These imposed patterns blend into a 'second nature' which becomes so ingrained in the person as to be perfectly 'natural' to him despite its 'artificiality'. It is this unthinking and almost effortless display of the 'second nature' which an individual can normally only

33

master through an upbringing in the group in which it is cultivated. Outsiders who try to imitate it rarely attain the perfection which conceals the effort, avoids mistakes, and sheds the air of embarrassing contrivedness. Thus it is the perfect vehicle for the discrimination of those who really belong from those who only pretend. As Warner and Lunt's (1941:131, 135) informants state it: 'We may not have much money, but we do have something that you can only get by being born into a long line of distinguished families – of people who just know instinctively how to do the right thing. That may be snobbish, but breeding does count.' For 'breeding is something that doesn't come out of a book or by imitating your betters'.

Weber's statements on estates are readily compatible with the considerations just presented. Implied in his observations on the emergence of a caste system is the idea that estate hierarchies have their social foundation in what might be called the 'natural ethnocentrism' of human groups: whenever a plurality of people, through feelings of affinity, think that they are of the same kind, belong together, and are somehow separate from others with whom they live intermingled or in juxtaposition, they develop a specific identity and, connected with it, a specific honor, i.e., a belief in the worthiness of everything that characterizes the group and its members. As long as these groups are not part of a larger political organization, each is in a position to consider its own honor the highest. Yet once they are integrated into a comprehensive ruling organization, the juxtaposition of equivalent honors is transformed into a hierarchical arrangement by those groups which are clearly more powerful than others and rationalized by a suitable theory about the basis of honor differentials, such as a group's functional contribution to societal survival. The subjective roots for the upper strata, Weber (1946:286; 1920:258) said, lie in the experience of worldly success which cannot but engender a conviction of their superior worth, or 'dignity'. The feeling of dignity of the positively privileged estates in the nature of the case is related to their immanent and self-sufficient 'being', their 'beauty and virtue'. Their kingdom is 'of this world' and lives for the present and off the great past. The feeling of dignity of the negatively privileged strata in the nature of the case can relate to a future which transcends the present, be it in this world or in another. In other words, as Weber suggested, it must feed on the belief in a providential 'mission', in a specific honor before God as 'chosen people' (1968:934; 1964:685).

Weber correctly realized that the principle underlying the structuration of society into estates involved, in contrast to the market, considerations of 'personal distinction'. Yet the precise meaning of this, and its implications, he left undeveloped. As a result, in spite of his extremely perceptive insistence on the significance of life style, the role of the latter remained unrelated to this principle and was considered basically only with regard to its function as an exclusionary device. Thus the inner unity and elective affinity between success in life, feelings of personal dignity, the attribution of social honor, charisma, and life-style elements as a symptom of gentlemanly pretensions (such as fashionable dress, the acceptability of a person as a dueling opponent, descent from famous ancestors, food taboos, and an active interest in the arts) is left obscure. He never exploits the insight contained in the statement that 'entailed by the predominant significance of the "style of life" for the "honor" of estates is the fact that "estates" are the specific carriers of all "conventions": everything in life which is "stylized", no matter what its manifestation, either originates in estates or is at least conserved by them'. Instead of raising the question 'Why this emphasis on style?' Weber ends with the obfuscating conclusion that underlying the estate hierarchy is the *consumption of goods* in the guise of specific styles of life (1968:933, 935–7; 1964:686–7).

On the basis of the analysis of social honor presented earlier, the emphasis on the pattern and style of people's life expressions and surroundings is easily understood. If what is honored in society is individuals' remoteness from animality, and if the latter is conceived as impulsive, chaotic, disorderly, and untamed, then distance from it must manifest itself as form, pattern, regulation, and harmonious configuration. Anything that resembles organic planlessness and an absence of orderly shape must therefore be banned and be replaced by pattern and regular formation.

Conclusion

Weber's statements on social stratification are, most overtly, organized in relation to three social formations, namely classes, estates, and parties. No explicit rationale for this approach is ever presented, yet it might be surmised that for Weber these formations represented the major collective 'actors' by reference to whose actions the major societal developments and processes could be explained. For not only did he engage in this kind of analysis but he (1968:929, 932, 938) also took care to identify the type of collective action characteristic of each (classes: individual adaptation on a mass scale, mass behavior; estates: communal action; parties: associational action). However this may be, underlying Weber's pronouncements is an analytical schema which, for the limited purpose at hand, could be interpreted as a view of the world as composed of three 'spheres' of action: the economic, the political, and the 'social'. Peculiar to each sphere is a particular type of goal (material possessions, political power, social honor), and each sphere is constituted by the totality of structurally conditioned activities to the extent to which they are primarily or partially concerned with the attainment of sphere-specific goals. The attempted attainment of these goals is conceptualized by Weber as a utilization of resources, and he distinguishes sphere-specific ones (goods and skills, ability to coerce, life-style elements in the economic, political, and 'social' spheres, respectively) from sphere-external ones.

The pursuit of goals in each sphere, i.e., the efforts of individuals attempting to realize their 'interests', necessarily involves people in competitive struggles. They participate in these struggles with very unequal resources and therefore are not equally powerful. As a result of these inequalities of power, the distribution of those things around whose appropriation the struggle in each sphere turns, is very uneven among the participants. The distributive structure manifests itself in social formations whose particular type is determined by the type of resource on which the competitors in each sphere predominantly rely. Weber distinguishes three formations which result from the prevailing reliance on sphere-specific resources, namely classes, rulers/ruled (domination), and estates.

Weber appears to treat the pursuit of sphere-specific goals by means of sphere-specific resources as somehow the core of a sphere, i.e., that set of processes which embodies its characteristic identity and which gives it a special inner 'logic'. Polanyi (1957:243–70) argues that in so doing Weber falls victim to the fallacious assumption that these modes of conduct represent the true 'essence' of each sphere, that it is in some sense 'natural' for people active in a sphere to engage in the corresponding type of 'pure' action. In any event, the distinction between the different types of resources permits Weber to distinguish the differentiating features of the types of power based on them, which is to say, the weaknesses whose exploitation they make possible. However, the insistence that not all power is alike and that individuals strong in resources specific to one sphere are not thereby automatically successful in other spheres must not be misunderstood. It does not entail a position which underestimates the possibility of using one's strength in one area of social life to reap benefits in another. Thus Weber's conceptual distinctions are not incompatible with some ruling-class view of society, and his empirical analyses actually embrace such a conception.

Notes

1 Weber (1968:302–7, 926–40). All quotations from Weber have been translated by the author of this chapter. Where his translations diverge from published ones, references to the German texts are also given after the English.

2 This is not one of Weber's terms; it is used here for convenience only.

3 This may seem to be a rather exaggerated claim and may therefore be somewhat elaborated. The vast majority of commentators have looked at Weber's statements in the context of an implicit or explicit comparison with Marx. While this is, of course, entirely legitimate and interesting, it is not necessarily the precondition most conducive to an understanding of the structure of Weber's thought. A pervasive assumption in the literature seems to be that Weber wrote about social stratification, if not with Marx constantly on his mind, at least on quasi-Marxian grounds as far as the definition of the problems is concerned. This author does not believe that the Marx-focused interpretation of Weber is particularly promising when it comes to understanding the inner logic of Weber's proceedings. This chapter attempts to follow this inner logic.

4 These ideas consist of a conceptual apparatus and a number of empirical generalizations expressed in its terms. The conceptual apparatus embodies a particular perspective on the empirical world. The 'inner logic' of Weber's approach consists in the systematic articulation of this perspective.

5 Weber's term '*Stand*' (estate) has usually been translated as 'status group'. This translation is defensible although there are no really strong reasons for preferring it to 'estate'. If the common meaning of the latter is considered too misleading or restrictive to cover adequately the range of phenomena to which Weber refers (Bendix, 1960:85; Dahrendorf, 1959:6–7), then the most appropriate English equivalent would appear to be the old-fashioned term 'order', as in the expression 'people of all orders and descriptions'.

6 Weber (1968:928–9; 1949:107–10). Almost certainly, however, Weber considers interests as defined by the acting individuals. Giddens (1975:43) is confusing when he states that ' "class", in Weber's terminology always refers to market interests, which exist independently of whether men are aware of them'. For discussions of some of the issues, see Plamenatz (1954:1–8; 1963:311–18), Benn (1959/60), Balbus (1971), and Connolly (1972).

7 Weber (1968:933, 938). 'Honor', 'prestige', and 'status' are used interchangeably in this chapter. There is some confusion in the literature due to Weber's careless use of 'power', which sometimes has the general meaning established by its well-known formal definition, i.e., all types of power, and sometimes refers more specifically to a particular subtype, namely political power.

8 Weber (1968:311ff). The notion of 'sphere' refers to a structured sector of social life, and what is structured in each sector is the pursuit

of a distinct type of goal by socially organized individuals. The lack
of systematic exposition of the general structure of each sphere,
and of their modes of interrelation as a whole society, is symptomatic
of the absence in Weber of an explicitly formulated image of
society. A few words about Hirst's (1976:60, 70, 76, 80, 92, 103)
interpretation:

> The Weberian categories of 'economic action' and 'domination'
> do not define specific and articulated structures of social
> relations, they are not equivalents of the Marxist concepts of the
> 'economic structure' and the state. . . . Weber's categories do
> not provide . . . an alternative theorisation of the social totality
> to that of Marx, more 'empirical' and 'multi-factorial', *they
> abolish the notion of social totality as such.* Social relations
> disappear into inter-subjective relations. Weber's categories are
> applied to a concrete human milieu without any general or
> necessary structure. There is no social topography in Weber's
> conception, social relations are reduced to the plane of inter-
> subjective relations.

Hirst's objection is not merely to the perceived *de facto* absence of
a 'social topography'; it is the claim of a disability *in principle,*
which is a consequence of Weber's supposed view of end-realizing
behavior as not caused by but freely chosen by the subject. Humans
are allegedly conceptualized by Weber as relating to each other as
freely willing, not as willy-nilly carriers of supra-subjective,
impersonal social relations with objective conditions of existence,
i.e., as 'objective social forms irreducible to the actions and
thoughts of human subjects'. The main problem with this
interpretation is the imputation to Weber of a free-will position.
Hirst's argument is extremely weak, relying to a good degree on
Weber's association with neo-Kantianism. Weber's own criticism
of the free-will position is disregarded. There is precious little
evidence that Weber championed a free-will reality-
constructionism. This view is not altered by the fact that he
considered ideas and values to be among the causal determinants
of social life, and categorized action according to subjective
meaning. Weber's apparent unconcern with something like Marx's
notion of 'totality' has probably more to do with methodological and
empirical reservations concerning 'totality' in general and Marx's
ideas about it in particular than with free will.

 9 Weber (1968:53); Weber's later definition of 'power' was as 'every
    chance to realize, within a social relationship, one's own will even
    against resistance, regardless of the basis for this chance' (Weber,
    1964:38).
10 Weber (1968:926; 1964:678). The last part of this definition has been
    criticized as misleading and superfluous. However, its inclusion
    makes sense on the assumption that Weber wanted to focus on the
    relational character of 'power' and defined the term in view of its

typical usage as 'power over'. For recent discussions of 'power', see Lukes (1974), White (1972), Baldus (1975).

11 Weber has come in for considerable criticism for his 'subjectivist' premise, i.e., the view that individuals are to be considered as 'actors' who create social structures rather than as the creatures ('supports') of social structures. This criticism, which is not based on any analysis of Weber's notion of 'interest', equates a conceptualization of human activity with reference to purposes and motives with a metaphysical tenet of individual freedom or autonomy. For a discussion of the issues, see Therborn (1976), Jones (1975), Scott (1974), and Turner (1977).

12 Many commentators argue that Weber considered classes as phenomena of the sphere of distribution while Marx located them in the sphere of production. See, however, Giddens (1975:109), who believes that both Marx and Weber view class as a 'phenomenon of production'. Weber does not appear to operate in terms of a production-distribution dichotomy.

13 Here is where one of the main differences between Weber's and Marx's concepts of 'class' lies, and not simply in the divergent emphases on the productive and distributive sectors. For Marx, *control* over means of production is decisive, regardless of its basis. For Weber, the *basis* of control is crucial; it must be economic, not political.

14 Runciman (1970). For a critique, see Ingham (1970).

15 Those who argue that, for Weber, 'power' is not a separate 'dimension' of stratification, since he treats all stratification phenomena as phenomena of power distribution, fail to make the distinction between 'power' in general (whatever its 'bases') and 'power of command'. Weber's three dimensions refer to distinct *sub*types of power, differentiated according to their distinct bases.

16 Further evidence for Weber's inconsistencies concerning the notion of 'estate' is provided by the following statements: 'A political organization in which the material means of administration are autonomously controlled, wholly or partly, by the dependent administrative staff may be called an association structured into "estates" ' (1946:81; 1964:1045). ' "Estate" is a quality of social honor or despicability and is, on the whole, determined as well as expressed by a particular kind of life style' (1958b:39).

3 Patrimonialism, modern and traditionalist:

a paradigm for interdisciplinary research on rulership and legitimacy

Vatro Murvar

The purpose of this chapter is to advocate and facilitate the greater use of the conceptual tool of patrimonialist rulership and legitimacy by examining its original context within the constructed typology as advanced by Weber seven decades ago and by suggesting some research-oriented modifications based on evidence instead of pure speculation. Indeed, recently the concept of patrimonialism has been successfully utilized in some empirical studies conducted in the developing world. Some other works, however, while dutifully acknowledging Weber's parenthood, have drifted toward a variety of speculative approaches with different degrees of abstraction which have not been based on solid evidence as postulated by Weber. In addition to going back to the original context and staying away from non-evidenced systematizations, this study will present from Weber's opus some as-yet-'undiscovered' clues to argue for the fullest applicability of the concept of modern patrimonialism.

Typology of rulership and legitimacy in general

On the whole, this much-celebrated but little-used typology ought to be considered an open-ended scheme to serve research needs as they develop, particularly when it is clear that Weber in two different periods of his intellectual growth made only some pioneering efforts in this area. His 1920 so-called revision of a much larger, very rough draft written between 1911 and 1914 is not actually a revision but a desperate effort under pressure from the publisher to streamline an introduction for that early draft which he never touched.

Since Weber consistently refused to create any grand social-scientific theoretical systems, he certainly did not intend to build this (in his judgment) modest, heuristic device into a dogmatic, all-needs-satisfying theoretical monstrosity. Instead, he anticipated empirical testing of this typology with newly accumulated evidence from history and the contemporary world. Curiously enough, with more than a touch of dogmatism as to its finality, this typology remains confined to the three usual types: legal-rational, traditionalist, and charismatic. Reinhard Bendix suggested at least nine types instead of the customary three, and, of course, future research can add, drop, or combine any of the constructed types on the basis of new materials, aspects, arrangements, and research needs as they develop. (For this very tentative proposition, see Chart 3.1.) Bendix said that Weber was concerned not only with domination and legitimacy, but also with the process of legitimation.[1] This is evident from his plans to write special studies on revolution and the usurpation of power, which he was unable to accomplish except (segmentally) on patrician and plebeian regimes in ancient Rome.

> Had Weber carried the design of this essay forward, he might
> have treated these themes in a modern context, on a national
> . . . scale. . . . It would be an interesting task to integrate
> Weber's approach to the Ancient and Medieval experience
> in this field with the knowledge now available about
> revolutions, *coups d'état*, and various types of oligarchic
> rule. . . . Weber's three types of domination must be
> supplemented by a typology of revolutions and usurpations
> . . . (1969:558).

The grand pontifical statement of a late sociologist that declared the typology of rulership the greatest event ever to occur in the social sciences did not foster any significant research results in spite of his considerable influence in the American sociological establishment. This seems quite logical for it is clear now that the school which he represented was responsible for many major misconceptions and misinterpretations of Weber's scientific and intellectual legacy, including this very typology. As documented below, Weber's typology, as well as some propositions outside of it, directly contradicts the fashionable modernization theories that are all based on the notion of the inevitability of progress through the stages of evolutionary development.

However, if Weber's typology of rulership and legitimacy had been inspected more closely in its entirety, the unfortunate consequences of the popular clichés, such as charisma and bureaucracy – two uneven, unmatched segments that were illegitimately carved out of the context of the entire typology – could have been avoided. Even a perfunctory examination of the works of Weber's

41

CHART 3.1
Typology of rulership
(tentative)

Charismatic	Revolutionary	Usurpational	Oligarchic	Patriarchal, patrimonialist, traditional and modern	Hierocracies (independent or self-ruling)	Feudal structures and sub-structures	Free city structures	Legal-rational
Monism: political or hierocratic	Monism: political or hierocratic	Monism	Monism: political (various ruling elites, 'Collective leadership' or hierocratic (priests, elders)	Monism: political (imperial, regal, dictatorial, caesarist, one-party, etc.) or hierocratic (papal, Dalai-Lamaist, etc.)	Interdependent with each other; limited pluralist experiences; autonomous, autocephalous, self-ruling or even independent at times; exempt – especially the free cities – from any other jurisdiction			Pluralism
Transitional	Pluralist goals at times	Pluralism at times						Democracy
	Transitional				These three types can also be considered pre-legal-rational – historic, traditional predecessors of the legal-rational type of rulership.			

three (slightly older) contemporaries, Rudolph Sohm (1841–1917) on charisma, Adolf Harnack (1851–1930) on legal rationality, and George Jellinek (1851–1911) on 'legal legitimacy' (with its three subtypes, patriarchal, patrimonial, and contractual) would have revealed the extent of his indebtedness to them. (This Weber expressed most graciously and humbly.) At the same time, it would have exposed the *tentative* character of Weber's major typological choices including labeling, which according to him should suffice until more and better evidence becomes available.

Repeatedly throughout his opus, Weber stressed as strongly as he could that charisma and rationality are two major revolutionary forces in history. He also spoke of the 'charismatic glorification of reason' during the French Revolution and of the charisma of reason as a revolutionary legitimation derived from the doctrine of natural law and basic human rights (1968:1209). This is significant for the understanding of the origin and limited occurrence of the charismatic and legal-rational types of rulership and legitimacy.

These constructed types as perceived by Weber are scientific models or yardsticks for the measurement of respective attributes and as such they appear universally applicable in all power configurations. Because Sohm did not take into account the historical diversity in which the charismatic phenomena frequently appeared, not only in religious but also in various political and economic structures, Weber objected to Sohm's limiting charisma – a potentially promising sociological tool – to one particular historical case, the early Christian church, however important and precious it was to the believers. Harnack's interpretation of the early Western church's legal-rational development presented Weber with a ready-made scientific model for constructing the legal-rational type of rulership and legitimacy.

By its conceptualization, the charismatic type cannot last: it is always highly transitional and inherently unstable. Whether revolutionary or non-revolutionary, charismatic rulership soon reverts to a more stable, durable patrimonialism or transmutes itself into an unsteady legal-rational power structure. Being of relatively recent vintage, the legal-rational rulership is confined to a few modern societies and is beset with serious difficulties and challenges, which frequently result in total failure. One of the best-documented cases of unsuccessful experimentation with legal-rational rulership and legitimacy is the unhappy experience of the Russian provisional government which lasted less than eight months, from March to November 1917, ending eventually with the resurrection of the traditionalist (tsarist) patrimonialism within the confines of the sophisticated modern (Soviet) patrimonialism.

When all the limited experiences with charismatic and legal-rational rulerships are recognized, it becomes starkly clear how much 'territory' is *not* covered by these two types, not only in history, but also in the world today. Then, the most striking characteristic of the allegedly remaining 'third' type manifests itself as an almost escapist sort of residue: whatever political experience within the rulership-subjects configuration does not qualify as charismatic or legal-rational automatically belongs in that big residual bag.

Patrimonialism: Residual major type with its own subtypology

As originally conceptualized by Weber, patrimonialism was located within the traditionalist rulership and legitimacy as a variant in sharp contrast to feudalism. His early rough draft (1911–14) presents patriarchal-patrimonialism as an almost universal human experience, while feudalism, limited to some western-European societies, is conceptualized as a Western deviation from that universal model.

Unfortunately, Weber never returned to this very early, very rough, and very preliminary draft loaded not only with such a richness of historical evidence but also with several theoretical propositions which should be brought to greater precision on the basis of new post-Weber data. In particular, the dichotomy of universalist patrimonialism versus particularistic feudalism has received considerable support in modern historical research. Of course, patrimonialism is featured prominently in both the draft and the 1911–14 'revision' of 1920. Weber presents two additional and, in this context, extremely relevant dichotomies which must be integrated within this typology: 'oriental' versus 'occidental' city and 'caesaropapist' (state) church versus hierocratic (autonomous or independent) church. In this last section, this author suggests some integrative conceptualizations for these two sets of supportive segments and structures, respectively, of patrimonialist and pre-legal/rational domination.

An additional rationale for the proposition that patrimonialism is a residual major type to be modified according to modern research data is discernible in the impact of and Weber's reaction to Jellinek's theories of legitimacy. Weber repeatedly expressed his admiration for Jellinek's work in political sociology and constitutional and public law. However, when Jellinek offered an ambitious, but highly speculative, set of five basic theories of legitimacy (psychological, ethical, religious-theological, naked-power-oriented, and legal) to account for all the logically possible origins of the state (1919:184–229), Weber rejected all five on

44

the grounds that there is simply no historical (or pre-historical) evidence for any of them. The facts on the origin of the state have been lost in the immemorial past of humankind. He accepted only from the last one, 'legal legitimacy', its division into three subtypes, patriarchalism, patrimonialism, and feudalism, because these constructs were supported by ample historical evidence. (Weber also relabeled Jellinek's 'contractual' subtype as 'feudal'.)

Patrimonialism considers the entire power structure the private property of the ruler; feudalism considers it a purely contractual relationship; and patriarchalism considers it a family matter rather than property or law matter. Some critics have suggested that it was inappropriate for Weber to derive feudalism as well as patrimonialism from the patriarchal model because of the uniqueness of feudalism and its interdependence with the extended network of free cities and hierocracies which originated in the West and the absence of these structures outside the West. According to Hintze, Weber actually attempted to conceptualize feudalism mainly as the final result of the routinization of the charismatic type. Hintze considered this a very fruitful approach, which needed more elaboration (1962:87).

Once again in this area, as elsewhere, Weber's efforts were directed toward getting away from Jellinek's or anyone else's speculative thinking on all the various logical possibilities of legitimizing the origin of the state. Instead, he attempted to construct an empirically evidenced typology of *both* rulership and legitimacy, not only the latter, for he insisted that the two are analytically inseparable.

In a more general commentary on Jellinek's versus Weber's typological conceptualizations, Engisch said that Weber accepted from Jellinek only the term 'ideal-type' but not the normative definition and contents of Jellinek's typology, which was: '*Der ideale Typus . . . ist kein Seiendes, sondern ein Seinsollendes*' (The ideal type . . . is not what exists in actuality, but what ought to be) (1966:80ff). In contrast to that of Jellinek, Weber's typology is not a normative construction of what an ideal, 'best', or 'perfect government' ought to be but only a record of what actual patterning is experienced in real-life situations of the ruler-subject relationships irrespective of the norm.[2]

The concept of patrimonialism, of course, cannot be limited to Asia and the orient as some terms used by Weber's predecessors for the same power phenomena would seem to imply. The so-called 'enlightened despotism' – as if there is such a thing – in the West offers uncontroversial evidence for the re-emergence of Western patrimonialism after feudalism was defeated at the hands of the French, Spanish, Austrian, and other patrimonialist 'enlightened despots' of the period 1660–1815. Ironically then, feudalism as a 'stage' was not replaced by the subsequent 'capitalist stage', but by the almost universal phenomenon of patrimonialism which had also preceded it.

By the force of evidence modern post-Weber research has removed another limitation: the concept of patrimonialism in its magnitude as perceived by Weber cannot and should not be confined to history as any particular stage of any 'barbaric past' as the evolutionists would have it. The unwarranted insistence on the progressive stages of universal development, which was once an article of faith, is what actually prevented the discovery of modern patrimonialism. It cannot be limited to traditional and neo-traditional societies. On this issue there seems to be a consensus of those who have used the concept successfully in their own work (Uricoechea, 1980; Sheikholeslami, 1978; Divine, 1977; Akhavi, 1975; Gellner, 1975; Gellar, 1973; Schwartzmann, 1973; Lev, 1972; Bendix and Roth, 1971; Willner, 1966; Faoro, 1958; and others).

Incredible as it may sound, one can argue that Weber's conceptualization does much better analytically with the modern widely diffused phenomena of patrimonialist rulership and legitimacy than with the traditionalist. The substantive characteristics of both seem identical. The perfecting of these substantive attributes as invariably achieved by the modern patrimonialist power structures neatly fits Weber's original assumptions, for they only represent the logical extension of the same. The patrimonialist type of rulership has not ceased to exist with the dawn of the modern age. Not only has patrimonialism refused to die; it is the overwhelmingly dominant type of rulership and legitimacy today, much more so than seventy years ago when Weber first conceptualized it.

Patrimonialism and societal monism

Patrimonialism rulership is located within the somewhat larger context of societal monism, which refers to the unity/identity of the entire power structure in a society. It approximates one end of the conceptual scale and societal pluralism the other. *Societal monism* is to be clearly differentiated from the philosophical concepts of idealistic and materialistic monism imputed frequently in Western European literature to Hegel's and Marx's respective intellectual legacies.

In addition to patrimonialism, societal monism includes the various ruling elites, oligarchies (including hierocratic), usurpational, charismatic, and some revolutionary non-charismatic rulerships. On the basis of historical and contemporary evidence, this author (1979) suggested that societal monism be analytically separated into two variants:

1 political monism: the unity/identity of a power structure under a basically political rulership (imperial, royal, caesarist, dictatorial, one-party, etc.)
2 hierocratic monism: the unity/identity under a hierocratic rulership (papal, Calvinist, Dalai-Lamaist, and other priestly or religious-elderly).

For most of human history, including the modern age, patrimonialism has been by far the most frequent and durable type of rulership within both monistic variants. Any notion concerning power diffusion or differentiation contradicts the concept of patrimonialist rulership and legitimacy whether celestial, deist (the patrimonialism of the deity's earthly vicegerent), global, or more particularistic as in the numerous nationalistic variants of *Pater Patriae*. In modern symbolism, Man of Destiny, the Brightest Star in Mankind's Firmament, Greatest Man Who Ever Lived, and similar descriptions seem to be successfully replacing the various deist and celestial claims of the past.

Until now, only a few philosophers and ideologists endorsed the usefulness of the monistic versus pluralistic dichotomy, Berdyaev being one of the most eloquent among them (1948:187 ff). Sturzo used interchangeably the terms political, social, and statal monism (1946:90). Jellinek referred to the power structures and political rulership in the ancient world as being typically monistic; this included not only the great empires of Rome, Greece, Persia, China, and others, but also the tyrannical city-states and various ruling elites. He emphasized that, despite being surrounded by dualistic politico-ecclesiastic arrangements in medieval Europe, the Italian city-tyrannies of the fourteenth and fifteenth centuries were monistic in their basic power structure and legitimacy. Jellinek also said that the Church contributed much to the attractiveness and values of the monistic model for all the political structures to emulate by insisting on a well-functioning bureaucracy for its own monistic rulership (1919:316–323).

In modern monistic societies, according to Fischer, 'monism stands for the identity of political and economic domination' (1968:179). However, the ideological or religious aspects of and 'contribution' to the same identity cannot be safely suspended or considered to be gradually vanishing from modern monistic societies and therefore deemed insignificant. In his analysis of modern monism, Apter speaks of

the messianic leader who points out the dangers and noxious

47

poisons of faction. Many such leaders are charismatic who represent the 'one'. They personify the monistic quality of the system. To achieve such oneness, mobilization systems begin by politicizing all political life. . . . This is in keeping with monistic political belief. Conflict is not only bad, but also counter-revolutionary (1963:78).

Apter added that there are high priests and that 'the texts themselves are a blend of ideology and theology'. When he refers to '*modernizing autocracies* within the framework of neotraditionalism, using ritual to institutionalize political religion', he seems to be getting very close in substance, if not in terminology, to the conceptualization of modern patrimonialism within the larger context of societal monism (1963:98-9).

Patrimonialism: two subtypes

As a major type patrimonialism is divided into two subtypes:

Traditionalist patrimonialism is an impersonal rulership based on the sacredness of tradition and legitimized by religious or philosophical doctrines and by the charismatic principle of success particularly needed for newcomers and new dynasties. Of course, there are effective compulsory organizations integrated within the differential distribution of rewards and penalties in addition to the 'caesaropapist' or patrimonialist state church, subservient clergy, and the patrimonialist city as the ruler's (or provincial governor's) headquarters, military garrison, and storehouses.

Modern patrimonialism is a highly personalized, 'detraditionalized', and modernized rulership. Sacredness is supplied by the most attractive, totalist, all-embracing ideologies, philosophies, and non-theistic systems of beliefs offered to the disenchanted masses of the modern world. The system of differential distribution of rewards and penalties in the ruler's hands is perfected to the greatest possible degree of sophistication, as is the charismatic principle of success. Extremely effective multiple compulsory organizations to control each other are created by the rulership as an instrument of total domination. Through the monopoly of all the sophisticated means of communication, modern patrimonialist regimes frequently and quite successfully manufacture the ruler's pseudo-charismatic and pseudo-revolutionary images to camouflage the unlimited exercise of his personalized power.

The suggested propositions modifying Weber's original typology also reflect his own personal anxieties over the events he witnessed during and after World War I. In those few years before his death in 1920, Weber became convinced (and bitterly disappointed) that the humanist expectations for growth of human rights, national self-determination, and liberty in the world, cherished since the Age of Enlightenment, would not be fulfilled. To him, the world was becoming more enslaved and totalist, less free and democratic. As noted below (pp.53–5), Weber always played down the impact of technology and an advanced economy as an automatic and self-propelled promoter of democracy, human rights, and freedom of creativity, which, in turn, would inevitably bring some sort of perfect society.

Weber did not live long enough to experience the full fury of the twentieth century's various patrimonialist power structures and legitimacies from contemporary 'oriental despotisms' to 'dictatorships of the proletariat' or 'race'. Still, on the basis of some evidence which perhaps escaped others, Weber almost prophetically visualized the mushrooming growth of non-democratic, non-legal/rational, and (without explicitly using the next two terms) non-pluralistic and patrimonialist regimes everywhere in the world. These global trends in the post-war era would spread and intensify, and the inevitable, undesirable result would be more oppressed people on earth, whether they be ethnic, national, or religious minorities, peasant or factory worker majorities, or entirely submerged, stateless, unfree nations under foreign occupation.

What distressed Weber was the stark, ever-growing tendency of his age to push toward political/economic/ideological oneness and the evident attractiveness of that unity/identity pattern to the subjects and the administrative staff as well as to the actual power-holders. The 'enlightened despotisms', as if there ever are any enlightened ones, always seem to go in the direction of more power unity and less diffusion instead of the other way around, as prophesied by many great liberty enthusiasts in the long history of social thought.

There is much support for these propositions in Weber's last, mostly untranslated, writings (including his five essays on the 1905 Russian revolution and the non-revolutions of 1917, written between 1906 and 1919 and analyzed by this author, 1984:237–72), in his correspondence, the memoirs of his friends and students, and the biography written by his wife (1975).

The first president of the German Bundesrepublic after World War II, Theodore Heuss, recalls (1971) how many leading intellectuals and statesmen were profoundly shaken by Weber's continuous and implacable attacks against the German establishment, the Kaiser, the Junkers, the industrialists and their foreign and domestic policies. In 1911 Weber wrote to Graf Keyserling that the Germans were not a civilized nation or people with a refined and politically sophisticated culture simply because 'we never have had the nerve to behead one of our monarchs', as the civilized nations had (presumably France, England, and others). He felt that such an emotional experience in the German cultural heritage would have been a good lesson for all the future rulers of Germany.

If Weber had known of President Wilson's secret decision, in direct contradiction to his celebrated fourteen points declaration on the rights for self-determination, to exclude its application to the numerous stateless nations within the Russian tsarist empire, Weber would have criticized Wilson just as bitterly and furiously as he did the German and Russian imperialist governments. As Killen shows:

> The protection of Imperial Russian territorial integrity was
> . . . one of the firmest and least ambivalent elements of
> Woodrow Wilson's Russian policy. . . . By 1919, reversing
> their earlier support of self-determination, the Bolsheviks
> had become staunch supporters of Russia's traditional imperial
> boundaries. Wilson feared that encouragement of
> dismemberment – in the form of peace conference support for
> the new nations – might alienate politically uncommitted but
> still nationalistic Russians and turn them toward the Bol-
> sheviks as symbols of Russian nationalism (1982:65, 67 ff).

There are also in Weber's opus several very significant intellectual and scientific clues which amply and specifically 'legitimize' the major modifications of the concept of patrimonialism as advocated here. Only three among several such specific clues are suggested:
1 Hobbes's and Locke's conflicting interpretations of the social contract theory and the complexity of their impact on Weber;
2 false 'beatitudes' of technological and economic growth;
3 patrimonialist mythology, apparently still vibrantly in demand.

Scientific and intellectual clues in Weber's opus on modernity and patrimonialism

Hobbes-Locke controversy and its impact

There is a frequent tendency to polarize controversial issues in social thought throughout the centuries and at least one such oversimplified polarization is directly correlated to certain major misinterpretations of Weber's propositions on patrimonialism and modernity which overlook the complexity of the impact his predecessors made on him. Machiavelli and Hobbes are usually placed on one end of the doctrinal spectrum to speak for all the political pessimists; Locke and Rousseau are located on the other end to represent all the incorrigible enthusiasts of humanity's inevitably bright future. In Weber's judgment, in contrast to many others, whatever the definitive evaluation today of their scientific contributions on liberty, legitimacy, and power, the ethical-normative ideas of these four philosophers are clearly a major part of their respective systems of thought. As Deutsch pointed out, some still overemphasize 'a definition of power which aligns Weber with Machiavelli and Hobbes, the idea that there is no other order in the world than that introduced by some external power. . . . But there is a second idea of the world which we find in Locke . . . that it is also possible to imagine a self-ordering system'. Noting 'that there are often, in Weber's ideas, notions of balance, counterbalance, and development toward rationality', Deutsch concluded: 'So the world is not a completely Hobbesian system for Weber – neither for his cognitive nor for his evaluative thinking – and the comparison of Weber's world with that of Hobbes is an oversimplification of his ideas' (1971:118–19).

Thomas Hobbes's disillusionment with humanity's alleged inability to live in liberty reflects quite substantively the almost universal experience with monistic, patrimonialist power, and no one can argue with that. It has been pointed out above that there is a consensus on the misery and poverty of human history concerning the rulership-subjects relationship. Only different labels have been used to describe basically the same phenomena. While accepting the evidence, Weber did not share Hobbes's ethical-normative judgment that only an absolutist power structure and legitimacy is capable of securing peace and tranquility, which is preferable to the allegedly only other alternative of anarchy and chaos. Weber also rejected Hobbes's norm that, in order to safeguard order and peace, the people's original sovereignty once transmitted to the ruler in the initial social contract can never be recalled by the people.

John Locke, in contrast to Hobbes's notion of a perpetual chaos without an absolutist sovereign, advanced the idea of a contractually conditioned exercise of limited political power based on the doctrine of natural law and a renewable social contract, which the people could withdraw any time the ruler violated the general well-being (*bonum commune*) and his other responsibilities as defined in the social contract. Locke was able to point to some unique evidence in his own country and era of various impositions of limits on the ruler's absolutist power.

Locke's unrestrained enthusiasm for the ethical-normative

inevitability that the future will be dominated by the total and durable victory of the people's sovereignty and the final disappearance of monistic, patrimonialist rulership was received by Weber with appreciation coupled with skepticism. In his view, Locke and his supporters did not have as much historical evidence as Hobbes, although Weber anticipated that the future, perhaps in some instances, would substantiate Locke's pluralistic democratic predilections.

Weber's special affinity for Locke's legacy is clearly documented in his analyses (unfortunately widely dispersed throughout his opus) of the West's multifaceted, independent, or autonomous and autocephalous, centers of power with their own particular legitimacies. These are independent or autonomous hierocracies, religious revolutionary movements, feudalist structures and substructures within their complexity, free cities with their multiplicity, free universities, small but powerful sodalities of legal professionals, and others. To depict the significance, the novelty, or the 'illegitimacy' of their non-traditional and recent origin, Weber uses the terms 'usurpation' or 'appropriation' for the capture by these new centers of power of chunks or spheres of power which 'normally' belong to the sacred monistic rulership. Nothing comparable to this ever happened outside Western Europe and not all of Western Europe experienced the same phenomena. These historically new centers of autonomous/autocephalous power are classified here, however tentatively, as pre-legal/rational or pre-pluralistic types of rulership and legitimacy (see Charts 3.2 to 3.4).

According to Weber (and as substantiated by recent research), the initial and very crucial steps in this slow developmental process were three early Western patterns:
1 the separation of Roman Catholic canon law from the church's theology;
2 the separation of non-church, political law from canon law; and
3 perhaps most significantly, the separation of procedural law from substantive law.

The reception of Roman law, the Renaissance and the Reformation augmented these charisma-of-reason revolutionary trends toward ever-increasing diffusion and potential separation of the various spheres of power in the West.

Through his historical-comparative methodology, Weber was able to isolate the tremendous cost of the absence of these separations for the growth of freedom, especially in Islam after initial attempts at separation of Islamic law from theology were not actualized (1954:226, 250ff). Instead, the growth of patrimonialism remained basically undisturbed (see pp. 211–13).

In contrast, the unique and novel sources of power and legitimacy as analyzed by Weber offer an entirely different concept of a *new* social order. His propositions on various multiple processes of rationalization within and between the new centers of power elucidate his perception of a new societal configuration. In addition in all Weber's dispersed analyses concerning the Western medieval, experimentally pluralistic, distribution of power, there also seems to be enough substance to formulate a new definition of power that at least supplements, if it does not correct, his celebrated definition of power which, however incorrectly, identifies him as a 'positivist'.

Indeed, Weber's conceptualization of liberty, legitimacy, and power closely approximates Locke's sense of social order, but without Locke's dogma of the inevitability of and the blueprints for a perfect society, without the myth of social contract as the origin of the state, and without other utopian notions of Locke and his numerous successors. This is certainly a scientific advance on Locke's original legacy.

'Beatitudes' of technological and economic growth

The enthusiasm for the inevitably perfect future society as generated by the Age of Enlightenment and reflected in the writings of all major figures of social thought except Weber, especially Condorcet, Turgot, Saint-Simon, Comte, Marx, and Durkheim, was popularized by literally thousands of their followers. While the contents and the labels in various evolutionary theories of progress toward higher and better stages may change from one author to another, the common firm anticipation was that, at the end of the road, there would be a final, perfect society from which there would be no more need to develop because the ultimate had been reached. The means recommended may vary but fundamentally they can be classified under the scientific, technological, and/or economic labels.

Eight decades ago, Weber, in sharp contradiction to all this literature, scathingly – if his sarcasm can be expressed in one word – attacked the dogma of evolutionary utopia in the first place and the component dogmas that economic or scientific-technological development would automatically produce democracy and basic human rights for everyone. He argued that regression is just as plausible, perhaps even more so, than steadily going forward. He seems particularly annoyed with the dogma that the final unavoidable societal perfection will eliminate need for change, consequently freezing forever any further human potential because the highest plateau of human achievement will have been reached.

In his unceasing concern, expressed in numerous places, with basic human rights *vis-à-vis* the modern state, Weber postulated that the practice and protection of democracy and individual human rights are not an automatic consequence of change in social and economic conditions, as had been visualized in various reform and revolutionary programs from the Age of Enlightenment on. He stressed that changes in economic conditions alone have the least chance of effecting such desirable practices or respect for the rights of individuals and that because of the many vicissitudes connected with improvement of the material conditions of life, the growth and actualization of human rights cannot be left to the mysterious magic of economic self-development. Repeatedly, he emphasized his scorn for the beatitudes of economic growth that seem to be an obsession with the proponents of both sets of modernization theories, capitalist or socialist, irrespective of what kind of fabulous economic growth they prophesy (1906:346–7).

After rebuking all shades of German conservatives who, no matter what, complained against too much democracy and not enough authority, aristocracy, and respect for high office, Weber assured them that they need not worry, for history is overloaded with rejuvenations of aristocracies, ruling elites, and authorities of various sorts and the trees of democratic individualism are not allowed to grow so tall as to reach heaven:

> When it comes to material conditions only, and through these material conditions the directly or indirectly created constellations of economic interests, any reasonable investigation must end with the following: all economic weather indicators [*Wetterzeichen*] point in the direction of increasing 'unfreedom'. It is utterly ridiculous to attribute to high (advanced) capitalism . . . some special (elective) affinity for democracy or even freedom in any sense of the word. The only question to be asked is how democracy and/or freedom are possible at all or in the long run under the domination of advanced capitalism? Democracy and freedom in actuality exist only where the determined will of a nation, refusing to be ruled like a herd of sheep, firmly and permanently stands behind them. We, the individualists and partisans (*Parteigänger*) of democratic institutions, must position ourselves against the stream and the pressures of material interest constellations (1906:347-8 translation by this author).

In contradistinction to Montesquieu, Locke and others, Weber feared that, for his own age as well as for the future, simple limitations on the supreme rulership and constitutional separation of power into various spheres were not sufficient to protect citizens' liberty and freedom of action for voluntary associations. The new power configurations, especially modern economic structures (both capitalism and socialism and all those in between), carried by their respective bureaucracies and legitimizing ideologies, can be limited and balanced only by equally powerful competing autonomous and autocephalous structures within the society. If these structures are not nourished, the democratic, legal-rational governments will drift toward monistic patrimonialist rulerships.

To the liberal economists and all sorts of technological enthusiasts, Weber issued a stern warning that the political power structure may and, indeed does, manipulate economic development and that frequently the political rulership uses the entire economy of the country, large or small, to serve political goals as perceived by the rulership. Of course, ample legitimation for this is found in the various political systems of belief. Considerably more documentation for this is available in the closing quarter of this century than in the first quarter when Weber lived.

Repeatedly and most emphatically, Weber played down the impact of technology. It is not a magic wand. Technology alone, without other factors supported and controlled by autonomous and autocephalous power structures, does not make for liberty. On the contrary, technology is used by the modern patrimonialist rulerships as another means for attaining the political goals as engineered and executed by the rulership, in addition to the entire economy of the country, education, communication, transportation, sports, and all other means. Today there is evidence – plenty of it – that modern technology performs the role of faithful servant of the patrimonialist political rulership.

It is only fair to say that Weber's criticism obliterated the modernization theories deeply involved with one or other evolutionary scheme decades before the social scientists embraced them most enthusiastically. In the meantime, some evolutionists even insist on claiming Weber as one of their own pathfinders in spite of the fact that it has been repeatedly suggested that Weber *cannot* by any stretch of the imagination be considered an evolutionist, functionalist, organicist, stage theorist, etc. It was, indeed, documented that just the opposite is true: he was a consistent and sharp critic of these persistent theoretical trends (Bendix, 1965; Simey, 1967; Freund, 1969). After all, Weber occasionally used the term 'development' (*Entwicklung*), which alone surely cannot be interpreted as Weber's implicit evolutionism.

All these modernization theories maintain explicitly or imply unmistakably the same formula: modernization results in and equals democracy; all modern societies are by definition pluralistic/democratic; and all societies that are not democratic at the present are expected to enter at some point in the future into the inevitable stage of modernity or the final stage of modernization development. Simirenko said that the current

> debate over the meaning of modernity and modernization seems to be a restatement of the 19th century debate over the concept of evolution. The time is ripe to recognize that such a debate is more ideological than sociological. There is nothing wrong with having ideological debates in the profession, but these should be clearly labeled as such and not as theory (1970:391–2).

Patrimonialist mythology

Most typical in all the evidence on patrimonialist power patterning is – to use Weber's term – the liturgical satisfaction of public needs, political, religious, economic, etc. This is how the patrimonialist ruler, the Father of the Universe or Father of the Fatherland, discharges his duties of providing for the well-being of his subjects, his children, as glorified in patrimonialist mythology and legends. At the same time the liturgical satisfaction of his public needs secures the fulfillment of the subjects' obligations to him, like children toward their father, through the instrumentality of compulsory heteronomous and heterocephalous 'associations'. These compulsory structures are 'associations' only formally or in name: in actuality they are governmental agencies, collectively accountable for the satisfaction of the public needs as perceived by the ruler.

The patrimonialist rulership can achieve tremendous political successes through all kinds of monopolies of fiscal enterprises that are at its disposal. In the well-developed money economies, patrimonialism has not experienced a loosening of the elements of political control (as the modernization theories incorrectly predicted), but has gained numerous additional fiscal and economic means for more efficient political management and use of the entire country's economy. Those means are state financing of the economy, state fiscal enterprises, monopolies of trade both foreign and domestic, direct monopoly and ownership of anything desirable at the time for producing monies. With these means, the ruler is able to support a well-functioning patrimonialist bureaucratic staff.

In contrast to many still-current misconceptions of bureaucracy, Weber forcefully documented that patrimonialism fosters a steady growth of various sorts of almost 'rational' bureaucracies in which, of course, 'rationality' is politically perceived and interpreted to serve the desired goals as selected by the rulership. As such, it could deceivingly appear very close to what the Western concept of rationality is supposed, though never precisely defined, to mean.

The patrimonialist ruler, indeed, set apart by the quality of sacred, unlimited, total power in his hands, is above and beyond bureaucratic reach. Since he defines 'rationality' as formalized and practiced in his domain, the rules of the bureacratic games apply to anyone below him, but not to him. As long as he successfully maintains himself on the top – the charismatic principle of success – he also maintains the ownership of the entire economy and distribution of the differential system of rewards and penalties, abetted by his own supreme ideological pontifications. For this proposition Weber offered an array of historical evidence. To order his data, he proposed a conceptualization which is cited here only as a significant *clue* in his opus on patrimonialism and modernity (1956:633–44). Within the concept of patrimonialism Weber distinguished two, positively and negatively, privileged kinds of liturgical satisfaction of public needs:

Patrimonial-state socialism typifies negatively privileged liturgical satisfaction of public needs by imposing on all the status groups various liturgical services based on the universal obligations of all the subjects to the exalted patrimonialist rulership/state.

Patrimonial-state capitalism typifies positively privileged liturgical satisfaction of public needs by giving concessions to private trade and craft monopolies, in return, of course, for a high concession fee limited in time and for a substantive share of the profit, both determined by the rulership alone and based on the universal obligations of all the subjects to the patrimonialist rulership.

In both the negatively and positively privileged satisfaction of public needs, patrimonial-state socialism and patrimonial-state capitalism, it is only the patrimonialist political power structure that really counts. Total control is in the hands of the political ruler, and the economic privileges, the goods, and services are the means to serve the purposes of the ruler; this is what is strikingly emphasized in Weber's repetition of the term 'patrimonial-state'. The liturgical satisfaction of public needs, positively or negatively privileged, has been practiced in the modern age more than ever before.

The total subordination of the entire economy, whether it is a socialist, capitalist, or mixed economy, to the political power structure is the core of this conceptualization. Weber's exceptionally strong emphasis on patrimonialist political domination over, if not absorption of, the economic structure and the total use of all economic, communicational, educational, artistic, etc., means for the purposes set by the political rulership cannot be limited to history and set aside as irrelevant for the modern age. The same conceptualization makes absorption and use of the economic power spheres or structures by the political rulership in modern non-pluralistic societies clearly recognizable beyond dispute. In spite of these awkward tripartite terms, or whatever appropriate nomenclature will be adopted by future research, there is a patrimonialist theoretical model applicable for the advanced and developing non-pluralistic societies of today. Without benefit of the actual existence of patrimonial-state socialist societies (and, of course, there are more patrimonial-state capitalist societies today), Weber in 1911 apparently anticipated and even attempted to solve some current conceptual difficulties.

Perhaps one of the major scientific intents or by-products of this conceptualization, lost among the deficiencies of his 1911–14 early draft to which he never came back, is a simple, but significant, theoretical inquiry: 'What is the difference between *patrimonial-state socialism* and *patrimonial-state capitalism?*' The emphatic answer is that the peculiarities of the economic structure, be it socialist or capitalist, whichever way it goes – more toward socialism or more toward capitalism – are actually insignificant, for the domination of the political rulers over the entire economy of the country is so overwhelming as to make the economic structure just its helpless subordinate tool for the political goals as defined by the rulership. Naturally, this is a painful issue with many who have a strong predilection for one or the other legitimizing ideology. For the believers in the utopia of a classless society, who are disappointed by the reality of rigidly stratified patrimonial-state socialist societies today, the saving thought is that 'if it is not socialist, then it must be a capitalist or at least a state-capitalist society'. 'If it is not capitalist, then it must be socialist' is the sad song of the anachronistic *laissez-faire, laissez-passer* doctrinaires.

In analyzing the advanced non-pluralistic non-democratic societies it appears that most researchers continue to experience some insoluble problems which Weber anticipated before the emergence of such societies. What is seemingly lacking is an emphasis on, or even awareness of, the centrality and overall dominance of the political power above all other aspects of the same power unity/identity: economic, ideological, educational, communicational, recreational, etc. And this power configuration is the most crucial feature. For all practical purposes the absorption by the political power of all other spheres of life is the chief attribute of the patrimonialist type of rulership. The decision-making in all the 'other' matters also remains unquestionably in the hands of the political decision-makers. The rationale is that all aspects of life are serious political affairs or public matters which cannot be considered *sui generis*, separate, or private.

An overwhelming majority of social scientists define the Soviet Union as a developed or advanced, large-scale urbanized and industrialized society. Under the influence of the (now discarded) evolutionary theories, it is still generally assumed that the Soviet Union is inevitably approaching the model of the Western industrial nations. If the principal criterion of definition is the country's economy, then in various approaches the term 'state-capitalism' is used to describe the Soviet Union. Petersen said:

> To designate the Soviet Union as 'capitalist', which would seem to deny official Soviet claims completely, is merely the other side of the same coin. Such a designation follows Marx's dictum that a society – any society – derives its principal attributes from its economy, and not from what he termed the 'super-structure' of politics, social relations and culture. (1963:12–13)

Depending heavily on Trotsky's analysis of the Soviet Union as the culmination of despotism, some writers stressed that in history 'state ownership of the means of production has prevailed (the so-called Asiatic method of production)' (Lane, 1971:43). Discussing the impact of evolutionary ideas in the current analysis of the Soviet Union's power structure, Lane uses the term 'state-socialism' in the title of his work as well as for a subtitle (1971:34).

In a carefully executed empirical study of 306 top officers of the one party in the Soviet Union, Fischer concluded that 'it makes no sense to judge the Soviet future in Western terms. Most immediately, this means that in an advanced monist society the Captains of Industry are apt to be, and to stay, in a subordinate place politically'. He cited Barrington Moore, who also argued that if the Bolshevik rule 'proves anything, [it] proves the possibility of treating industry as a political instrument to serve political goals'. And they both reiterated that evidence indicates 'industry can be forced to continue in the role of servant' (1968:16ff), just as it has performed this role exceedingly well for almost seven decades.

In total contradiction to the modernization theories, so-called westernization and industrialization are not simply two names for the same process of development from pre-modern to post-modern (and modern in between if one insists on three 'evolutionary' stages). The history of tsarist and Soviet Russia demonstrates quite vividly that industrialization/modernization can be most successfully separated from 'westernization', pluralism, and democracy (see this author's 1971a:281ff, 304ff). This is increasingly applicable to post-Maoist China and all other patrimonial-state socialist and patrimonial-state capitalist power structures. The evidence for the entire set of propositions offered here can be derived from the recent history of several rapidly industrializing/ modernizing, but not democratizing, countries irrespective of their economic pretenses, programs, or labels.

In summary, one of the most significant and also frequently ignored propositions within Weber's intellectual and scientific legacy is his correlating the loss of freedom and growth of enslavement with the excessive rationalization of the new monistic patrimonialist power structure and legitimacy. It has been casually said that Weber in disagreement with the liberal economists had no doubts about the state's ability to command the economy in the future. The political power can be and frequently is in total control over the economic growth of an entire nation and of a multi-national empire, as nurtured by ideological values, beliefs, and sentiments. While the political power structure can take command over the economy and all other means available, the economy, of course, can take command over the polity. By applying the adjectival term patrimonial-state Weber recognized, whenever warranted by evidence, the primacy and dominance of the political power over all other aspects of power to the point even of total absorption of the economy. Today there is more evidence for it than ever before. Moreover, in some durable cases it is not only the economy and economic development that is used for political goals but also the media, education, prestige, sports, housing, the arts, mobility, occupations, and all other means available. And perhaps it has not always been well understood that this command is immensely enhanced when the blueprints for a perfect society and its corresponding ideologies legitimize the entire syndrome.

Weber's postulate and the test of validity was to present the evidence alone and there is no argument against sufficient evidence. Again the decisive question is simple: 'in which direction does the evidence go?' But this postulate and test were not shared by those who accused Weber quite unjustly of trying to dismiss economic determinism by pleading for political determinism instead.

Past and present apologetics for 'enlightened despotism'

Reference to the extensive literature glamorizing 'enlightened', 'benevolent', or even 'virtuous' despotism, which has been produced continuously from the Age of Enlightenment to modern times, dramatizes the irresistible appeal of the modern-patrimonialist type of rationality to some educated strata. The apologists for the various sorts of modern patrimonialism use almost identical arguments to legitimize their favorite rulership as Voltaire, Mercier, Mirabeau, Grimm, Helvétius, d'Holbach, Bentham, and many others did when they glorified their own particular 'enlightened' despot, such as Peter the Great, Frederick, Catherine, Gustave III (of Sweden), and especially the Roman emperor-philosopher Marcus Aurelius. They argued that history offers many examples of despots who were neither cruel nor stupid. To them 'enlightened despotism' remains defendable as an ideal instrument for progress, because the ruler can use his unlimited power in a rational way to serve the best interests of the state, which is too frequently but unjustifiably identified with the interests of the people.[3]

One of the most eloquent apologetics from the late enlightenment period was offered by Linguet, who expressed his preference for this type of rulership for the reasons of 'well-being and happiness of the people, who are the most numerous and most helpless (weakest) segment of the nation'. Absolutist rulership is the only one capable of imposing reforms. To Linguet sovereignty is property. Proprietor sovereigns 'can do everything in their states that a *paterfamilias* can do in his own household. Linguet criticized some liberals of his era who displayed their thoughtlessness by stigmatizing progressive and benevolent rulership with the odious name of (oriental) despotism. D'Holbach argued that '*le pouvoir absolu*' is very useful when the ruler 'removes abuses, abolishes injustice, corrects vices and reforms the customs'. And he exclaimed, 'Give the world more Trajans, Antonins, Marcus-Aureliuses and there will be no need to limit their power'. Others describe some 'benevolent' rulers as aging slowly surrounded by the admiration of their people 'as a father with his children' (Lortholary, 1951:138, 143).

A comparison with modern patrimonialist mythology is hardly necessary. A few recent works are Tumarkin (1983), Supek (1983), Djureković (1983a, 1983b, and 1982), and Tudjman (1981). In modern patrimonialism some legitimizing mythologies including the supreme leader's manufactured charisma (or pseudo-charisma) are usually debunked immediately after his overthrow. But if death removes him, his successors desperately try for

61

decades to keep his mythology alive in spite of overwhelming evidence to the contrary in order to secure their own legitimacy. It is not generally accepted that similar if not identical mythologies are major attributes typical of any modern patrimonialist power structure and legitimacy. However fantastic, these mythologies are not singular instances of deviation or personal aberrations of an individual ruler as the apologists have attempted to explain them away.

There is an ever-growing literature based on memoirs, diaries, observations, interviews, correspondence and the like, written by the closest associates of the Supreme One, some of them heirs presumptive, number two or three in line of succession. According to such documents the reality of power enjoyment and excesses are quite different from the fabricated glorifications of his alleged fairness, revolutionary idealism, and total dedication. In all instances the precise details of actual events in major decision-making, also supported by other participants, are incontrovertible. In practically all cases of modern patrimonialist rulership the palaces and extensive preserves inherited from the royal and other predecessors were not sufficient rewards for the worshipped Supreme One. While utilizing all these 'homes' with their full domestic service staff, enormous security details, and instant mobility equipment ready at all times, the modern patrimonialist rulers have added to this long list several formerly private and public estates and have built new ultra-extravagant palaces for their exclusive though rare habitation.

Modern and traditionalist patrimonialism compared

From patriarchal to patrimonialist rulership

Patriarchalism is defined by Weber as the personal rule of a master over his household based on the sacredness of tradition. The whole tribe or country is considered to be his household and the administrative staff is recruited from his extended family (1956:550). Patriarchalism is the most significant type of rulership among the pre-bureaucratic types. This is the rationale, perhaps not the only one, for the differentiation between patriarchal and patrimonial subtypes with the original traditionalist type. Patrimonialism uses a sophisticated bureaucracy to achieve its goal: patriarchalism does not need it at all.

Some norms limiting the patriarch's rule were not enacted in tradition, but only sanctified by it. The informality of these limits, however, makes them less effective, Weber said, particularly when the patriarch is a powerful personality loved or feared by his tribe.

For all practical purposes, personal subjection is what is crucial. Weber stressed that it is always uppermost in the subjects' minds that this actual living patriarch is their master. This makes his rulership unrestrained and any possible limits are left to his own discretion (1956:588). Patriarchalism and patrimonialism share this major attribute in common.

In larger territorial political units, however, the ruler needs a more complex administrative staff than the limited number of sons and sons-in-law available in a patriarchal household. As soon as such a staff under the strict personal control of the ruler develops, patriarchalism is of necessity transformed into patrimonialism. The former members of the patriarchal household are now treated as subjects. The rulership, previously understood to be exercised on behalf of and for the benefit of the members of the household, becomes the ruler's unlimited and unchecked domination. According to Weber, patrimonialism then is the political rulership 'over the masses by the Single One' with a personal, highly dependent, and strictly subordinated administrative staff (1956:659).

Needless to say, the former members of the patriarchal household do not always become patrimonialist subjects without a struggle. Therefore, the ruler must have the necessary means at his disposal to make the transition successful. Weber underlines that military force under the complete control of the rulership is the most efficient, if not the only means in the process of transformation from patriarchalism to patrimonialism (1956:595–8).

Patrimonialist ruler's bureaucracy: universal servant nobility

An elaborate system of differential distribution of rewards and penalties is the most significant means used universally by patrimonialist rulers through the instrumentality of a servile administrative staff, the servant notables. Weber repeatedly emphasized the universality of highly centralized patrimonialist bureaucracies: the interests of a patrimonialist ruler everywhere are the same and just as universal are the means available to assure the absolute loyalty of his servant nobility. Equally crucial for the continuity of patrimonialist rulership are religious/ideological doctrines, whether new or (more frequently) only shrewd reinterpretations of traditional dogma.

The traditional patrimonialist ruler creates his own personal staff for administration and support of his policies out of various groups of people extremely dependent upon him, people who will always be grateful to him for dramatically improving their lot: slaves, *coloni*, conscripted subjects, prisoners of war or unpaid debt, foreigners, members of persecuted national or religious minorities, persons of 'low birth', outsiders, strangers, and all other out-group members. In historical societies, after dissolving their previous relationships of bondage or indebtedness by virtue of his universal ownership of land, the patrimonialist ruler, according to his needs, elevates them irrespective of their past into the various ranks of his servant nobility. In addition to these abundantly available sources, if and when necessary, the ruler hires mercenary bodyguards or entire mercenary armies. Adventurers of all shades are welcome at his court and the self-interest of these people is carefully enlisted in opposition to the subjects.

His monopoly of trade, domestic and foreign, and the automatic and unquestioned possession of precious metals, furs, stones, woods, etc., provide the patrimonialist ruler with the cash to pay for the administrative and mercenary services he needs. Weber sharply criticized contemporary scholarship for persistently overlooking trade as historically an almost constant factor in the building and strengthening of patrimonialist centralized bureaucracies. The primary surge of a patrimonialist rulership without trade playing a significant role occurred only in the Mongol empire and a few other similar kingdoms. The patrimonialist (royal, imperial) trade monopoly can be found over the entire world from Polynesia to Africa just as much as in the great ancient and more recent oriental empires (1956:649).

Weber repeatedly made his major theoretical proposition based on solid evidence: in patrimonialism the economic means are firmly subordinated to the political power structure. When the ruler is the owner of the whole country, trade monopoly is not the foundation or origin of patrimonialism; just the opposite is true: the monopoly of trade is the consequence of the ruler's unchallengeable possession of political power (1956:650ff). With several interposed sentences here, as well as in other sections of his work, Weber tries to dramatize the universality of patrimonialist ownership in many historical societies. Through his political power position the ruler also has all possible advantages in the acquisition of various sorts of movable property, just like land, as he needs them: chattels (not only cattle, but in many instances human beings, especially women and children), precious metals, furs, etc. Neither are the beginnings of patrimonialist power structures anchored by necessity in trade monopolies nor did patrimonialism appear whenever there was trade. Weber also warned that if the term 'landlord' is used when discussing the patrimonialist ownership of the whole country, there is a need to emphasize that feudal overlordship is in substance quite different from and contradictory to patrimonialist ownership of the whole country's land and industry.

In spite of the recognized economic aspects of the compulsory organizations, no theories of economic determinism or even of economic domination over the political structure (whether feudal, traditional patrimonialist, or modern patrimonialist) are warranted. Critically focusing on the theorists of economic determinism, whether vulgar or non-vulgar, Weber emphasized that there is actually a consensus that military and/or judicial, whether separated from each other or not, are substantively political attributes.

The successful rulership simply continues over the ages to use all the economic means and values as they become available for the further solidification of the entire, basically political power structure. It is the rulership's absolute inseparable military-judicial-fiscal power structure which makes possible the decision-making in all vital matters.

In modern patrimonialism this political-economic-ideological identity, legitimized by popular doctrines of liberation, nationalism, egalitarianism, socialism, or some other non-theistic system of beliefs, is immensely enhanced by the facilities of modern technological advancement and media sophistication. Today there is a proliferation of political means far above the more limited means in traditionalist patrimonialism to achieve the political goals as determined by the rulership.

The next sections will analyze some typical attributes of patrimonialism, traditionalist and modern. Regrettably, it is not within the scope of the present chapter to examine all of them and their ranking, but some major attributes will be selected that will sufficiently indicate their communality.

Heteronomy and heterocephaly

The administration of the servant notables is heteronomous and heterocephalous. The ruler is their only lawgiver and their only chief. The members of the administrative staff have no right to hold office, no legal status, and, consequently, no independence from the ruler. Without giving a reason, the ruler has the power to withdraw from them the means of their livelihood which are at the same time the means of administration: they belong to the rulership.

Compulsory state agencies regulate the administrative staff and all other occupational groups as they develop. The liturgical satisfaction of the rulership's public needs through the instrumentality of compulsory heteronomous and heterocephalous state agencies is the central feature of patrimonialism. Frequently in the pre-patrimonialist past (patriarchal, tribal, or whatever classification is adopted) the kinship groups were the most ancient compulsory organizations that were collectively responsible to the ruler for obedience and more specifically for meeting the liabilities within their own group. However, Weber recognized that the most radical liturgical innovation/enlargement of these traditionally sanctified practices takes place when the patrimonialist ruler, on the basis of his already successfully established sacred and total power, imposes on all occupational groups the same kind of hereditary collective responsibility as that of the kinship groups. Frequently various mythologies of kinship extension on the newcomers are employed, but in any event the practical results are the same.

The ruler has the unquestionable power to accept or approve the old responsibilities, create or legalize new ones, or make them all compulsory for everyone. The ruler can give or withdraw from the organizations his monopoly on any products or raw materials in accordance with how satisfactorily they perform their obligations.

In modern patrimonialist societies, the so-called professional 'associations' of professors, artists, scientists, writers, physicians, lawyers, and workers' labor unions are not associations, in spite of the persistent use of the term. It implies some degree of voluntary sociation, freely associating with or equally freely dissociating from it; also it implies a degree, however variable, of autonomy and autocephaly for their members. There are none of these characteristics in a patrimonialist structure: all activities are political activities. In actuality, as well as in their constitutional provisions and bylaws, these groups are compulsory state agencies that were modeled from a variety of past patrimonialist experiences to regulate all the activities of all the subjects engaged in all the occupations.

These state agencies decide on the number, sex, age, and family background of prospective candidates before they enter school or training facilities. The agencies control the size and quality of professional schools, run the entire job market, and make all the appointments to all the positions for all the localities for there is only one employer, the rulership. Furthermore, as a matter of routine, the same state agencies use police or fiscally punitive measures against any offenders as well as manipulating the entire system of rewards through promotions, prestige, salaries, fringe benefits, including retirement, vacation spots, etc. To accept these state agencies, or even to label them, as labor unions or professional associations, is absurd.

It is quite a foolproof system capable of achieving the prescribed goals, which, needless to say, are not the goals of the 'members', but are the political goals formulated by the rulership for the *subjects* in the various professional and working areas.

Absence of ownership

Being personal servants of the ruler, the members of the staff are supported and equipped from the ruler's stocks, first in kind and later through various land privileges. These means of livelihood are also means of administration and are only temporarily given to the servant notables while their services last. Weber contrasted *benefices* and *fiefs*, the institutionalized means of administration and staff's support in patrimonialism and feudalism respectively (see Chart 3.3). Benefices are almost universal non-hereditary land-usufruct privileges on the patrimonialist ruler's land to support the patrimonialist administration. Income from the benefice is attached to the patrimonialist office and service and not to the person of the servant notable. All benefices are conditioned and terminated by the arbitrary will of the ruler. The servant notable is not entitled to any protection or reciprocity. It is always a one-way street, in sharp contrast to feudalism, which is a reciprocal relationship based on legal contractual stipulations. The patrimonialist ruler generally succeeds in repressing any attempts to make benefices hereditary.

Whenever the land, however, ceases to be the only or the most significant means of administration and support for the servant nobility, the ruler without endangering his patrimonialist power can safely afford the luxury of granting formal hereditary rights to his servant nobility on that chunk of land enjoyed by them previously as usufruct. Precisely at that historical moment the prestigious and salaried services – military, civil, or industrial – already made attractive earlier, become the only or the most significant source of support. As industrial enterprises become politically desirable (primarily those that manufacture military hardware), state-owned and state-managed industries multiply intensively. Some of the mercantilist regimes (patrimonial-state capitalist) in the West are remarkably similar to non-Western politically dominated rulerships, whether they are patrimonial-state socialist or patrimonial-state capitalist. Monopoly of banking, financing, and foreign trade are dominant features of patrimonialism entering the nineteenth and twentieth centuries as it moves toward accelerated technological development.

In modern patrimonialist societies the absence of non-political, i.e., non-public or private ownership, remains a major attribute.

And in comparison with traditionalist patrimonialism this absence of ownership is all the more comprehensive and oppressive. Djilas (1957) in a disarmingly simple way expressed his personally disturbing discovery of this universal experience in his own patrimonialist society which he helped to create and in which he held the number two position of power until arrested. While supporting Weber's major propositions (without knowing it), Djilas emphasized again and again the centrality and overwhelming domination of the political power over the economic and other aspects of life in the modern – to use his own term – 'totalist state' power structure. Djilas's question was 'Whatever happened to the principle of the withering away of the state?' The state was never before so powerful. He insisted that political power always plays a major role in *all* phases of the development of modern 'total statism' and that it will inevitably continue to do so: 'It is only through power itself that ownership can be exercised'.

In modern 'total statism' Djilas perceives a unique achievement (which is questionable), because according to him no other power structure, past or present, was able to deliver a complete fusion or total inseparability of (political) rulership and (economic) ownership: 'Other classes may be able to maintain ownership without a monopoly over power, or power without a monopoly over ownership.' Djilas then suggested the concept of sophisticated modern slavery that is put into practice when the rulership – 'the one and only party' or 'the new class' – monopolizes 'three basic factors for controlling the people': power, ownership, and ideology (1957:166–9).

In analyzing various definitions of ownership from Roman jurisprudence to modern legal systems, Djilas and similar dissenters in modern patrimonialism concluded that whatever the terminology and however it is laced by ideological images projected into the future, the owners are the persons who make the crucial decisions in acquisition, use, disposition, and other conventional acts by handling the entire economy of the country as their own private property. This is precisely what Weber had in mind when he constructed the concept of patrimonialism. The entire economy of the country, including the people as natural resources, is legitimately considered the private property of the rulership.

Dependency and discipline

Several critics of modern patrimonialist structures which they helped to build and ruled, for some time at least, agree that the new ruling elite including themselves is totally and hopelessly subordinated to the ruler as long as he successfully maintains himself on top. In the interest of preserving his own power and legitimacy, untouched and unchallenged, he must continuously struggle against any tendency of his closest associates to achieve a degree of prestige or power independent from him. Any manifestation of personal pride or feeling of personal dignity on their part is suspect to the ruler as potentially directed against his absolute domination and legitimacy and it must be suppressed as an act of treason.

Only the religionlike absolute devotion and loyalty of all, the common people as well as the members of the ruling elite, to the Father of the Universe (or of the Fatherland) is accepted as a supreme virtue. The ruler cleverly exploits the hostility against the members of his ruling elite: they are used as 'scapegoats' and blamed for the suffering of the common people and the shortcomings of the administration. By falling from grace they have lost not only those segments of power delegated to them and luxurious living according to rank, but also their place in history.

As a matter of fact these typically patrimonialist characteristics, as suggested above, were formulated by Weber in his analysis of the relationship between the traditional patrimonialist ruler and his servant notables (1956:661ff). Seven decades later the same characteristics still summarize extremely well the experience of many members of the modern patrimonialist ruling elites. The ruler's discipline over them and their dependency on the ruler are immensely strengthened by ever-growing technologically sophisticated systems of instant and continuous control in the ruler's hands. Moreover, in modern patrimonialism double- or even triple-control systems are designed to check on each other's delivery, whereas in traditional patrimonialism there was only one.

The instant replacement of any ruling elite member (including the heir presumptive selected by the ruler) is one of the major attributes that disenchanted former members report extensively and with the greatest personal pain. Almost identically with the tsarist *mjestničestvo*, Confucianist literati, and Islamic ulama from the past (see pp. 199–201, 211ff), today's patrimonialist rulers have not only large pools of candidates anxious to replace the disgraced ones, but also several institutionalized pools of aspirants instead of the single one in traditionalist patrimonialism. Although they have been noticed by others, Derek Scott has more systematically analyzed some of the parallel pool systems of eager candidates (1961:152–75).

Weber noticed the historically frequent occurrences of total oblivion of formerly powerful members of the patrimonialist ruling elite who became unpersons – persons who never existed in the first place. However, the modern literature (see pp. 61–2) reports in great detail many instances witnessed throughout the twentieth century – to use Weber's words once again – of such sudden jumps from nothingness to the precarious omnipotence of being the ruler's favorite followed by a dramatic downfall.

It would be a gross oversimplification to dismiss some of the recent media-belabored cases of downfall as a consequence of an unsuccessful succession game for the disgraced individual. The pattern is, indeed, universal and it potentially covers all the members of the patrimonialist ruling elite equally from the highest to the lowest ranks. Lane (citing Aron and others) said that instead of the general liberation predicted as inevitable by Marx the modern patrimonialist power structure and legitimacy reduces the entire society to a total obedience *vis-à-vis* the exalted ruler: 'The elite must be monistic because otherwise all economic and political power will not be concentrated at one source which is a necessary condition for planning in a collectivized economy' (1971:51).

The convergence of the three interdependent dichotomies within the types of pre-legal/rational and patrimonialist rulerships and legitimacies

Karl Jasper, Paul Honigsheim, and other close associates of Weber have noticed his abhorrence of hasty conceptualizations, superficial labeling, and unsound definitions, particularly when in his cautious judgment there was not sufficient evidence to warrant conceptual and theoretical settlement. Instead he attempted to avoid all these 'temporary fixes' whenever he could, believing that his 'substance' was powerful enough and that it could be classified or labeled by implication or perhaps later.

> Weber did not care about the systematic presentation of his thinking. . . . And he attached no importance whatever to the form in which he presented his wealth of ideas. Once he got going, so much material flowed from the storehouse of his mind that it was often hard to force it into a lucid sentence structure. And yet he wanted to be done with it quickly and express himself as briefly as possible, because new problems from the realm of reality constantly crowded in upon him (Marianne Weber 1975:309).

All three of the closely interrelated dichotomies to be presented now –

1 hierocratic church versus patrimonialist church (religion) and clergy
2 feudalist versus patrimonialist (political) administration
3 free city versus patrimonialist city
– have a number of terminological, definitional, and at times some (minor) conceptual problems. Here this author proposes to resolve them by suggesting certain modifications in the light of post-Weber research.

One of the three dichotomies is relatively explicit, the other two are more implied and have to be unearthed from unlikely places. All three display varying degrees of finalization, but they all represent logically and substantively inseparable aspects of Weber's intellectual and scientific search for the basic 'whys' in cultural and societal contrasts. As essential elements of the same configuration they converge to support the notion of achievement of Weber's typology of rulership and legitimacy, reinforcing his extensive research on the presence of patrimonialism and the absence of viable and lasting alternatives in many historical and modern societies.

Dichotomy 1: Hierocratic church versus patrimonialist church (religion) and clergy

The basic characteristics of hierocratic churches, which have varying degrees of freedom from the political power structure and its legitimacy, are in sharp contrast to the basic characteristics of those groups of servant notables who run for the ruler his religious department of state, his state church. A conceptual scale, in which hierocratic independency, autonomy, autocephaly, or self-rule and patrimonialist non-hierocratic dependency of the state churches occupy the opposing ends, appears scientifically warranted.

To capture analytically all the religious power structures that challenge or at least attempt to differentiate themselves as *sui generis* from the power unity/identity under political rule, Weber suggested a conceptualization of hierocracy as a rationally and bureaucratically streamlined religious or priestly/elderly power. He defined it in general as the religious authority to rule supported by the sole right to administer, distribute, or withdraw sacred or religious values. There is no report here on certain deficiencies in Weber's impatient attempts to relate the more traditional concepts such as 'church' and 'theocracy' with his own, certainly most promising, 'hierocracy'.

However, Weber repeatedly emphasized that Western medieval hierocracy was uniquely differentiated or even independent at times from the political power and frequently crossed its path, in the sense of contradicting it. At least for sociological considerations, he said, Western medieval culture was much less monistic (*Einheitskultur*) than were the totally monistic cultures of Egypt, Tibet, Israel, China, Japan, Russia, Islam, and with certain modifications, the ancient Hellenistic and Roman cultures (1956:721–2). He also attempted to specify certain events in the histories of these countries as the actual beginning of the unity/ identity patterns.

Weber was aware of, but did not bother to separate analytically, the monistic hierocracy, the power structure which absorbs the political aspects of power unity/identiy, from the hierocracy which, whether independent or autonomous, is continuously at least attempting to challenge the co-existing political rulership. He speaks of a few cases of Calvinist hierocracy in the West on one side and of the Western powerfully monistic states (*Einheitsstaat*) of the Lutheran and Anglican Reformation and of the Catholic Counter Reformation, foremost in the monistic states of Spain and Bossuet's France, on the other side. Both the Reformation and Counter Reformation monistic states were dominated by the decisive attributes of the power unity/identity under political rulership (1956:721ff). The early modern 'enlightened despotism' successfully destroyed the hierocratic achievements of the previous centuries. But Weber implied that even in these instances of religious subordination, historical memories of the once-independent hierocracy still represented some kind of potential revolutionary inspiration.

According to Weber a strong indicator of independent hierocratic development, the existence of an independent or at least autonomous hierarchy of offices with its own hierocratic system of education, is a basic condition for the development of rational theological speculation. The emergence of rational theology and theological priestly education is the strongest bulwark of a hierocratic power structure.

A fully developed church hierarchy with its dogmatic structure and especially its penetrating educational system (including universities) cannot be uprooted, because the hierocratic power is based on the principle that one must obey God rather than man for the sake of one's well-being in this life and the afterlife. This is the oldest and, until the time of the Puritan revolution and 'human rights' by far the most permanent and invulnerable limitation on all political power structures. Weber frequently elaborated the points that only Western hierocracy, bureaucratically most rationalistic and streamlined, developed, in its own interest to be sure, a rational procedural law in addition to the rational and frequently changing contents of canon law; and that above all hierocracy threw its total weight in favor of the reception of rational Roman law. He also emphasized the continuous formation of law on the basis of rational jurisprudence by the hierocracy in the West (1956:716, 721ff).

Supporting Weber in light of new historical research, Brunner repeatedly stressed the need for precise evaluation of the total cultural context: not only must economics, law, and constitution be scientifically investigated, but the relationship of the church and the worldly order must be carefully taken into account as well. This relationship is probably of much greater significance than is commonly thought (1956:115). Brunner also suggested that in the West the undecided war between the hierocratic and political power structures finally leads in the long run to a cultural context in which law and liberty retain validity (*Geltung*) and in which a rationally formed law continues to grow (1956:71–2). He pointed out that while the conflict between religiosity and rationality is a matter of relatively recent concern, Western Europe early in its development experienced ever-increasing rational trends in the church, her constitution, her canon law, and in scholastic philosophy. All these trends toward greater rationalization were lacking everywhere else including the loci of Christian cultures outside Western Europe (1956:18–19).

In spite of the rarity of this type of peculiarly labile and fluctuating state-church relationship as compared with the almost universal unity/identity of power under a political or hierocratic head, Weber argued that, in the West at least, this type did gradually impose a peculiar dualism, which was the first step toward the rise of *plural* autonomous and diffused power structures. This long developmental process displayed several varieties, from the earlier structures, in which the claims for hierocratic supremacy were successfully materialized for a period of time, to later structures, in which the hierocracy was not able to avert defeat by the political rulership. But this experience of independence and ability to struggle created ineradicable memories and strong cultural values that offered differential ideologies and a choice of loyalties.

The term 'hierocracy' should not be used (Weber himself was not always consistent on this) when a specifically autonomous structure is absent, even though a group of the ruler's servant notables who specialize in religious affairs are differentiated, though only formally, from the rest of the ruler's bureaucracy and designated as a clergy. In that context they are the 'religious specialists', an extension of the same patrimonialist bureaucracy. To speak of a 'dependent hierocracy' is a contradiction in terms:

'-cracy' means power to rule. An outstanding Russian ecclesiologist Anton Kartašev, who was the minister for religious affairs in the Russian provisional government of 1917, said that Peter the Great, in spite of his success in technologically modernizing old Russia,

> was unable to break and completely destroy the deep
> Orthodox tendencies toward a sacral-historic theocracy.
> Paradoxically the image of the Russian tsar appears two-faced.
> According to the letter of the constitutional legislation and
> his actions he is at one time a worldly absolutist monarch,
> then at another time a theocratic *basileus*. However, the
> church, faithful to the old Byzantine ritual of consecrating her
> own tsar, looked upon him solely from the oriental monistic
> point of view as a charismatic biblical tsar, as the head of the
> . . . Orthodox theocracy, which ideally should embrace all
> nations (1948:97 translation by this author).

Casey's statement that the Tsar 'was *de iure* and *de facto* supreme arbiter in all decisions affecting faith and morals' (1946:18) is one of the major characteristics applicable to all patrimonialist rulers. Obviously, from the point of view of liturgical preservation of patrimonialism the ruler is never interested in or sympathetic toward systematic, rational, or changing interpretations in either theology or ethics. The ruler's decision-making in purely religious matters is just as absolute and unlimited as it is in all political and economic affairs. The patrimonialist ruler is the head of the church, the head and lawgiver for the clergy, which exists formally and in name only; he is the deity's vicar on earth, if not the incarnate deity himself. Consequently the designation 'patrimonialist church (religion) and clergy' appears logical and warranted, because it is supported by evidence.

The non-hierocratic state churches are almost universally present in a number of well-documented case studies throughout history. (For a case study on Russia, tsarist and Soviet, see this author's 1968 article, and for more specific characteristics see Chart 3.2). When Weber discussed substantively the numerous non-hierocratic cases in Christianity or elsewhere, he never failed to emphasize the absence of various hierocratic attributes in every one of them. His concern with both actual and formal facts was the most persistent feature in his entire research.

CHART 3.2

The conceptual dichotomy: hierocratic church versus patrimonialist church (religion)

Hierocracy	Patrimonialist church (religion)
A	
Differentiation of religion (church) from the rulership/ ownership: hierocracy – independent or autonomous/ autocephalous power structure, deviation from patrimonialism	Identification of rulership, ownership, and religion (church) – universal patrimonialism
Peculiarly labile relationship between hierocracy and rulership	Stability in structural patterns and relationships
Hierocracy continuously crossing the path of political rulership, challenging political decisions and imposing limitations on the ruler's power	Rulership's total domination over religion (state church)
Religious affairs belong to the ecclesiastic sphere or competency.	Religious affairs belong to the political sphere or competency.
B1	
Hierocracy: international, national, regional, local	Universal spiritual bureaucrats of the ruler: religious officials a part of political machinery, a department of state
Autonomous	Heteronomous
Autocephalous	Heterocephalous
Economic self-rule	No economic self-rule
Bureaucratic organization of their own	No bureaucratic organization independent of the ruler – patrimonialist bureaucracy
Specific style of life for the clergy	No specific style of life for the ruler's religious specialists
Ideology of their own	No ideology of their own, patrimonialist ideology only
Formal education, ecclesiastic universities the only universities in existence, and a high degree of academic freedom	No formal education, no universities, and no academic freedom
B2	
Patterns of twofold areas of conflict and consensus	No conflict: if any conflict develops, it exists only until the

Hierocracy	Patrimonialist church (religion)
B2—*continued*	
1 Outside the church: between hierocracy and rulers, feudal lords, vassals, subvassals, free cities, etc.	ruler makes his choice by siding with one or other conflicting group.
2 Within the church: between the hierocratic clergy with their charisma of office and various religious movements, revolutionary and reform-oriented, with the charisma of their founders	
a) Monasticism: new reform and revolutionary structures within the church	No monastic structural and functional variety: a single monastic order only
Rationality in monastic practices	No rationality in monastic practices
Monastic ability to impose radical reforms	No monastic ability to impose any reforms
b) Sectarianism: new structures outside the church, but still within society, underground sectarianism highly exceptional	Underground sectarianism only: messianic, millennial, utopian, escapist
C	
Religious and metapolitical legitimacy controlled and at times denied by hierocracy by imposing ethical or moral limitations and fostering rational and revolutionary doctrines and ideologies against the political ruler	Moral, spiritual and metapolitical sanctification (and also magical support) for the patrimonialist rulership not only unchallenged but actively reinforced by new or reinterpreted traditional monistic/patrimonialist ideologies and doctrines
Systematized rational theology and ethical systems	No rational theological or ethical systems
Independent and rational canon law	No canon law independent or differentiated from the ruler's laws
Procedural law emerging from canon law and theology	No procedural law: no differentiation from substantive law
Fusion of ecclesiastic, religious, and political power seen as gradually less appropriate pattern and of decreasing societal or cultural value	Identity of ecclesiastic, religious, and political (economic) power-image of celestial harmony and unity – perhaps the highest societal or cultural value

Traditionally in European studies the power unity/identity in which the (Christian) church is subordinated to a political rulership, especially in the Eastern Orthodox empires, Byzantium and Russia, was labeled 'caesaropapist'. Weber inherited this, what he called 'inadequate,' term. Although in Germany Ziegler (1953:81–97) and Beck (1954:94–5) enumerated significant objections to its continuous use, the term remains current in the English-speaking world. When discussing absorption of religious structures by political rulerships, Morrison (1969) used the term 'regal pontificalism' and still occasionally 'caesaropapism' to replace the terms 'royal' and 'imperial theocracy'. His 'regal pontificalism' is certainly an improvement when the fallacies of 'caesaropapism' are considered.

It is proposed here that this term be discarded because it presupposes dualism and a division or separation of powers, which were unknown in the structures labeled 'caesaropapist'. It projects the conceptual tools of modern man – religion and world, church and stage, religious and 'secular' or temporal – backwards into the centuries in which these conceptualizations did not exist. Further, putting these two words together would imply the potential quality of two offices imperial and papal, while the generally accepted meaning of the term assumes the complete subordination of the church to the state. The Byzantine and Russian rulers, for example, never assumed the title of 'pope' and could not possibly do so, because the papal office was not recognized. Especially after the 1054 division into Western and Eastern Christianity it was considered heretical usurpation. From the time of the belated and still very much reluctant acceptance of dualism in the medieval West, 'caesaropapism' appears to be a Western-culture-oriented value which expresses Western contempt for the assumed artificiality of uniting two allegedly incompatible forces into one entity, while in total contradiction the power unity/identity in patrimonialist societies represents a harmonious solidarity of all equally subordinated groups of people united in liturgical service to the exalted ruler. The contrast between the presence and absence of hierocracy in its fundamental features is almost identical with the other two typological dichotomies to be introduced next.

Dichotomy 2: Feudalist versus patrimonialist (political) administration

Rejecting the dominant theoretical assumptions of his era, especially the various evolutionary and stage theories, Weber kept contrasting some basic attributes of patrimonialism and feudalism. His insistence on the significance of this contrast for theoretical purposes seems today even more justified by new historical research that either followed him or was independent of him.

Without any sequential or numerical ordering, perhaps even without determining the final selection of the attributes, Weber offered a well-honed typological contrast of the feudalist, almost independent, autonomous, autocephalous political administration of the feudal lords, 'the king-makers', and their vassals, subvassals, and knights versus the totally subordinated, heteronomous, heterocephalous political administration of the ruler's servant notables, patrimonialist bureaucracy, or patrimonialist administrative staff. The contrast is most striking at the top: a figurehead king totally at the mercy of his feudal lords, vassals, etc., versus the unlimited, absolute patrimonialist ruler, the owner of all the land and all the people, the head of religion. In his early (1911–14) rough draft he contrasted *ständisch*-feudalism and patriarchal-patrimonialism as the two variants or subtypes of his traditionalist type of rulership (1968:1006–1110).

In the early Western development the patrimonialist means of administration, owned by the ruler, were gradually appropriated and eventually became legally owned by members of the feudal aristocracy including vassals, subvassals, and knights. Weber emphasized how crucial was this appropriation of hereditary ownership in the early Middle Ages (1956:149). In contrast to benefices in patrimonialism, *fiefs* were the Western feudal aristocracy's hereditary land-ownership grants which supported its military, judicial, and legislative rulership.

This successful imposition of hereditary rights by the incipient feudal aristocracy against total land ownership by the patrimonialist ruler did not take place universally as is frequently assumed. Just the opposite is true: it was a highly exceptional, particularistic deviation from universal patrimonialism that occurred in some Western European countries, not in all of them. Elsewhere the land remained the property of the ruler. The Western medieval usurpation of the ruler's power represents for the first time in history a major durable diffusion at the same time of ownership as well as rulership in the hands of the feudal lords, vassals, subvassals, and knights. Outside the feudal hierarchy there was additional appropriation of rulership and ownership by numerous free cities and by independent or autonomous hierocracies. This gradual segmental appropriation of the ruler's power structure ended in the long run with the collapse of patrimonialist rulership in all those particular areas of Western Europe where the structures of feudalism, hierocracy, and free cities emerged.

In all the historical-comparative cases such as the Byzantine, Japanese, and other empires (see Appendix) that various historians at times considered marginal to either patrimonialism or feudalism, the most recent research has documented that in most instances the patrimonialist rulers of these great and durable empires when challenged, succeeded in remaining the sole owners of the land and formally or informally prevented the members of their patrimonialist staff from becoming hereditary owners. (For Russian patrimonialism, modern and traditionalist, see this author's 1984 and 1971b respectively.)

The fundamental polarity runs consistently through a wealth of research materials accumulated by Weber (1956:552–3, 639–40, 658–61ff). The separateness (*Scheidung*) between patrimonialist and feudalist societal structures was to him of fundamental significance for the entire sociology of rulership before the emergence of the modern legal-rational state (1956:554). The contradictory characteristics of the two dominated the totality of the respective cultures most emphatically. So basically contradictory are their characteristics that they may be located at the opposing ends of a continuum where all of historical reality fills the scale between the two extremes (see Chart 3.3).

CHART 3.3
The conceptual dichotomy: Feudalism versus patrimonialism

Feudalism	Patrimonialism
A	
Quantitative diffusion of political power and of ownership in the hands of many feudal and hierocratic lords and the free cities' elected burgomasters, judges, etc.	Totality of all power in the ruler's hands undifferentiated or only formally differentiated/separated: no free cities; no independent (autonomous) hierocracies
B1	
The administration of the feudal aristocracy is autonomous and autocephalous.	The administration of the servant notables is heteronomous and heterocephalous.
The right to hold office is a legal title, usually transmitted by a legal act, including privilege, concession, rent, purchase, etc.	No right to hold office
The ruler has no power to withdraw the title, once transferred, except for treason as judged by his peers.	The ruler has power to withdraw the land for no reason.
This legal status enhances the political and economic independence of the feudal aristocracy.	No legal status or independence for the servant notables

Feudalism	Patrimonialism
B1—*continued* No compulsory state agencies	Compulsory state agencies regulate the administrative staff and all other occupational groups.
B2 All means of administration belong to the feudal lords (also vassals, subvassals, knights) as their private property (fiefs).	All means of administration belong to the ruler (benefices).
B3 The ruler's discipline and the feudal lord's dependence are non-existent. The ruler's arbitrariness severely undermined or permanently blocked.	The servant notables' dependence on the ruler and the ruler's discipline over the notables are absolute. The total personal dependence of the servant notables eliminates any limitations or checks on the ruler's arbitrariness.
B4 The ruler's helplessness against the impersonal aristocratic solidarity based on their own social status and honor. The status honor of the feudal lords and their loyalty to purely contractual mutual obligations are the only security the ruler has.	Absolute personal power of the ruler; no solidarity of the servant notables against him; no social status or honor of their own without the ruler's grace. The ruler's security unlimited; no contractual and no mutual obligations: only one-way obligations.
B5 Minimization of the ruler's power and a decrease in the number of administrative functions. The elaborate hierarchical structures are correlated to the differentiation of offices. Diffusion of power. Derived not from patriarchal model, but from routinized (family or office) charisma and possibly other sources	Maximization of the ruler's power and an increase in the number of administrative functions. Extreme simplicity of the entire social structure: no power diffusion/separation. All administrative offices develop from the ruler's household. Derived from patriarchal model.

Feudalism	Patrimonialism
C	
The dominant political and societal ideology is centered in the knight, vassal, and (rarely) in feudal lord, never in the king.	The dominant political and societal ideology is centered in the omniscient, omnipotent, godlike ruler or God's substitute on earth, Lord of the Universe, owner of the globe and humankind.

Dichotomy 3: Free city versus patrimonialist city

Both conceptual scales, patrimonialism versus feudalism and patri-monialist versus free city, should reinforce the general proposition against the cherished myth of societal evolutionism – a myth that strangely survives in spite of so much damaging evidence against it. In contradiction to various evolutionary schemes using sequential stages, the free cities *did not replace but co-existed for centuries* with feudalism. To Brunner (1956) the free city represents a special aspect of the feudal societal type. To Bloch (1961:354, 355) it is 'a foreign body in feudal society':

> It was there . . . that the really revolutionary ferment was to be seen, with its violent hostility to a stratified society. Certainly these . . . urban groups were in no sense democratic. . . . But by substituting for the promise of obedience, paid for by protection, the promise of mutual aid, they contributed to the social life of Europe a new element, profoundly alien to the feudal spirit properly so called.

The free city as it developed in the medieval West accumulated considerable economic power over the centuries which was used to bargain for political gains, especially for the exemptions from papal and royal jurisdictions granted by various city charters. But independent or autonomous economic power was not the only or the most dominant feature of the free cities. Since there were so many of them in relatively small political territories, the free cities displayed considerable political power, including military, which was based on religious sodalities of all their citizens and their personal military obligation to defend the city walls. Religiously inspired brotherhoods and equality of all citizens were probably a source of immense gratification for the citizens in their continual struggle against political and hierocratic monism.

Any potential alliance of the free cities could be a deadly affair for a Western rulership, imperial, royal, feudal, or hierocratic, and the free cities frequently and successfully used this threat.

81

The support that the free cities provided to the various actually revolutionary religious movements (before and after the Reformation) against the political and hierocratic establishments was one of their major achievements, which in the long run contributed toward eliminating for several centuries societal monism and promoting the growth of nascent pluralism in Western Europe. Frequently the citizens refused the religious services of the members of the hierarchy and diocesan priests, whom they accused of corruption and betrayal of Christian ethics, and insisted that only the members of the mendicant and other reform-oriented religious orders were welcome as their ministers and confessors. And they financed or granted them permission to build their monasteries and churches within the city walls.

CHART 3.4

The conceptual dichotomy: Free city versus patrimonialist city

Free city	Patrimonialist city
A1 The free city is sharply differentiated in procedural and substantive legal, as well as in constitutional, documents from all other spheres of power structures: political, religious, and economic.	The patrimonialist city is juridically indistinguishable from the rest of the patrimonialist power structure; it is the ruler's headquarters and a dwelling place for the ruler's servant notables, storage, military garrisons, etc.
A2 Various differentiations between religious and political dominations and quantitative diffusion of political and economic power produce a change in value-systems.	No differentiation of political, religious, or economic power spheres; all united in the ruler's hands; no change in value-system unless the ruler introduces it.
A3 Interdependence of the free city with other supporting power structures outside the city: hierocracy, various revolutionary religious movements, free universities, legal professionals, feudal structures with the substructures of vassals, subvassals, and knights.	Absence of the free city's institutions and other supporting power structures outside the city.

Free city	Patrimonialist city
B1	
Autonomy and autocephaly are taken for granted and frequently lead to independence, factual and informal, at times also formal.	Heteronomy and heterocephaly are absolute: the patrimonialist ruler is the city's lawgiver, supreme judge, and chief executive, and the only one.
B2	
Elaborate diffusion of economic power structures within and outside the free city.	Ruler's ownership of land, people, and their industry; pre-rational patrimonial-state capitalism.
B3	
Independence of the free city from the ruler, feudal lords, or church hierarchy; in practice total exemption from their respective jurisdictions.	Total subjection of the patrimonialist city-dwellers (including merchants and artisans) to the ruler, who is also the supreme merchant and the head of religion in addition to his monopoly of political and economic power.
B4	
Considerable military power accumulated over centuries through almost regular alliance of many cities against their antagonists, based on the religious sodalities of the free citizens with obligations to serve and to supply their own equipment.	Absence of the patrimonialist city's own military or police power as a consequence of the ruler's unlimited power: it is a dwelling place for his military and police forces.
B5	
Absence of tribal and kinship ties based on magic in the value-systems of the free cities; among others, 'the free city's pure air makes a man free' irrespective of his serfdom or bondage of any kind.	Presence of magical ties of the patrimonialist city-dwellers to their respective clans, tribes, or castes; various value-systems and institutions dominated by magic.
C	
An ever-increasing variety of religious, political, legal, economic, philosophical, and	Absence of hierocratic, feudal, bourgeois, revolutionary religious movements' and legal

Free city	Patrimonialist city
C—*continued*	
other doctrines (including rationalism vs. voluntarism) fostered by the free city through city-sponsored free universities and other supporting power structures outside the city; legitimation of the rulership frequently challenged, at times successfully.	professionals' ideologies; only one ideology sanctified by religion: the glorification of the ruler and of his divine or superhuman attributes and achievements. It supplies a powerful legitimation.

In patrimonialism there are no free cities; its cities are only the capital cities, headquarters of the patrimonialist ruler or his provincial governors with the courts, military garrisons, storehouses, trade outposts, etc. The city is juridically indistinguishable from the rest of the patrimonialist power structure. Diffusion or separation of the economic power sphere from the patrimonialist unity/identity configuration is as inconceivable as the separation of the religious sphere. The ruler successfully claims all spheres of power as his own absolute domain.

Certain specific and limited tasks can be delegated to the servant notables charged with certain technical aspects of 'political' or 'economic' affairs, but the differentiating lines here are even less clear than those specifying 'religious' affairs. Since they are only conditionally and temporarily appointed agents, they have no power to make any important decisions nor any chances to challenge the ruler by organizing themselves into an autonomous/autocephalous power structure of their own. Appropriation of even a segment of the ruler's power for a limited territory is highly unlikely because of their extreme vulnerability in relation to the omnipotent, all-owning sacred ruler. The exceptions are limited to short periods of time during the general breakdown of an established rulership, as between two dynasties or after a conquest. Historical sources indicate that frequently the subjects, well socialized by the religious/ideological doctrines of the particular culture, reject these experiences of deviation as 'times of trouble' and express their longing for a return to a stable, indivisible, and 'normal' patrimonialist power structure and legitimacy.

Notes

1 This significant commentary by Bendix as well as the one by Simirenko (1970) (quoted on p. 56) were published only as book reviews perhaps because the American sociological establishment at

that time still would not tolerate any higher ranking peer-evaluated publication of outlets for such heresies. In another review, Arthur Schweitzer, an economist, expressed his puzzlement that Weber's 'steady attempt of linking social theory with the relevant facts is not appreciated' by some European critics of Weber.

2 Curiously enough, the late Howard P. Becker's energetic and frequent efforts to replace the term 'ideal-type' or 'ideal-typical', which caused so much misunderstanding, with the term 'constructed type' has not caught on (1940; 1945; 1956; Becker and Boskoff, 1957).

3 The conviction generally shared by the Enlightenment enthusiasts of all ages that history is simply an account of the achievements of great men helped immensely to perceive 'enlightened despotism' as the only way to secure good society. This is significant in relation to one of the major misinterpretations of Weber's concept of charisma, which was that it was just another great-man theory of history, in spite of his insistence that extraordinary societal crises involving intense suffering for masses of people is one of the three basic prerequisites for a successfully functioning charismatic power structure.

4 Law and society in Max Weber's sociology*

Edith E. Graber

For Max Weber, law was one of the key explanatory variables in the understanding of society, as significant as were economic, religious, and political variables. But there has been little acknowledgment among American sociologists of Weber's view of the significance of the role of law. Much attention has been paid to Weber's discussion of the influence of economic variables (particularly capitalism) and of the interaction between religious and economic variables. There are a number of important works on Weber's political sociology. But there is little commentary on Weber's writings on law, rules, and norms.

The purpose of this chapter, therefore, is to examine Weber's view of the relationship between law, society, and sociology and to evaluate the significance of his work on the role of law for the understanding of his interpretive sociology.

Law and rules in sociology and society

Weber's writings on law form a conceptual unity. Yet for analytical purposes, it is possible to draw a distinction, for their approach and focus is somewhat different. Law is the dependent variable and Weber investigates the influence of social factors and other societal institutions on the development of law (1968:641–875). Elsewhere, his general thrust is toward the explanation of society itself or of specific institutions such as the economy and religion, or he is delineating the scope and method of his interpretive sociology. Here he focuses on the role of law as independent variable in development and change or on specifying the relationship between sociology and law (1968:3–62; 1981).

The theme which informed Weber's writings on law is the same as that which occupied him in his other work. Like other social theorists of his day, Weber saw in the process of modern Western development fundamental changes from societies of the past. He was interested in accounting for these changes and in tracing their ramifications on various societal institutions and, particularly, on the interface and interaction between social institutions. Hence, on a universal-historical canvas reaching across time and space, he investigated the interplay of causal, contributory, and facilitating factors, indicating how the nature and pace of change had been hindered or helped and characterizing the kind of change which had taken place.

In general, he depicted this process of change as one of increasing rationalization. There had been the development of a methodical way of thinking and methodical conduct of life. Action was oriented to the most economical and direct means by which to achieve desired ends. The trend was toward a greater reliance on reason as against an earlier dependence on tradition, values, and emotion. It was this process which, in Weber's thinking, in large measure accounted for the particular and unique development of the West.

In the process of his analysis he explored the thoroughgoing rationalization of social phenomena across a wide range of socio-cultural fields: science, historical scholarship, religion, music, art, economic activity, institutions of learning, and government administration.

Hence, it is necessary but not sufficient to say, as Trubek does, that the focus of Weber's writings on law was to explain the rise of capitalism in the West and he therefore 'identified unique features of Western legal systems which are especially conducive to capitalistic activity' (Trubek, 1972:722). Weber does incorporate discussion of legal institutions facilitating the rise of capitalism but his range of analysis is broader. Capitalism was for Weber the prototype of contemporary rational economic activity but it formed a subset of the institution of the economy. And Weber's analysis was broader than the economic institution. Just as he traced the rationalization of procedure in organizations which resulted in bureaucracy and the rationalization of religion from the practice of magic to the theological and doctrinal salvation religions, so in his writings on law and particularly in the sociology of law chapter, he was interested in explaining the systematic forms of thought, procedure, and action essential to the rational jurisprudence. 'Our interest is centered upon the ways and consequences of "rationalization" of the law, that is the development of those juristic qualities which are characteristic of it today' (1968:775–6).

Attention is first given to Weber's references to law in his general writings. Two areas will be explored: first, Weber's perception of the relationship between law and sociology and, second, his view of the place of law, norms, and rules in the social order. Next, the thesis of Weber's sociology of law is examined. Finally, an assessment of Weber's writings on law is offered.

The relationship between law and sociology

Law is a crucial subject for any social theory. This is true if one views the social world from the order perspective as held together by consensus and allegiance to common values. It is particularly true if one views the social world from the conflict perspective, where the coherence and stability of the social order must be accounted for despite the ubiquity of competition, domination, coercion, constraint, and hegemony.

Like other subdisciplines of sociology such as the sociology of medicine, the sociology of religion, and the sociology of education, the sociology of law is formed by the overlap of the two parent disciplines, law and sociology. But, as is often true with the joining, there are inherent tensions and contradictions in their confluence.

Weber was especially cognizant of such tensions. His rigorous training and practical experience in law had taught him to distinguish and delineate legal concepts and facts with clarity and care. He was entering upon and giving definitive shaping to the new discipline of sociology. Here too he saw the need for concise and disciplined thought in a field where, in his estimation, early work was characterized by imprecise thinking and careless definition. The awareness of differences, contrasts, and antinomies led him to sharpen distinctions between the legal and the sociological approaches to law.

Weber specified three problematic areas in the overlap between sociology and law: the conflict between the normative basis of law and the empirical basis of sociology, the range of materials considered by each, and the divergent meanings attributed to jointly used concepts.

First, Weber held that sociologists and jurists view their joint subject from varying perspectives. Law is a normative discipline; it concerns itself with what *should* be. It evaluates certain kinds of behavior; it prescribes some actions and prohibits others. It designates the boundaries of acceptable conduct. But its designations are not merely normative in that certain standards are set. Law is also imperative; at certain points, there is a *must* behind the *should*. Hence, a staff of people who are designated to use coercion to enforce the law help ensure that the normative becomes the imperative.

The jurist tests whether a particular law or legal order is valid (has legal efficacy or force) by ensuring that it was issued by the proper authorities in the prescribed manner. He or she scrutinizes legal propositions to determine the interrelationship of each with the other and their placement in a system which is logically coherent and free from internal contradictions. The jurist then tries to define the facts to which this order applies and the way it bears on them (1968:311). This, for Weber, determines the validity of the law from a legal point of view.

Sociology, on the other hand, was for Weber an empirical science of social action and of society. It focuses not on the logically correct meaning of legal propositions but on what actually happens in society when a certain legal order is issued. It focuses on what role the ideas which persons hold about the meaning of certain legal orders play in the determination and outcome of their behavior. Hence, it may ask to what extent people actually know about the law; it may consider how the fact that one can with reasonable probability rely on conformity to law provides certain expectations about the behavior of others, toward which one can orient one's own behavior (1981:159). For sociology the validity of a law depends on whether it *actually* governs the actions of persons and how and to what extent it does so.

The legal observer is concerned with the *Sollen* of behavior (the *should* and the *must*); the sociological observer focuses on the *Sein* (what actually *is*). The *Sein-Sollen* dichotomy is prominent in Weber's discussion of the interface between law and sociology. These are ideal types consisting of pure norm and pure fact. As such, they are non-existent. Weber keeps the distinction conceptually crisp but concedes that reality is made up of fluid and varying mixtures of both.[1]

In order for a norm to be empirically valid in the sociological sense, Weber held that it is not necessary that all or even a majority of those under its jurisdiction comply with the law simply because of the threatened coercion. The broad mass of those subject to legal norms may comply not out of a sense of compulsion to what is regarded as a legal obligation but perhaps because their social milieu encourages compliance or because of unreflective habituation to certain patterns of conduct or because of convenience or because conformity is viewed as reasonable. Nor is it necessary that an individual comply at all times. To the sociologist, what is determinative for the validity of a law is that the individual can depend, with varying degrees of probability, that others will comply with the law, whatever their individual motives for doing so.

Second, law and sociology differ in the range of materials they take into consideration. For the jurist, those propositions designated as legal by persons in positions of authority (legislators, judges, lawyers, officials) are of primary interest. These formally enacted or designated rules form the context within which officials can mobilize the enforcement apparatus. The ancient Latin canon holds *Nullum crimen, nulla poena, sine lege* (no crime, no punishment except as a law prescribes it). The formal statement of a rule provides authority for enforcement and hence for action on the part of legal officials.

But Weber indicated that sociologists are interested not only in formally enacted laws but in all social phenomena which regulate behavior. This includes customs, usages, conventions, and interests which structure the social order. So he discusses the role of law but also differentiates law from custom and convention. He incorporates into his discussion both rules which were explicitly formulated and rules which may result from unconscious consensus and are therefore not stated or enacted but which still regulate behavior.

Third, law and sociology also differ in the divergent meanings attributed to concepts common to both. Weber held that law and sociology view the same phenomenon but from different perspectives, so that confusion arises. One area where this is apparent is in the different ways they define a shared vocabulary. Both disciplines, for instance, use the concept of the 'state'. Jurisprudence deals with the state as if it were a single entity or, in Weber's terms, as if it were an individual person, a 'legal personality'. But for Weber's interpretive sociology, such collective concepts are not valid. For sociology as he defined it, the action of the individual as it is oriented to that of others is the basic unit of analysis. the individual, he says, is the only carrier of meaningful behavior:

> Concepts such as the 'state', 'association', 'feudalism' and the like generally indicate for sociology categories of certain kinds of joint human action; it is therefore the task of sociology to reduce these concepts to 'understandable' action, meaning without exception, the action of the participating individuals (1981:158).

Hence, for sociology, the state is not a 'legal person' or a unitary collective entity. It is rather the simultaneous action of a multitude of interacting individuals who are orienting their action toward each other.

Even in cases of such forms of social organization as a state, church, association or marriage, the social relationship consists exclusively in the fact that there has existed, exists, or will exist a probability of action in some definite way appropriate to this meaning. It is vital to be continually clear about this in order to avoid the 'reification' of those concepts. A 'state', for example, ceases to exist in a sociologically relevant sense whenever there is no longer a probability that certain kinds of meaningfully oriented social action will take place. This probability may be very high or it may be negligibly low. But in any case it is only in the sense and degree in which it does exist that the corresponding social relationship exists (1968:27).

Weber is here concerned with avoiding the use of static or reified constructs in his interpretive sociology in order to reflect faithfully the moving, dynamic, constantly changing nature of the social world. And he is concerned with specifying the irreducible unit of analysis in sociology, which is not large-scale social group-ings but the action of the individual taking cognizance of the actions of others. Here sociology diverges from law. Hence, though the two disciplines may use the same terminology, one must be aware that the meaning attributed to those concepts may vary considerably and in significant ways.

In summary, the two disciplines approach the study of law and the legal order from divergent viewpoints. One is a generalizing science engaged in causal explanation of human behavior: it focuses on the empirical interactions of individuals and probes the role of law as both determinant and result of human behavior. The other is a dogmatic discipline which proclaims authoritative legal orders for behavior. It is thus a normative discipline whose propositions have an underlying imperative quality. It compares individual instances of behavior with its normative and imperative requirements.

The place of law, norms, and rules in the social order

It is apparent that, for Weber, rules and regulations both legal and extra-legal, form the core of the social order. Life is regulated by rules; order is imposed on the social world. Otherwise, social interaction would be impossible.[2]

For Weber, such rules for social ordering were of interest precisely because of their recurring and patterned nature. They involved courses of action which were repeated among individual actors and groups of actors and were therefore of particular interest to a generalizing science. Further, the use of sanctions to enforce expected behavior provided a guarantee that the actor(s) could rely on compliance and therefore chart a course of action.

Weber classified this regulation of the social in several different ways. One classification had to do with the degree of coercion implied in the regulation; the categories were custom, convention, and law.

Custom is 'a typically uniform activity which is kept on the beaten track simply because men are "accustomed" to it and persist in it by unreflecting imitation' (1968:319). In distinction to convention law, custom refers to rules lacking external sanction or a coercive apparatus. An example is eating a breakfast which conforms to a certain pattern.

Convention, by contrast, involves the sanction of an evaluative reaction by one's social milieu. 'An order will be called convention so far as its validity is externally guaranteed by the probability that deviation from it within a given social group will result in a relatively general and practically significant reaction of disapproval' (Weber, 1968:34).

Law is characterized by the probability that action is deemed binding on the individual. 'An action will be called . . . law if it is externally guaranteed by the probability that physical or psychological coercion will be applied by a staff of people in order to bring about compliance or avenge violation' (Weber, 1968:34). Where such enforcement of conformity to the norm exists, Weber spoke of 'guaranteed law'.

Over time, the state had increasingly monopolized the use of violence in legal coercion. However, law could also be guaranteed by milder forms of physical or psychological coercion. And it need not be guaranteed only by the state; extra-state law was also a pervasive and effective factor in the regulation of the social world. It was not unusual, particularly outside European Continental legal systems, that modern state law treated as valid the rules of non-state organizations (such as labor unions) and reviewed their decisions. Hence

> for the sake of terminological consistency, we categorically deny that 'law' exists only where legal coercion is guaranteed by the political authority. . . . A 'legal order' shall rather be said to exist wherever coercive means, of a physical or psychological kind, are available (Weber 1968:316–7).

From a sociological point of view, the belief in the validity of an order is paramount. Persons may disregard or disobey an order which they believe invalid. Legitimacy must be ascribed to the order; lawgivers assume that they have the right to govern, and the governed, at least in part, acknowledge that right. Weber held that persons may ascribe legitimacy to a social order on the basis of tradition, affect, value-rational faith, or legal enactment. 'Today the most common form of legitimacy is the belief in legality, the compliance with enactments which are formally correct and which have been made in the accustomed manner' (1968:37).

Hence, one way of classifying the regulation of the social world is based on the degree of coercion and is conditioned by the belief in the legitimacy of the order. But Weber recognized that society was also regulated by the inner ordering which occurred through the rules and structures of voluntary and imposed groups. In another taxonomy, Weber classified social regulation by the social action which had produced the ordering. The categories were the consensual group, association, organization, and institution (Weber, 1981). As Roth (1968:lxii) suggests, Weber elaborated 'a continuous typology of social action along the line of increasing rational control, persistence and legal compulsion'.

At one end of the continuum, Weber described that conformity to rules based not on enactment but on an implicit consensus (*Einverständnis*). There was no rational conscious agreement on rules, yet compliance existed 'as if' such agreement had occurred. In an act of exchange involving money, for instance, 'one's own action is oriented toward the expectation that makes the use of money possible; that others will also "accept" money . . . that net result is, in many respects, normally fashioned "as if" it had been reached through orientation by all participants to an order' (1981:166).

In contrast to consensus, a group of persons may decide to form an association (*Vergesellschaftung*) for a specific purpose. The rules toward which they orient themselves have been consciously formulated to govern their joint action. No formal group need have been established; the relationship may be *ad hoc* or enduring.

That action of several persons is oriented to the same set of rules does not mean that the action is identical. They may have varying conceptions and interpretations of the rules. But there is usually enough similarity of response that actors know approximately what kind of behavior to expect of other participants and can determine their own action accordingly. These rules thus structure or order the interaction and the individual action.

'Orienting one's actions to rules' does not necessarily mean complying with them; the card player who cheats still orients his action to the rules by concealing his act. And his cheating is possible only because he expects the others to comply in an approximate way to the rules. An association may continue or be discontinued depending on the action of individuals. As soon as all card players know the rules will not be observed, the association ceases.

The ideal type of the associative relationship is the 'voluntary association' in which all participants have rationally agreed on the rules of their association and have acquired a staff. When fully developed, the voluntary association is an enduring structure. Thus, despite the turnover of members, the 'same' association exists. Rules can be changed or their meaning altered without breaking the continuity.

The voluntaristic and consensual nature of this action has been emphasized. But Weber does not minimize the imperative dimension in social action: 'coercion, physical or psychic, somehow lies at the root of nearly all social relationships' (1981:173).

Members of an organization (*Verband*) also orient their action to rules. In addition, a greater degree of formality exists. The group is either closed or limits the admission of outsiders. The definitive criterion, however, is that a person or persons are in a position of authority. In their executive capacity, they enforce the regulations or order of the organization. Such an order may be the result of explicit consensual agreement or may be imposed by the executive with the acquiescence of members. There is thus not merely action oriented to an order but the guarantee of potential enforcement (1968:48).

Finally, there are social relationships in which one participates without one's volition. In these, the individual is obligated to participate and to observe the rules (law) of the group. The normal manner of entrance into such relationships is that one is born or socialized into participation. A community in which these circumstances obtain is a compulsory organization or institution (*Anstalt*).

For Weber, an order was always considered 'imposed' when it did not result from 'a voluntary personal agreement of all the individuals concerned' (1968:51). In institutions, laws are rarely enacted through autonomous agreement. Rather, they are imposed from above. This obtains despite the common conception of majority rule. Even where a majority of members gave assent, the action is imposed on the minority. More often imposition occurs through the action of certain persons who were elected by majority vote and who impose rules without the deliberate assent of members to the particular action. Weber traced 'an ever wider ranging rational ordering of consensual action by means of statutes, and, especially, an increasing incidence of transformation of organizations into rationally ordered institutions' (1981:177).

Thus Weber (1968:876) affirmed the 'rule-boundedness of the

social order', whether this occurred through conscious or unconscious and formal or informal rules or whether by the inner ordering which occurs through the joint participation of individuals in social group action.

The social determinants of legal development

In his sociology of law, Weber's focus is narrower than it is in the writings just discussed. Instead of dealing with society as a whole, Weber here centers on the legal system as one of the social systems and examines how changes in other social institutions and in the legal institution itself affected the nature and character of law. He specified that the task at hand was 'to find out how the various influences which have participated in the formation of the law have influenced the development of its formal qualities' (1968:657).

Weber suggested that both 'lawmaking' and 'lawfinding' (the application of law) can be either rational (guided by general rules) or irrational. On another dimension, law can be either formal (guided by general facts of the case and by legal propositions) or substantive (guided by extra-legal principles). This leads to a cross-classification. Law is:

1 irrational
(a) *formally* irrational when the lawmaker or lawfinder applies means which cannot be controlled by the intellect, such as oracles or ordeals;
(b) *substantively* irrational when the decision is guided by an ethical, emotional, or political evaluation of the factors in the individual case rather than on the basis of general norms.
2 rational
(a) *substantively* rational when the decision is influenced by articulated general norms, i.e., by ethical imperatives, utilitarian and other expediential rules, and political maxims.
(b) *formally* rational
    (1) influenced by *extrinsic* factors, such as the utterance of certain words or the execution of a signature; this constitutes the most rigorous type of legal formalism.
    (2) *logically* formally rational 'where the legally relevant characteristics of the facts are disclosed through the logical analysis of meaning and where, accordingly, definitely fixed legal concepts in the form of highly abstract rules are formulated and applied' (1968:656-7).

Weber found that the legal science of his day, especially that influenced by the civil law of the Pandectists, German legal scholars of the nineteenth century, most nearly approximated the ideal

95

type of logically formal rationality. Their legal science proceeded from five postulates:

> first, that every concrete legal decision be the 'application' of an abstract legal proposition to a concrete 'fact situation'; second, that it must be possible in every concrete case to derive the decision from abstract legal propositions by means of legal logic; third, that the law must actually or virtually constitute a 'gapless' system of legal propositions, or must, at least, be treated as if it were such a gapless system; fourth, that whatever cannot be 'construed' rationally in legal terms is also legally irrelevant; and fifth, that every social action of human beings must always be visualized as either an 'application' or 'execution' of legal propositions, or as an 'infringement' thereof, since the 'gaplessness' of the legal system must result in the gapless 'legal ordering' of all social conduct (1968:657-8).

The development of law was, for Weber, an example of the rationalization process which he had traced in religion and economics. In early history and in pre-history, law was irrational; it was informed by oracle and lawfinding was often carried out through ordeal and blood feud. But in the process of development, there had arisen trends toward formally logical rationality which had culminated in the jurisprudence of the Pandectists. What factors influenced and directed this development?

Weber's analysis does not begin with a clear statement of his development scheme. In fact, it is in the final section of this chapter that he explicitly specifies the conceptual scheme he has been using. The general development of law and procedure, he asserts, may be viewed as passing through the following stages:

> first, charismatic legal revelation through 'law prophets'; second, empirical creation and finding of law by legal honoratiores, i.e., law creation through cautelary jurisprudence and adherence to precedent; third, imposition of law by secular or theocratic powers; fourth and finally, systematic elaboration of law and professionalized administration of justice by persons who have received their legal training in a learned and formally logical manner (1968:882).

Weber emphasizes that this is not a developmental scheme in the Comtean sense: it has not everywhere been only unidirectional. In his final section, he indicates a number of anti-formal and irrational tendencies in modern law. But the general movement had been in the direction noted.

As in his sociology of religion, it is the organizational 'carriers' or notables and the strata which support them who are instrumental in shaping a period of development. Rheinstein (1954:xlvii) asserted that Weber's 'interest in law came to be centered around that problem which in this country is usually referred to as that of legal thought or of the judicial process'. Similarly, the focus here is on social action in the legal institution as influenced by extra-legal factors or by factors within the institution itself.

In his analysis, Weber addresses the following questions:

1 What is the general sequence of legal development: types, regularities, recurring patterns?
2 What legal actors are principally involved in the socio-legal action at each stage and what strata support them?
3 What specific social action factors (political, economic, educational, religious, or factors within the legal institution itself) are responsible for producing characteristics and change?
4 What qualities did this produce in law?

His findings are based on empirical instances which are described with such specificity, delimitation, and precision that they do not lend themselves to ready generalization. The following discussion can only hint at the wide-ranging scope of Weber's exploration.

In his analysis, Weber weighs the contribution of the various institutional sectors – economic, religious, political, and legal – to the process of the rationalization of law.

Economic factors

Weber begins by drawing the distinction, significant in Continental law, between subjective and objective law. The latter refers to those rules which are applicable to all members who live within the jurisdiction of a particular legal system. Subjective law refers to the opportunity for an individual to appeal to the apparatus of coercion for the legal protection of his interests. He suggests that a 'right', sociologically speaking, simply means that there is an increase in the probability that one's claim to such protection will be honored to the extent that it is guaranteed by law. The subjective expectation is undergirded by the legal promise. Freedom, for Weber, consists in being in possession of such rights, either actual or potential.

The freedom of contract is one such right, significant because of the decisive role it played in the development of modern capitalism. Weber found that, in contrast to older law, the most essential feature of modern law was the greatly increased significance of legal transactions, particularly contracts; indeed, it was proper to designate modern society as a contractual society. And the money contract was, for Weber, the archetype of the modern purposive contract (1968:674). Such a contract creates special law between parties; in that sense, it involves a decentralization of lawmaking. However, modern legislatures regulate various types of such special law, putting limitations on contractual agreements in such areas as marriage, estate law, and work relationships.

The needs of the economic sector had, at various points in history, facilitated the systematization and rationalization of law. The extension of the market economy had necessitated stability and certainty in law so that the future legal protection of economic interests could be calculated and relied on. But such economic influences were indirect and secondary. Weber found that economic situations do not necessarily give birth to new legal forms; the impetus for new forms comes from the political or legal sectors. However, the economic sector can give opportunity for the dissemination of such forms, once invented. Hence, economic factors played an important but not determinative role.

The argument that seems to have been most persuasive to Weber that economic factors were of secondary importance derived from his examination of the relationship between the rationalization of law and the development of modern capitalism. He found, as we shall see, that English law was characterized by a greater degree of 'irrationality' than was Continental law, in which the logical formal rationality of law had reached its highest form. Yet it was England that had furnished the most favorable milieu for the development of capitalism. Indeed, 'England achieved capitalistic supremacy among the nations not because but rather in spite of its judicial system' (1968:814). Hence, he concluded that 'capitalism has not been a decisive factor in the promotion of that form of rationalization of law which has been peculiar to the continental West ever since the rise of Romanist studies in the medieval universities' (1968:892).

Religious factors

Weber focused not only on the emergence of subjective law (the claim to the legal protection of personal and group interests as in the case of contracts) but also on the creation of objective law. In the emergence of common or 'customary' law, such new legal norms have three sources. The first is extra-legal; it involves the standardization of certain consensual understandings:

The psychological 'adjustment' arising from habituation to an action causes conduct that in the beginning constituted plain habit later to be experienced as binding; then, with the awareness of the diffusion of such conduct among a plurality of individuals, it comes to be incorporated as 'consensus' into peoples' semi- or wholly conscious 'expectations' as to the meaningfully corresponding conduct of others. Finally these 'consensual understandings' acquire the guaranty of coercive enforcement by which they are distinguished from mere 'conventions' (1968:754).

Changes in the external conditions of social life are partly responsible for such new law. But the really decisive factor, according to Weber, is a new line of conduct which then either produces a change in the meaning of extant rules of law or results in the creation of new rules (1968:755). Hence, social action is the causal factor producing new law. Very often the social action arises out of the desire to protect or promote individual or group interests. A selection process is at work, determining which of several courses of action will survive and be protected by new law. Where one such course of action has the approval of religious groups this is sometimes the factor determining its selection for survival.

A second source of customary law is judicial precedent (to be discussed later). Finally, new customary norms could also arise through charismatic proclamation or imposition. This constitutes the first stage of Weber's historical sequence of legal development. In a tradition-oriented society, the notion that new rules or law could be established by deliberate enactment was largely absent. Law was 'an inert mass of canonized custom' which was deemed quite immutable. But a revelation of new law by a charismatic leader was a revolutionary element which broke the crust of tradition and provided for the emergence of new law. Such revelation was often, though not necessarily, of religious origin. Particularly in early history, the charismatic leader was often a magician, prophet, sage, or priest of an oracular deity. He proclaimed new rules which superseded the old: 'You have heard that it has been said. . . . But I say unto you. . . .' Members, imputing charismatic qualities to the leader, would communicate the revelation to others and begin to alter their conduct to comply with the new rules. Weber finds that 'legal prophecy seems to have been universal. Everywhere the power of the priests rested largely upon their activities as dispersers of oracles or as the "directors" of the procedure in ordeals' (1968:769–70).

Weber is interested in the effects which this method of legal action had on its formal characteristics. The presence of magic in the creation and application of law led to a rigorous formalism. The question of law at issue had to be stated in a precise way for even the slightest deviation would result in nullifying the legal transaction. 'The formal character of the procedure thus stands in sharp contrast to the thoroughly irrational character of the technique of decision' (1968:762).

Charismatic legal personnel were involved in the proclamation of law and in the issuing of legal decisions in the individual case. They were seldom involved in its application or enforcement. This contributed to the rudimentary separation of powers into distinct spheres for lawmaking and lawfinding. Secularization and the processes of social change, especially those initiated by war, and the varying degree of reception of charismatic declarations of law contributed to the decline of charismatic revelation of law.

The first stage of Weber's treatment of the relationship between religion and law was thus that of charismatic legal revelation. Another type of legal development was that of the imposition of law by theocratic powers. Where sacred and secular law remained undifferentiated, theocratic or religious powers were able to wield a decisive influence on legal development. But where the *fas* or divine law was early separated from the *ius*, the established law for the settlement of secular disputes, the latter passed through an independent course of development into a rational and formal system.

In his analysis, Weber explored the varying mix of sacred or secular law in early Roman, Indian, Chinese, Islamic, Persian, Jewish, and early Christian law. In India, for instance, a dominant priesthood was able to institute a ritualistic regulation of most areas of life and thus to control the entire legal system (1968:816). The canon law also aimed at regulation of the whole range of human conduct but it did not ultimately determine the nature of secular law. 'The reason was that Canon law had found in the Roman law a secular competitor which had achieved an extraordinary formal perfection and which, in the course of history, had become the universal law of the world' (1968:830). Further, where Canon law tried to extend its dominion, it found resistance from vigorously developing economic interests.

These varying circumstances affected the nature of law. Where religious law was based chiefly on revelation, it tended to maintain flexibility and adaptability to changing circumstances. But where it was based chiefly on a transmitted sacred tradition, it remained much more rigid; when adaptation was sought, such theocratic law tended toward an extremely formal casuistry.

Weber discusses this second stage of religio-legal development, the imposition of law by theocratic powers, in conjunction with the similar imposition of law by political powers.

Political factors

The second authoritarian power which sought to impose its stamp upon the primitive irrationality of early forms of justice was the *imperium* of princes, magistrates, and officials of secular politics. Of direct significance was the mutual power relationship between the imperium and the social strata on whom the continuation and support of power depended.

In cases where the power of the imperium was clear-cut and acknowledged, the prince might issue decrees which were deemed to have a validity equal to that of the existing common law. Usually, however, it was necessary to secure the assent of the notables or *honoratiores*; where this was withheld, it constituted a considerable obstacle to princely legislation.

Rationalization occurred, again, in many forms and with varying results. Generally, the power and duty of the prince to protect the peace meant that a rational penal law was one of the first products of the *imperium*. Private law was not accessible to the peace-keeping power of the prince to the same degree, with the result that rationalization in that sphere generally occurred later.

The systematizing and ordering of the law was an important step in its attaining a logically formal character. Various forces coincided to produce such a codification. Monarchical officials, desiring order and unity in their realms, were interested in the systematization of law to further their own interests and those of their administration. The creation of new political entities encouraged codification as new groups sought legal security. Political and economic interest groups as well as permanent organizations sought calculability and legal certainty; for these groups, the stability and dependability of rational rules and procedures were of paramount importance. Often these interests coincided with those of the king or ruler who wanted the support and development of commercial interests for his own political and fiscal purposes. But, as we shall see, Weber contended that the greatest impetus to codification came from the legal sector itself.

Legal factors

The function of charismatic law prophets has been to reveal law. As their determinative influence declined, lawfinding or application increasingly demanded the skills of legal specialists. It was

101

'the increased need for specialized legal knowledge [which] created the professional lawyer' (Weber, 1968:775).

The growing demand for experience and knowledge led to the demand for legal training for notables. And it was the method of training which was a paramount factor in the rationalization of law. Weber held that the development of formal qualities in law was conditioned primarily by 'intrajuristic' conditions, that is,

> the particular character of the individuals who are in a position to influence by virtue of their profession the ways in which the law is shaped. Only indirectly is this development influenced, however, by general economic and social conditions. The prevailing type of legal education . . . has been more important than any other factor (1968:776).

Weber contrasts two divergent methods of training of which the English and the Continental modes are fairly pure illustrations.

Law as craft

The guild-like social organization of the legal profession in England led to a monopoly in legal training and to an autonomous and independent profession. Legal training was pursued at the Inns of Court in London where trainees learned from legal practitioners in an apprenticeship arrangement. For a time, some lecture courses were introduced to counter competitive training courses in universities. However, in the fifteenth and sixteenth centuries, the lawyers were able to secure the monopoly on legal training and subsequently dropped formal academic training.

Such empirical and practical training produced a characteristic kind of law. The emphasis was on the particular case and how similar previous cases had been decided. This led to a 'formalistic treatment of the law, bound by precedent and analogies from precedent' (Weber, 1968:787). The evolution of law was directed not to the creation of a rational systematization but to pragmatic responsiveness.

Weber insisted that 'From such practices and attitudes no rational system of law could emerge, nor even a rationalization of the law as such' (Weber, 1968:787). Decisions governing such cases were not obtained through logical generalization of abstract general rules but were influenced by concrete factors in the particular case; decisions were guided by utilitarian or political rules or by principles of the common law and legal precedent. The argument was from particular to particular rather than from particular to general propositions. Hence, such training through apprenticeship by a monopolized and autonomous profession led to a kind of law which contained strains of substantive irrationality.[3]

Law as a science

Modern legal education in universities, as found on the Continent, presented the purest example of training in which legal rules were expressed by use of abstract concepts and distinguished from one another by 'a rigorously formal and rational logical interpretation of meaning' (Weber, 1968:789). Pedagogical demands necessitated systematic classification and clarification. Such law was more divorced from the pragmatic everyday needs of the public and more oriented to theoretical and conceptual elaboration. It represented to Weber the ideal type of logically formal rational law.

Where such formal legal education was located in seminaries or in universities connected with such seminaries, the resulting law was characterized by substantive or material rationalization, i.e., it was guided by religious or ethical principles rather than by formal principles. Such law, because it was based on a sacred book or tradition, generally possessed a rational and systematic character.

In Germany, the decentralization of the administration of justice prevented legal guilds from monopolizing the professional training as in England. Hence, lawyers were regulated by the government rather than by professional autonomy.

Among the classes of legal notables which were influential in contributing to the rationalization process were the Italian notaries who were specialists in drafting real estate conveyances and commercial documents. They needed a rational law to meet the needs of the rapid expansion of trade. Roman law, which was being taught in Italian universities, was increasingly drawn on by the notaries and adapted to current needs. But it was the Byzantine bureaucracy which finally systematized existing law (1968:797). The task was aided by juriconsults, legal experts who were consulted on points of law by both private parties and magistrates. Their opinions were collected by jurists and, with explanatory commentary, taught in law schools. The necessity for systematic juristic studies was further increased by the bureaucratization and rational administration of justice. Weber asserted that the systematic rationalization of the law in England was retarded because bureaucratization did not occur there to a similar degree. Hence, while political and other social factors facilitated codification, the paramount factor was the need within the legal profession for the systematization of law.

Strains of irrationality in modern law

Weber traced a general trend toward formal and logical rationality in Western law over the period of its development. In his final section, he examines the continuing tension in law between substantive justice considerations and the formal rational 'purity' of logical rules. He had previously explored two great systems of law: Roman law, a product of 'theoretical-literary juristic doctrine' (1968:865), and Anglo-Saxon law, the product of juristic practice. He now introduced the French Civil Code, 'the third of the world's great systems of law', the product of rational legislation. The French code was a 'child of the Revolution' and, because it contained strains of 'natural law', was of revolutionary character itself. Such law approached the type of substantively rational law for it was guided by general rules but the principles which informed the law and the claims of individuals were derived from extra-legal sources:

> Natural law is the sum total of all those norms which are valid
> independently of, and superior to, any positive law and which
> owe their dignity not to arbitrary enactment but, on the
> contrary, provide the very legitimation for the binding force
> of positive law. Natural law has thus been the collective term
> for those norms which owe their legitimacy not to their origin
> from a legitimate lawgiver, but to their immanent and
> teleological qualities (1968:867).

Natural law might serve as a normative standard for or a limiting factor on positive law. Over time, however, axioms of natural law lost their capacity to serve as the fundamental basis of a legal system. Theories of evolution and the impact of modern power politics were among the factors which helped relativize and disintegrate axioms based on metajuristic considerations and encourage the spread of legal positivism.

But Weber found other anti-rational tendencies in modern law. Several causes were given for the dilution of legal formalism. First, there is a reaction by laymen against the rationalism and 'specialization' in modern law; the layman wants a system of justice which is intelligible to him. Second, ideas and ideologies of the legal profession itself contain strains toward anti-formalism; some Continental jurists admire the higher professional status of English judges and suggest that their more 'creative' and less formally logical role is responsible for that increased status. Third, modern law has decreased its dependence on externally tangible formal characteristics of the case and on abstract logical reasoning; rather it has depended for proof on the 'real' intention of the parties or on their expectations of the behavior of others or on such considerations as 'good faith'. Fourth, there is a general recognition that the notion of the consistency and gaplessness of the law is a fiction and not a reliable assumption. There is thus the continuing conflict between formal and substantive principles of justice and a desire to achieve a settlement which would be expeditious, utilitarian, 'fair', and 'just'. From this standpoint, legal considerations are seen as secondary to such substantive goals as 'social justice', 'human dignity', or 'liberty' (1968:883–9).

In some quarters there may be an attempt to re-establish some objective standard of values which underlies and informs all law. The old natural law has been discredited, it is true, but natural law springs up in new guises. Weber considers such tendencies 'a flight into irrationality'. Though on the whole he maintains the stance of the objective social scientist, he here advances the opinion that 'the juristic precision of judicial opinions will be seriously impaired if sociological, economic, or ethical argument were to take the place of legal concepts' (Weber, 1968:894). Inevitably, he suggests, 'the notion must expand that the law is a rational, technical apparatus, which is continually transformable in the light of expediential considerations and devoid of all sacredness of content' (1968:895).

Conclusion

The rules for social ordering create, sustain, and enforce order in the social world, both when imposed by the state or organization and when evolved through voluntary agreement by consensus or by association for some group purpose. The sociologist, says Weber, is involved in making generalizations about social phenomena and in ascertaining causal relationships among such phenomena. Hence, it is of vital importance to ascertain those factors which give stability, predictability, and patterned regularities to individual and group social action. One needs to know what to expect from others, not only as an individual actor but also as a sociological observer. One needs to ascertain how action has become standardized, stabilized, institutionalized, and routinized.

Not only social action but also social institutions are shaped around the rules for social ordering. The sociologist is continually faced with the 'rule-boundedness of the social order' (1976:876). Weber, at the intersection of the two disciplines of law and sociology, understood this; for him, rules for social ordering were of paramount importance. This was particularly true in modern societies which were characterized by rational-legal domination and in which the role of law was more central and determinative than in societies ordered by traditional or charismatic relationships.

Given the significance of law to Weber's sociology, it was also important to him to analyze how it developed and how its nature and character were shaped by the other major social institutions: the economy, the polity, and religion. And it was important to probe how the nature of law was conditioned by the requirements within the legal institution itself. Hence, in his sociology of law he explored the social determinants of legal development (thus examining law as a dependent variable).

For the sociology of law, Weber furnishes a theoretical and historical context in which to anchor empirical research. Much of the middle- and close-range empirical work in this newly emerging subdiscipline could benefit from the contextual mooring which a closer study of Weber's sociology could provide. Further, many of the problems which Weber posed have yet to be explored in a systematic way. Weber's sociology of law thus serves both as a key to his interpretive sociology and as a model for inter-institutional sociological analysis.

Notes

* The author is indebted to the German Academic Exchange Service and to Washington University for grants supporting a period of research at the Max Weber Institute of the University of Munich and the Max Weber Archive at the Bavarian Academy of Sciences during the summer of 1976. The criticisms of Michael Weinberg, Richard Ratcliff, and the editor of this volume were helpful and constructive.

1 Other specialists developed somewhat similar distinctions between the legal and the empirical view of law. Ehrlich (1862–1922), a contemporary of Weber, spoke of the 'positive law' and the 'living law'. The positive law refers to enacted or legislated law and to judge-made or case law. The 'living law' is that which actually governs life itself, even though it may not have been incorporated into legal propositions. One ascertains the latter by direct observation of life, customs, and usages and of social interaction (Ehrlich, 1970). An alternative formulation is that of Roscoe Pound (1870–1964), who spoke of the 'law on the books' and the 'law in action' (Pound, 1910).

2 The word which Weber used in speaking of this core of the social world is *Ordnung*. It has no simple English equivalent. It refers to the arrangement and structuring (order) and to the regulation of a society or group (rules). Weber applied it to something as simple as a card game and as complex as the regulations of an international cartel. It is applied to ordering as informal as the rules governing the use of

language, which may not be articulated and of which the individual may not be conscious but with which he nevertheless complies.

3 Max Rheinstein contends that Weber overstated the difference between the English and Continental legal systems and understated the stability, continuity, and certainty in English law (1954:xlviii, lviii).

5 Max Weber and the causality of freedom

William W. Mayrl

Weber's dilemma

Throughout his intellectual life, Max Weber maintained a commitment to two values which seem quite contradictory. On the one hand he had, in Shils's words, 'a strong belief that man's dignity consists in his capacity for rational self-determination' (Weber, 1949:v). Yet at the same time, he believed that as a scientist he must reject 'all concern with practical (ethical, religious, political, esthetic, etc.) goals of any kind' and concentrate instead on the development of objective, i.e., causally adequate, explanations of social action.

Great thinkers rarely ignore obvious contradictions. Weber confronted the 'antinomy' of human liberty and scientific objectivity in several, quite different areas of his work. His most well-known and influential 'solution' to the dilemma was presented in his writings on value neutrality and on science and social policy. In these, he maintained there is and should be an unbridgeable distinction between 'arguments which appeal to our capacity to become enthusiastic about and our feeling for concrete practical aims or cultural forms and values' and 'arguments which appeal to our capacity and need for *analytically* ordering empirical reality in a manner which lays claim to validity as empirical truth' (1949:58). Values can play a legitimate role in scientific inquiry, Weber continued, as long as their *pre-scientific* character is recognized. In brief, such values 'always will be decisively significant in determining the focus of attention of analytical activity'. However, the procedures used to define the contours of that activity, i.e., the nature of the data, the means by which they are gathered, and the 'proofs' to which they are subjected, must be freed of any practical concerns. There is only one value to which the methods of science can relate: the desire to achieve objectively valid empirical truth.

There is something unsatisfactory about this solution. It is true that on one level it offers a remedy for certain rather obvious forms of bias. However, as a resolution of the conflict between the advocate of human dignity and the practitioner of social science, it raises more questions than it answers. In a sense, Weber's formulation reminds us of the caricature of the famous rocket scientist in a popular protest song of the 1960s: ' "Once the rockets go up, who cares where they come down. That's not my department," says Werner von Braun.' We know, of course, that Weber was not recommending moral indifference. But that only makes the conflict between his two values more intense. In a way, the natural scientist is more fortunate than the social scientist in this regard. Regardless of the epistemological difficulties involved in the separation of facts and values, the moral rocket scientist can at least argue that knowledge about rockets is, in and of itself, a good thing for humanity. Since the anti-human uses of rocketry originate outside the realm of physical science, it is logically possible to separate oneself from such uses without compromising one's integrity as a rocket scientist. The moral social scientist is not so fortunate. Objectively valid empirical truth which is relevant to a system of social scientific knowledge would seem, in principle, a violation of human dignity. Auguste Comte's well-known rationale for social science – 'To see, in order to predict, in order to control' – implies that while the discovery of social laws may benefit humankind, it does so only in a realm beyond dignity and freedom. Indeed, it could be argued that social science is successful to the extent it can demonstrate that human liberty is a functional myth. If this is the case, then a simultaneous commitment to liberty and scientific exploration would require a leap of faith much broader than a person of Weber's intellectual integrity could make. The separation of values and science is not enough. The antinomy has to be dealt with by a direct assault on one of its principles. This, we will suggest, Weber did by introducing the contradiction between human freedom and causal necessity into science itself by means of his demand that explanation in sociology must be adequate at the level of meaning as well as causality. In Weber's words:

> Sociology (in the sense in which this highly ambiguous word is used here) is a science concerning itself with the interpretive *understanding* of social action and thereby with a causal *explanation* of its course and consequences (Weber, 1968:4, emphasis added).

109

The terms 'meaning' and 'causality', at least as applied to the subject and method of science, are usually considered to be incommensurable. The realm of subjective meaning is characterized by purposeful activity, by intentionality, and ultimately by analytic indeterminacy. The realm of causality, on the other hand, is one of necessary relations, of occurrences which are predicted by antecedent conditions, and ultimately by analytic determinacy. Weber was certainly aware of this dilemma and although he could not avoid it – to do so would have been to reject one or the other of his fundamental values – he did devise a solution. That solution, we will show, was similar in many respects to Immanuel Kant's resolution of the third antinomy of human reason: the simultaneous affirmation of freedom and necessity in the empirical world. Our analysis will start with a brief review of Kant's explication of the problem. That review, in turn, will provide a framework for our discussion of Weber's approach to causality in the social sciences.

Kant's dilemma

In one of the best-known episodes in the history of modern European philosophy, Immanuel Kant was awakened from his dogmatic slumbers by the skeptical empiricism of David Hume. It is not necessary to review that episode in any detail, except to note that in his effort to anchor causality in the universal categories of subjectivity, Kant was forced to establish a radical dichotomy between the worlds of appearance and reality. The separation between phenomena and noumena, in turn, unfolded into a series of oppositions including those of nature and morality, fact and value, and necessity and freedom. While both sides of this dichotomy were empirical, the investigation of each involved a special methodology.

Within the realm of phenomenon it was possible to make the kind of judgments necessary for the construction of deterministic explanatory models. The various elements of this sphere were understood to relate to one another in temporal sequences wherein changes in one resulted in alterations of the others. Furthermore, particular events or processes were conceived as instances of general laws or principles. The notions of existence in time and universal regularity are, of course, the essential ingredients of causal explanation which, in turn, is the keystone of modern natural science. Neo-Kantians Wilhelm Windelband and Heinrich Rickert referred to the methods of inquiry into the phenomenal world as nomothetic in order to emphasize their quest for causal laws. Talcott Parsons, on the other hand, in his

110

discussion of neo-Kantian sociology, used the more general concept *positivistic empiricism* in order to allow for the analysis of phenomena in terms of functional as well as causal relations (Parsons, 1949:418). However, regardless of whether relations are analyzed in terms of causality or functionality, ideally they are *necessary*. They leave no room for the freedom which, for Kant, characterizes the practical, moral activity of human beings. In fact, functional or nomothetic methods cannot be applied to the moral realm without destroying its essential character. 'If freedom were determined in accordance with laws', Kant observed in his proof of the antithesis in the third antinomy, 'it would not be freedom; it would simply be nature by another name' (1929:411).

Kant did not reject altogether the notion of causality in the realm of human action. He simply revised its focus. When Kant spoke of 'the causality of free actions' he was referring to consequences rather than antecedent conditions. In brief, what is being caused is not intent, *per se,* but the actions – direct and indirect – which flow from it.

> The idea of freedom finds a place solely in the relation of the intellectual as cause to the appearance as effect. . . . Only when *something* is to *begin* through an act and the effect is to be encountered in the time sequence, consequently in the world of senses (e.g. the beginning of the world) does the question arise, whether the causality of the cause must itself begin or whether the cause can start an effect without its causality itself beginning. In the first case the concept of this causality is a concept of natural necessity, in the second case of freedom (1953:109–10n).

The implications of Kant's position for research in history and sociology are clear. While it is possible to study the 'course and consequences' of human action and thereby to pursue objective empirical science, the origins of action remain ineffable. Human dignity rests safely in the mystery of timeless causality.

Weber and the causality of freedom

Max Weber did not consider 'freedom' to be an essential component of his methodology. Indeed, he explicitly rejected the use of this term, at least in its moral sense, in scientific discourse.

> all modes of introducing the philosophical problem of freedom into the procedures of history would suspend its character as an empirical science just as much as the insertion of miracles into its causal sequences (1949:123).

111

On the other hand, Weber also rejected the notion of necessity in the human sciences on the ground that, like freedom, it lies 'beyond any "observational experience" employed by [the human sciences] for purposes of verification' (1975:197–8).

It would appear that Weber's agnosticism on the metaphysical question of freedom and necessity places him outside the Kantian problematic. This is exactly the position taken by Talcott Parsons, who argues that Weber never really concerned himself with the philosophical issue of whether 'valid empirical science in the field of human meaning and motivated action is possible'. He took it for granted, Parsons suggests in much the same way the physicist does not bother with the question of whether the world exists (1977:54). However, if we examine more closely what Weber 'took for granted', it appears he was less of an agnostic after all. In what follows, we will show that human freedom and dignity clearly have an important place in Weber's methodology. In spite of the great pains he took to point out that freedom is an unnecessary hypothesis for the human sciences, both Weber's definition of the subject of sociology and his conception of the procedures of 'valid empirical science' manifest a commitment to a form of metaphysical libertarianism which is entirely consistent with Kant's conclusions on the nature of practical reason.

In the remainder of this chapter, Weber's methodology will be examined with particular attention to the concept of causality. It will be shown that despite his frequent use of terminology from the 'nomothetic' side of the Kantian dichotomy, and his occasional claim that 'the special role of the "interpretively" understandable in "history" . . . does *not* concern differences in the concept of causality' (1975:186), Weber carefully and systematically outlined procedures for the analysis of human action in terms of what Kant called 'the causality of freedom'.

Causal explanation: Two views

The key to Weber's thinking on both interpretive understanding and causal explanation can be found in his conception of 'nomological knowledge'. For it is in his assessment of the proper role of lawlike regularity in causal analysis that we find Weber's strongest affinities as well as his sharpest differences with the nomothetic or positivistic tradition in the human sciences.

For the positivist, propositions which indicate either a universal or highly probable regularity in the interaction of two or more variables constitute the fundamental features of deductive explanatory formats. Particular events or processes are 'explained' when they can be subsumed under one or more propositions of this type. Thus, for example, the fact that the suicide rate in Spain is consistently lower than that of, say, Sweden, is explained by showing that the former society possesses certain features not found in the latter which we understand, on the basis of our nomological knowledge, to be associated with low suicide rates. Our nomological knowledge, in this regard, consists of propositions indicating that there is an inverse relationship between the degree of social solidarity in a group and its suicide rates and that groups with a high incidence of Catholicism manifest a high degree of solidarity. The fact that Spain has a high incidence of Catholicism enables us to subsume its suicide rate under the more abstract and general propositions.

There are several formal similarities between the positivist notion of nomological explanation or prediction and Weber's discussion of the role of nomological knowledge in causal analysis. For both Weber and the positivist the explanandum is a 'historically given individual configuration'. The actual process of explanation in both cases consists of two components: (1) knowledge of certain facts pertaining to the phenomenon under study ('ontological knowledge' for Weber; knowledge of particular circumstances or initial conditions for the positivist) and (2) knowledge of particular empirical rules or laws ('nomological knowledge'). Following Carl Hempel (1959), we can present the positivist and Weberian explanatory format schematically:

Positivist (Hempel, 1959:273)		Weber (1949:174)
	$L_1, L_2, \ldots, L_n$	nomological knowledge
Explanans	$C_1, C_2, \ldots, C_n$	ontological knowledge
Explanandum	E	causally adequate explanation

The horizontal line in the above scheme represents, in both cases, an operation whereby the general laws and statements of particular fact are combined to produce the explanation.

These formal similarities between Weber and the positivists seem to have confused (or given false comfort to) some writers who find in Weber's methodology 'a partial return to the positivistic tradition of the founders of sociology' (Martindale, 1959:69). While Weber's use of concepts like 'nomological knowledge', 'empirical rules', 'causality', and even 'explanation' would appear to support such an interpretation, the differences which underly the similarities between Weber and the positivists are so profound as to remove any doubts as to Weber's relationship to the founders of sociology. Three of these differences are of special importance to the present discussion. These pertain to: (1) the nature and origins of nomological knowledge, (2) the operation whereby factual and nomological knowledge are combined to produce an explanation, and (3) the goal of explanation in social science.

The nature and origins of nomological knowledge

Within the positivist tradition, the propositions which constitute nomological knowledge can be of two types: *deterministic propositions,* which provide 'strict and precise predictability of individual events', or *statistical propositions,* which provide 'predictability on the basis of stable frequency ratios or according to strict laws governing frequency distributions' (Feigl, 1953:409). Although the two forms of proposition have different origins – deduction and induction respectively – the explanation yielded by both types is deductive in that, as we saw above, the explanandum is subsumed under general statements and thereby 'predicted'.

From the perspective of the positivist, Weber's discussion of nomological knowledge must seem rather confusing. According to Weber, such knowledge consists of 'general empirical rules' which are expressed as *probabilities* that human beings are prone to react in certain ways in given situations (1949:174).

It is customary to designate various sociological generalizations, as for example 'Gresham's Law' as 'laws'. These are, in fact, typical probabilities confirmed by observation to the effect that under certain given conditions an expected course of social action will occur, which is understandable in terms of the typical motives and typical subjective intentions of the actors (1968:18).

Although this type of knowledge is based on induction, few positivists would recognize the procedure as such. Weber is not talking about enumerative induction – 'stable frequency ratios or according to strict laws governing frequency distributions' – but rather about a kind of interpretive operation which is based ultimately on judgments of everyday life or what the phenomenologists would call 'common-sense knowledge'. Thus, Weber suggests that the empirical rules which make up our nomological knowledge are 'derived from our own experience and our knowledge of the conduct of others' (1949:174). Although Weber does not spend much time on the specific question of statistical analysis (i.e., positivist induction) in his methodological writings, what he does say leaves little doubt that he did not feel this was a fruitful approach for social scientists. For example, in his essay on 'Knies and the Problem of Irrationality', first published in 1905, he wrote:

Suppose that somehow an empirical-statistical demonstration

of the strictest sort is produced, showing that all men everywhere who have ever been placed in a certain situation have invariably reacted in the same way and to the same extent. . . . Such a demonstration would not bring us a single step closer to the 'interpretation' of this reaction . . . it follows that even an ideally comprehensive empirical-statistical demonstration of the regular recurrence of a reaction will still *fail* to satisfy the criteria concerning the kind of knowledge which we expect from history and those 'socio-cultural sciences' which are related to history in this respect (1975:128–9).

Later, in the notes which were published as a methodological introduction to *Economy and Society* he referred to the 'rare ideal cases' in which statistical analyses might be appropriate in sociology (1968:10,12).

If positivists find Weber's notion of probability without statistics confusing, they will certainly be perplexed by his claim that his type of nomological knowledge gives rise to causal imputations in which we can have more confidence than in those based on statistics.

A judgment of 'possibility' [which, as we will see in the following section, is the critical operation for the establishment of causality] in the sense in which the expression is used here, means, then, the continuous reference to 'empirical rules'. The category of 'possibility' is thus not used in its negative form [as it would be in statistics]. It is, in other words, not an expression of our ignorance or incomplete knowledge in contrast with the assertive or apodictic judgment. Rather, to the contrary, it signifies here the reference to a positive knowledge of the 'laws of events', to our 'nomological' knowledge, as they say (1949:173–4).

We will have more to say on judgments of possibility in the following section. At this point, it is enough to note that Weber's confidence in probabilities based on nomological or 'positive' knowledge stems from the fact that such knowledge is the result of *verstehen* (interpretative understanding). In order to get a clearer picture of the role of interpretation in the formation of causal generalizations, we will take a brief and highly selective look at this extremely important component of Weber's methodology.

Although the concept of interpretive understanding appears in all of Weber's methodological works, the most extensive and clearest treatment is found in his essay on 'Knies and the Problem of Irrationality' (1975:125–91). Since our present concern is with the relationship between *verstehen* (interpretative understanding) and nomological knowledge, it will not be necessary to recount Weber's elaborate discussion of interpretation and the cultural sciences. For our purposes, the important features of that discussion include Weber's critique of empathy, his notion of interpretation as an analogical procedure, and his insistence that 'whenever interpretation is employed in empirical science, then . . . it is a form of causal knowledge' (1975:154–5).

Scholarly opinion seems polarized on the question of the role of empathy in Weber's interpretive methodology. One extreme is represented, for example, by Theodore Abel, who has suggested that 'the operation of *verstehen* is performed by analyzing a behavior situation in such a way – usually in terms of general "feeling-states" – that it parallels some personal experience of the interpreter' (1948:218). There is support for this interpretation in several of Weber's writings. For example, in *Economy and Society* he suggests:

> The more we ourselves are susceptible to such emotional reactions as anxiety, anger, ambition, envy, jealousy, love, enthusiasm, pride, vengefulness, loyalty, devotion and appetites of all sorts, and to the 'irrational' conduct which grows out of them, the more readily can we empathize with them. Even when such emotions are found in a degree of intensity of which the observer himself is completely incapable, he can still have a significant degree of emotional understanding of their meaning and can interpret intellectually their influence on the course of action and the selection of means (1968:6).

On the other side of the issue, Guy Oakes argues that Weber's interpretive understanding is 'not a peculiar kind of intuition . . . nor is it a diffuse, unanalyzable feeling, the alleged results of a putative ability to "participate sympathetically" or "empathetically" in socio-cultural phenomena' (Weber, 1975:28). As is the case with Abel's formulation, there is ample support for Oakes's position in Weber (cf.1975:159–60);

The reason for the apparent contradiction here is that while Weber did recognize there was a role for empathy in interpretive understanding, such an understanding, in the service of science, is not exhausted by empathy. The major limitation of empathy, in this regard, is that it presents itself to us as an object of immediate experience. I have an empathetic understanding of an action when I can place myself 'inside' the actor and participate directly in his or her thoughts and feelings. The problem with this type of direct inner experience is that it does not, in and of itself, constitute nomological knowledge. In Weber's words, 'the object of immediate experience . . . cannot be the object of a proposition – that is, an empirical explanation of facts' (1975:160).

For purposes of scientific explanation, empathy must undergo a process of *abstraction* and *analysis*. First, certain aspects of the experience in question have to be *selected out* according to the purposes of the research (1975:166). For example, the fearful thoughts and anguished feelings of Brutus the conspirator may be accessible to the sensitive observer. However, these may not be as relevant for an understanding of Caesar's death as Brutus' sense of patriotic duty or his feelings of loyalty to the other conspirators. Once the relevant aspects are selected out (more will be said on this later), they are, by means of analogy, compared with the experiences of others who have been involved in similar, or in some other way comparable, situations (ibid., 162). After we have been able to establish on the basis of the facts that Caesar's assassination was 'political' (as opposed, say, to 'personal'), then we are able to compare it to other acts of patriotism or loyalty. Relying on 'our own experience and our knowledge of the conduct of others', we are able to conclude that people who are strongly committed to a cause are prone to attempt to eliminate obstacles they perceive to be standing in the way of its realization. We, thus, have an 'empirical rule' under which to 'subsume Brutus' act. And Caesar's death has been accounted for in a 'causal' manner.

Nomological knowledge and causal explanation

The key to any causal assertion is the manner in which a fact or set of facts is justified as accounting for another fact or set of facts. For the positivists, justification is based on a 'covering law'. X accounts for Y because we are in possession of a law, in which we have confidence, which states that type Y events necessarily follow the occurrence of type X events. In our previous example, the account of the low suicide rate in Spain, in terms of the high incidence of Catholicism, was justified by the nomological statement that 'in any social group, the rate of suicide varies with the rate of Protestantism'. The operation, signified by the horizontal line in Hempel's scheme, by which an abstract proposition justifies the necessary linking of concrete events is deduction according to the rules of logic.

We have already suggested that, for Weber, nomological knowledge is not related to the event to be explained as a series of covering laws but rather as an analogical context which makes a causal judgment reasonable. Our general knowledge that patriots seek to eliminate tyranny along with our ontological knowledge that Brutus considered himself to be a patriot and Caesar to be a tyrant enabled us to explain Caesar's death. However, our explanation is neither *necessary* nor probabilistic (in the statistical sense). Rather, it is adequate or sufficient to satisfy our need to understand the specific event in question.

The notion of adequate causality did not originate with Weber. It was developed in the 1880s by the Freiburg physiologist, J. Von Kries, whose explorations in the theory of probability led him to advance the notion of 'objective possibility', a notion which he felt might be applied to the human sciences and to the law. Von Kries's ideas on adequate cause had a significant impact on German legal theory. By the time Weber turned his attention to it, it had been discussed extensively, and therefore modified and developed by a number of legal scholars (Hart and Honoré, 1973:417). Although any complete discussion of Weber's construal of Von Kries's theory would require an analysis of the various modifications which were available to him, we will simply focus on the key elements of the theory and then proceed directly to Weber's own thinking in this regard. The following discussion of Von Kries is based on an analysis offered by Hart and Honoré (1973:411-41).

According to Von Kries, an action or event is considered to be the adequate cause of a particular occurrence if two questions can be answered in the affirmative: 1) is the action or event a *sine qua non* of the occurrence? and 2) did the action or event significantly raise the objective probability of the occurrence? If the answer to both is 'Yes' then the action is an *adequate cause* of the occurrence. If an affirmative answer can be given only to the first question, then the causal relation between the act and the occurrence is non-adequate or coincidental. The example Von Kries offers of non-adequate causation is of the coachman who falls asleep, permitting the coach to deviate from the original route. During the course of the new route the passenger is struck by lightning. While 'falling asleep', in this instance, was a *sine qua non* of the occurrence, it did not increase the probability of being struck by lightning, which is extremely small regardless of whether the coachman is awake or asleep. Thus, the somnolent breach of duty was a coincidence, rather than a 'cause' of the passenger's unfortunate experience (Hart and Honoré, 1973:416).

Although the notion of probability in Von Kries was inspired by mathematics, he was aware that judgments of objective possibility in history and in everyday life could not always be applied with mathematical precision. However, this did not affect the validity of the approach. Indeed, it is evident from the example of the sleeping coachman that Von Kries's approach to causality is quite consistent with the procedures of common sense. He felt that the layman could make similar judgments by appealing to 'the teachings of experience and the regular course of events' (1973:415). The notion of adequate causality was simply a rational reconstruction of the common man's intuitive approach.

The legal concept of the 'regular course of events', which, according to Hart and Honoré, was given both a justification and a more precise formulation by Von Kries, served as the starting point for Weber's analysis of objective possibility. In legal discourse the notion of the 'regular course of events' refers to a theory of causality which holds that an event is responsible for a particular consequence if its occurrence departs from a regularly expected course of events. For example, in seeking the cause of an automobile accident, investigators look for 'what went wrong', i.e., what *unusual event* caused the driver to lose control.

It is evident that the two 'tests' applied by Von Kries (that of *conditio sine qua non* and that of objective possibility) would both formalize and, in those rare ideal cases where numerical probabilities can be stated, increase the precision of legal as well as common-sense approaches to causality in everyday life. Like Von Kries, Weber reconstituted the intuitive approach to adequate causality. In so doing, he retained the notion of objective possibility but presented it through the procedures of the intellectual experiment by means of 'imaginary constructs'. Briefly, the event or process in question is reconstructed as an ideal, typical sequence of occurrences (i.e., a 'regular course of events') *without* those features to which we have attributed causal significance. We then contrast what actually happened with our constructed type. Our purpose in this is the establishment of the reasonable conclusion that the outcome under study would not have occurred had the exceptional circumstances to which we have attributed causal significance not been present (cf. Weber, 1949:174ff, esp. 180–1). This experiment is essentially the posing in the negative of the question raised by Von Kries: Did the action in question raise, according to our knowledge of the course of empirical events (i.e., nomological knowledge), the probability of the outcome?

Causality and the goals of social science

The foregoing discussion of the constitutive elements of Weber's causal analysis has demonstrated (again!) that his approach to sociology was quite different from that of the founders of the discipline and their epigones who dominate modern social science. To consider Max Weber to be a precursor of modern, enlightened positivism, as do many in the Parsonian tradition for example, is to reduce the corpus of his substantive work to a reservoir of interesting hypotheses and to ignore his extensive methodological writings altogether. Let us quickly review our discussion of the operations and constituent elements of causal analysis in Weber's writings.

The goal of social science for Weber is the interpretation and explanation of concrete social actions and their consequences. Although we did not focus our attention on interpretation in and of itself – that would have taken us into the nature of meaning and the typology of motives – our discussion of nomological propositions led us to conclude that they are products of *verstehen* combined with the operations of abstraction (isolation, selection, generalization) and comparison (analogy). In brief, we concluded that interpretation and explanation are *not* differing and opposing processes. They are one and the same method applied to different levels of abstraction. Interpretation involves the comprehension of the intended meaning of an individual action or the significative structure of transindividual activity (e.g., a religious movement, a school of art, etc.). Explanation involves the insertion of the interpreted event into a larger context by means of abstraction and comparison and the development of judgments of objective possibility. Thus, the interpretation of the concrete event of Caesar's assassination as a type of political activity enables the research not only to understand Brutus' motives but also to explain subsequent events in Roman history.

The suggestion that interpretation and explanation in the human sciences are essentially the same may seem confusing in light of Weber's claim in several of his works that the concept of causality in the social and historical sciences is no different from that in the natural sciences. There are two dimensions to this claim, both of which can be clarified by means of Kant's notion of the uncaused causality of freedom. The first relates to the explanation of concrete events and will be taken up presently when we comment on idiographic causality. The second relates to Kant's notion of the intellectual as cause and appearance as effect.

Kant would agree with Weber's suggestion that the question of whether 'someone through his action has "caused" a certain external effect, is purely a question of causation' (1949:168). Kant would also agree with the opening lines of the methodological introduction to *Economy and Society* where causal explanation is directed toward the 'course and consequences' of social action. In brief, the focus of causal analysis for Weber, as for Kant when he dealt with the realm of morality, is not on the *origins* of social action but on its *effects* in the external world. Once this focus is

120

established, then the *logic* of causal attribution is the same in both the human and the natural worlds. For example, it does not really make a difference whether the suspected cause of an automobile accident resides in the realm of human action or 'blind nature'. In both cases we have what is, in Weber's words, 'purely a question of causation'. And in either case, the attribution of a causal connection could be made by means of an assessment of the accident in terms of an ideal, typical conception of the normal course of events and the establishment of a judgment of objective possibility.

This leads us to the primary dimension of Weber's claim, namely that the most crucial distinguishing feature among the sciences is not their subject matter but the *goals* they establish for explanation. Sociology and history are, for Weber, idiographic sciences. Their goal is the interpretation and explanation of concrete historical events. While nomological knowledge is indispensable to sociological explanation as a 'heuristic means' (1949:76), the development of abstract propositions, whether in the form of empirical rules, statements of probability, or ideal, typical descriptions, should never be confused with the goal of sciences (cf. for example, 1975:150; 1949:75ff, 168; 1968:13).

Weber's position on the goals of science stands in sharp contrast to that taken by proponents of the nomothetic sciences. The latter group, which includes non-positivists (e.g., Karl Popper) as well as positivists, maintains that the goal of science is the development and testing of universal-type propositions. From this perspective, research which generates explanations of concrete, individual events such as an earthquake or a riot or a suicide rate is actually a heuristic means to the goal of the establishment and verification (or falsification) of nomological knowledge. Seen in this light, for example, Durkheim's study of suicide was simply a means to the establishment of universal laws about anomie and social structure. In any event, the continuous quest for highly abstract propositions which state universal and *necessary* relations between empirical processes (conceived as *variables*) is the distinctive feature of the purely generalizing, i.e., nomothetic sciences. This is the case regardless of the subject matter of the science in question. The idiographic sciences, on the other hand, regardless of their subject matters, search for the *sufficient grounds* for concrete events rather than their necessary relations (1975:194). In Weber's words, 'whenever it is a question of concrete events, the judgment of necessity is by no means the only or even merely the major form in which the category of causality can appear. There is . . . in this respect, no distinction from particular natural events, and even in explanation in the sphere of nature. . . .' (1949:128)

Idiographic science and the causality of freedom

It can be seen from the foregoing that Weber's approach to causal analysis did not depend, in a logical or conceptual sense, on the fact that what is being explained is social action. Rather, it arose out of his interest in accounting for concrete, individual events. The point here is not that Weber did not believe that idiographic approaches to causality were the most appropriate form of analysis for the human and cultural sciences. It is quite clear that he did. What is important for our purposes is that Weber was able to justify his appeal to the causality of freedom on 'empirical' rather than metaphysical grounds. Whereas Kant and his epigones in the human sciences had arrived at idiographic science from the ineffability of the 'intellectual as cause', Weber started with the analysis of concrete events and was led thereby to indeterminacy and freedom, in what he called the empirical sense of those terms. Weber used two arguments here, one which dealt primarily with indeterminacy in the natural world and the other which focused on the 'freedom' of rational action.

The indeterminacy of particular natural and human events arises from the fact that on an empirical level we can never isolate the many complex processes which led to their occurrence. Generalization, which is the key to positivist assertions of causality, 'has no meaning from the point of view of an absolutely unique cosmic or quasi-cosmic development' (1975:195–6).

> Both human and non-human ('living' or 'dead') *entities,* conceived as finite aspects of the totality of cosmic events, can never be exhaustively 'deduced' from exclusively 'nomological' knowledge. This is because a concrete entity is invariably (and not only within the domain of the 'personal') an intensively infinite multiplicity of properties. From the point of view of the logic of causal relations in history, these properties become the object of a scientific investigation only as 'given' verifiable components that are causally significant (1975:194).

In other words, the researcher selects from the multiplicity of contributing factors those which are significant in terms of the interests of the study. In light of the factors which must inevitably be ignored, there is no way in which those so selected can be considered to have determined the event in question. Thus, Weber maintained that for history or any other idiographic discipline, 'the postulate of the strict "necessity" of the concrete . . . event is not only an ideal. It is in principle unattainable' (1975:197).

With respect to Weber's discussion of freedom and social action, it might be useful first to recall his suggestion that the introduction of the philosophical concept of freedom into the causal sequences of sociology is about as sound as the introduction of miracles. Compare that suggestion with the following statement which appeared in 'Knies and the Problem of Irrationality' (1975:194):

> Every purely rational interpretation of a concrete historical process obviously and necessarily *presupposes* the existence of 'freedom of the will', in every sense of this expression which is possible within the domain of the empirical.

Earlier in the same essay, Weber had defined the 'empirically "free" actor' as one 'who acts on the basis of his *deliberations*' (1975:193).

In order to determine what was for Weber the scientifically legitimate use of the notion of 'freedom of the will', it will be useful to discuss briefly those uses he wanted to exclude. This latter category includes two interpretations which were fairly common in nineteenth-century Germany. The first identified freedom with morality. In the words of Kant, 'a free will and a will under moral laws are identical . . . if freedom of the will is presupposed, morality together with its principle follows from it by the mere analysis of its concept' (Kant, 1976:102). Weber's most explicit rejection of this position came in his arguments against the historical evaluation of particular actions and in his carefully stated distinction between scientific and legalistic uses of the notion of adequate causality (cf. 1949:123ff and 168ff).

While the first of the 'philosophical' uses of freedom was criticized on the grounds it violated ethical neutrality, the second was objected to for its distortion of empirical reality. Opponents of positivistic determinism in late nineteenth-century Germany had argued that freedom can be demonstrated by the existence of irrationality. Irrational acts, it was maintained, are by definition unpredictable and therefore are indicative of an undetermined or free will. This position, which had strong romantic as well as reactionary overtones, found an articulate expression in the philosophy of Nietzsche wherein the madman was often portrayed as the messenger of truth. Within the human sciences this position implied that freedom and unpredictability were synonymous. The free actions of historical personages were, in principle, incalculable and, therefore, beyond the scope of scientific interpretation.

Weber's response to these arguments was rooted entirely in the empirical domain of phenomenological analysis. If we reflect on the feelings associated with our various actions, he suggested, we find we are most likely to experience a sense of freedom when we behave rationally. Rational action, of course, is in its purest form the most understandable and, indeed, 'predictable' type of behavior (cf. 1975:186ff). On the other hand, it is when we act on the basis of emotion or impulse, i.e., irrationally, that we feel we have lost control of our will. Therefore, Weber concluded, we are *empirically* most free when our behavior is most predictable and most subject to analysis in terms of nomological knowledge (1949:124ff; 1975:192ff). It is evident that, as with his position on indeterminacy, Weber's notion of the free will is rooted in his idiographic approach to social-science. The freedom of rational action is not grounded on the highly abstract formulations of the theoretician but on the empirical attitudes of everyday life.

Conclusions

Max Weber's commitment to human liberty through rational self-determination presented a potential conflict with his equally strong commitment to scientific explanation. His best-known effort to eliminate this conflict is in his writings on value-neutrality in science. However, his most effective solution was in the development of a system of scientific explanation which utilized a form of causality which did not contradict the possibility of human freedom. Although similar in many respects to Kant's 'causality of free acts', Weber's non-deterministic causality was justified by an appeal not to metaphysical principles of moral freedom but to the concrete empirical realities of everyday life. Thus, we saw in our discussions of nomological knowledge, adequate causality, and objective possibility that Weber never strayed far from the judgments of common sense. Although it would be an oversimplification to regard Weber's approach as phenomenological in this respect, there is no question that his conception of the human sciences as essentially idiographic disciplines enabled him to utilize criteria for causal explanation which were rational reconstructions of those found among ordinary people. This, in turn, made it possible for Weber to avoid the abstract and deterministic models proposed by the founders of modern social science and at the same time offered him a seemingly non-tendentious way of affirming his belief in the possibility of human freedom.

6 Sociological demystification of the arts and music:

Max Weber and beyond

K. Peter Etzkorn

In memory of Alex Simirenko (1931–79)

There is hardly an area of social life in the early part of the twentieth century which did not attract the interest of Max Weber. Many of his analyses of contemporary issues employ illustrations that are derived from his own personal experience. Prominent amongst these are contacts with a wide range of friends and intellectuals who provided him with information and stimulation. These were supplemented by his enormous capacity for digesting the scholarly literature and newspapers of his day. In the realm of the fine arts and music Max Weber, the comparative historical sociologist, enriched his personal life through direct encounters with these arts whenever the opportunity arose.

In this chapter, the author will attempt to set Weber's dialogue with the arts into a perspective with characteristically Weberian accents. A dominant threat that appears to be woven through all of his scholarly endeavors is the question how the eternal dialectic between *Sein* (being) and *Sollen* (what something should be) applies to a given phenomenon. In the author's view, his way of working out this dialectic can be considered as the driving impulse of his scientific career as it is embodied in his very person. This dialectic, while deeply personal, is thereby a crucial part of Weber's response to the early history of German sociology.

The history of the reception in the United States of Weber's contributions to the social sciences can also be seen as having been afflicted by a lack of appreciation for this perspective. It is difficult to gain an understanding of the complexity of Weber's total work unless one recognizes it as his deeply personal struggle with the normative bases and the sensual nature of human values as they are expressed in individual lives. This difficulty for Americans with gaining access to and appreciating Weber's writings was initially increased by the highly selective and not always successful translations through which he came to their attention. Until recently most American sociologists had been exposed to only a segment of Weber's total work. In these selections Weber appeared to be preoccupied with developing a set of analytic tools by which modern society could be described in a value-free manner.

A realization of the tendentious interpretation that Weber's work had received, for example in the area of bureaucracy, was unmistakably driven home after this author had spent several weeks studying the administration of German higher education support in the Bonn government. Some American sociologists had faulted Weber's work for not elaborating more fully the 'informal' in contrast to the 'formal' aspects of bureaucratic organizations. Yet Weber's texts on bureaucracy still applied to the empirical bureaucratic world that this author encountered in Bonn in the mid-1970s as if they had been written then rather than half a century ago.

These writings dealt with developing a methodical understanding of bureaucracy, which was derived from his personal observations of administrative organizations. Weber's ideal type (constructed as a methodological tool for measuring the *Sein* of administrative organizations) was closely enmeshed with the legal requirements, that is, the *Sollen* of the Prussian state bureaucracy. These normative assumptions survived changes in the forms of government from the Weimar democracy through the Hitler dictatorship and the post-World War II government reforms. Administrative processes in the Bonn government of the 1970s are still highly legalistic and, thus, empirically close to Weber's ideal type.

This is different from what one would expect if one were to rely on American critics of Weber's treatment of rationalized administrative organizations. Many of these criticisms failed to appreciate that Weber was dealing with particular situations. The sociologist's observations of the ideal-typical construct are an analogue of the 'legal' norm for the operation of government bureaucracy; Weber's ideal type of yore (constructed as a value–free yardstick for measuring the *Sein* of administrative organizations) appeared to be reified in the ongoing operation of the government machinery.

The reception in the United States of Weber's studies on the arts has also been haphazard (Weber, 1958c; Honigsheim, 1968; Marianne Weber, 1975; Etzkorn, 1973b). The overall picture within German research on the sociology of the arts is very similar.

It is illuminating to consider Weber's own comments on the social situation that influenced the reception and application of his methodological perspective to the sociological study of the arts. He suggests that the typical reader of art-historical discourses expects to find expressions of evaluation and suggested interpretational points of view rather than empirically causal or aesthetically value-referential discussions; yet the very logics of these perspectives are distinctly different. The personal-value-interpretational approach is in no way identical either with the scientific empirical or with the aesthetic perspective. He holds both of these perspectives, however, to be indispensable for disciplined inquiry into matters artistic. In Weber's (1973:524) words: 'Whoever wishes to produce results (findings) in art historical, empirical investigations must have the additional capacity of *understanding* artistic productions. This is unthinkable without the capacity for aesthetic judgments; that is, without the capacity for evaluation.'

In his personal life, Weber developed such a capacity. His appetite for artistic encounters appears to have been insatiable. As a youth growing up in upper-class German society, he was surrounded by piano music, availed himself of good reading, participated in the reading aloud of dramatic literature and attended theatres and concerts with subsequent discussions about these events in his cosmopolitan family. During his university studies, away from his family, and later during his days in military service, he continued his search for artistic experiences. Once he was married and travelling with Marianne, they would hunt for the unusual in the musical, theatrical, and fine arts, wherever they were. During their visit to the United States they attended the Yiddish theatre in New York. Marianne reports that, unlike some of his fellow travelers, 'he rejected for the time being any criticism of new things which was based on unfamiliarity with them. He was on the side of the new and empathized with it, as it were, in order to do it justice.'

Wherever the Webers traveled, they would partake of the arts – visit the home of Shakespeare, attend the music festivals in Bayreuth, admire the ancient temples in Rome, view the modern galleries in Berlin, and visit the Opera Comique in Paris. Theirs was an active personal interest in the gamut of the arts from painting to music and literature (1975:282, 497). Weber's personal association with artists was close. Indeed, he dedicated one of his volumes on the sociology of religion to a pianist who had opened up the complexities of reading orchestral scores to him. This musical lesson was to find reflection in his frustrated comment: 'If I could only display sketches of my [sociological] data in such a manner!'

A wide range of literature from Tolstoy, Dostoevsky, and Henry George, to the regular members of the Weber's Heidelberg discussion circle prior to World War I, dominated much of the Webers' intellectual lives. Weber himself wrote poetry, collected prints, and bought a piano. On this instrument he was able to illustrate the principles laid out in his musicological studies. In describing his reactions to these experiences he frequently employed terms of a very personal (*wert-interpretierend*) nature – as when he judges that the operas *Die Meistersinger* and *Tristan und Isolde* are the only 'eternal' works of Wagner (1975:503). Similarly 'personal' were their reactions to Paris, as Marianne writes: 'as an expression of modern decay there was every evening in several theatres the mixture of lust and sentimentality contained in dramas of adultery; only Maeterlinck's symbolistic fairy-tale plays were pure and serious' (1975:500).

The very first book that Weber studied after recovery from his illness was a history of art. As Marianne reports: 'He fetched one volume after another from the library of the [Roman] artists' association' (1975:25). From what can be learned, especially from Honigsheim (1963), there is every indication that Weber enjoyed many and varied opportunities for experiencing the arts, that he searched out the unconventional and the new, and that he utilized these occasions for gaining first-hand information on the production of all types of artistic creations, that he inquired about employment and working conditions as well as the remuneration of contemporary artists, and about other economic data such as the price of paintings, or their re-sale value.

Keeping this personal relationship to the arts in mind, what, then, is Weber's sociological (empirical) treatment of the arts? An appropriate point for starting this inquiry is Silbermann's (1973) bibliography on the sociology of the arts. Failing to find anything there of Max Weber's except his fragmentary notes on music and the section on Chinese literati, this author recalled a conversation with Honigsheim in which he said that Weber's sociology of religion contained the essence of his sociological views on aesthetics and the arts. For the purposes of this exposition the author refers principally to Weber's discussion of the arts in various contexts of his sociology of religion and of progress in his discourse on *Wertfreiheit* (value freedom) before the *Verein für Sozialpolitik*. These contexts allow a broader view of Weber's concern with the arts than can be gained from dealing with his fragmentary text on music. Such more limited exposition has already been provided by Etzkorn (1960:232–4) and Silbermann (1963).

In this section the author constructs a synthesis of what might be considered Weber's broader views on aesthetics. Naturally this attempt will drastically simplify his wide historical sweep.

Artistic productions are intertwined with religious practices for most periods of human history. Only under specified conditions of religious practice, namely with the rise of ethical religion, does a self-conscious separation between religion and art (or for that matter sexuality) occur. With the separation of art from religion, when art becomes an autonomous sphere, art tends to acquire its own constitutive values. Artistic values may even form the foundation of social communities to be built on them – and these may then develop into a self-conscious aesthetic system – climaxing the process leading to the separation and independence from religion. From that point on, the aesthetic value system, as it emphasizes the intellectual and subjective, comes in conflict with both traditional (religious) values and with communally supportive ethical principles. For Weber the aesthetic system maximizes the values of the individualized and subjective elements in human experience. Thus it turns into the antithesis of community (1968:608):

> Every unreflectively receptive approach to art starts from the significance of the *content,* and that may induce formation of a community. But the conscious discovery of uniquely aesthetic values is reserved for an intellectualist civilization. This development causes the disappearance of those elements in art which are conducive to community formation and conducive to the compatibility of art with the religious will to salvation. Indeeed, religion violently rejects as sinful the type of salvation within the world which art *qua* art claims to provide. . . .
>
> But this unappealable subjectivity of all judgments about human relationships that actually comes to the fore in the cult of estheticism, may well be regarded by religion as one of the profoundest forms of idiosyncratic lovelessness conjoined with cowardice.

Art, as it were, attains an independent aesthetic, or value system, which governs its substance (the relationships of artistic matter), its practitioners, and its functioning in society *vis-à-vis* other institutional sectors, but especially religion. While Weber does not analyze extensively how this artistic-aesthetic value system articulates with other realism, his analysis indicates that the eventual supremacy of aesthetics over religion and ethics is reached when (1968:608):

> This tension increases with the advance of intellectualism, which may be described as quasi-aesthetic. The rejection of responsibility for ethical judgment and the fear of appearing

129

bound by tradition, which come to the fore of intellectualist periods, shift judgments whose intention was originally ethical into an aesthetic key. Typical is the shift from the judgment 'reprehensible' to the judgment 'in poor taste'.

Art, at this stage of self-conscious development, attains a position in social life with both a series of distinct occupational (artistic) activities *and* a body of 'theoretical' (ideological?) – i.e., aesthetic – pronouncements concerning these activities, their results (art objects), and certain relationships to the social setting in which this is embedded.

In order to appreciate more fully Weber's views on the developmental relations between artistic practices and the establishment of a governing secular aesthetic, a look at his discussion of the methodological issue of studying social change and social development, and the appropriate methodological criteria for the scientific discovery of 'progress', will be illuminating. An exclusive focus on Weber's discussion of the dialectic between art and religion might be methodologically disappointing. These discussions, though rich in historical detail and immensely impressive in the display of scholarly erudition, sometimes do not analyze the treatment of various *practices* (music, pictures, and poetry) separately from discourse on what *is* art, as when Weber states how 'orgiastic religion leads most readily to song and music; ritualistic religion inclines toward the pictorial arts; religions enjoining love favor the development of poetry and music' (1968:609). In concluding his discussion of links between religion and the arts Weber writes, 'the one important fact for us is the significance of the marked rejection of all distinctively aesthetic devices by those religions which are rational [i.e., Judaism, ancient Christianity, ascetic Protestantism]. . . . Their rejection of aesthetics is either a symptom or an instrument of religion's increasingly rational influence upon the conduct of life' (1968:610).

Methodological questions of the study of historical processes occupied Weber's attention throughout his scholarly career. Besides selecting topics for his substantive studies, the methodological issues of how such studies could be conducted in a 'scientific' manner – and how he, the scientist, could objectively deal with the differences between *Sein* and *Sollen* in empirical analyses – dominated Weber's moral being.

On rare occasions the arts attract this specific methodological attention outside the context of religion. Early in the century, soon after his recovery from illness and his extensive study of art history in Rome, he devotes space in the essay on Knies and Roscher to the discussion of what types of reaction works of art call forth, and how works of art can be appreciated beyond the purely sentimental level (*Gefühl*). In this context he contends that art can be demystified – that it can be brought to a level of discourse through which personal experience of art can be shared (1973:120).

Weber differentiates here between two basic types of response to works of art:

1 *Nacherleben* (re-experiencing) of historical events which does not guarantee that there will be any correspondence with the historical event; it generates highly personal, evaluating responses of limited scientific use. It may even be outright dangerous in denying the difference between the sensations of the creative artists and those of the beholders;

2 *wert-beziehende Interpretation* (value relational interpretation) imposes an order (*Formung des 'historischen Individuum'*) from our contemporary perspective on historical data. This type of interpretation may proceed in two separate ways:

(a) what we can find of value in the object; and

(b) what we should find of value (aesthetic value judgment).

Through both of these approaches, although the direction of the 'values' varies, the experiencing of artistic phenomena can be differentiated from purely emotional responses; it becomes rationalized. Through determining the respective value, the object is raised above the level of the emotional (1973:24). A few years later Weber squarely addressed himself to this methodological issue in his presentation on the 'Meaning of Value Free Positions' before the *Verein für Sozialpolitik* (Baumgarten, 1964:129). This lecture became the basis for an augmented 1917 version, '*Der Sinn der Wertfreiheit der soziologischen und oekonomischen Wissenschaften*' (The meaning of value freedom in sociology and economics). In between these events may be placed Weber's systematic studies of the musicological literature on tonal systems. These form the basis of the 1921 posthumous edition of *Die Rationalen und Soziologischen Grundlagen der Musik,* materials from which he had used in presentations to various audiences, ranging from his weekly gatherings in Heidelberg to his seminar in Munich in 1919 and the 1920 preface to Volume 1 of *Sociology of Religion* (Baumgarten, 1964:483–4; Honigsheim, 1963:248).

In the 1913 text Weber raises the question of the conditions in which the concept artistic 'progress' can be used in a neutral, value-free manner. He points up the necessity of differentiating between progress (a) in the meaning of continuation as an ongoing process and in the meaning of increase in value. Progress in both these meanings in turn can be analyzed as being an aspect of either (a) the irrational-emotional affective spheres of psychic *(seelische)* behavior, or (b) the rational sphere, i.e., in action situations in which 'subjective desires for a planned course of action are directed through means which are considered appropriate for the given purpose' (Baumgarten, 1964:129). Weber illustrated this discussion by references to the way in which art historians (like Wölfflin in his *Klassische Kunst)* treat the concept of artistic progress. Further he shows how the majority of significant contributions to aesthetics developed evaluations of works of art that elaborate the mere contrast between art and non-art by applying further analytic dimensions. Some of these are the distinction between attempt at and solution of an artistic problem, the differential evaluation of various solutions or the treatment of partial versus fully successful solutions, or the exemplification of single works of art as contrasted with those of entire artistic periods. In the expanded 1917 treatment of this topic Weber offers additional illustrations for his thesis that empirical art history and the sociology of the arts will equally profit from 'an entirely technical, rational, and because of that unambiguous, concept of progress. The origin of Gothic architecture is first of all the result of the technically successful solution of the civil engineering problem of covering space by vault construction *(Überwölbung).'* Once this technological achievement had been attained, appropriate applications to other artistic fields such as sculpture could be made. At the same time, Weber observes, his new technological rationalism came into conflict with religiously and sociologically conditioned sentiments *(Gefühlsinhalt)* that found expression in the artistic creations of this period.

For Weber the sociology of art can unmask the substantive, technical, societal, and psychological conditions of new art styles. In so doing its scientific contribution is completed. There is no need to assign additional value judgments to the Gothic style in comparison to, say, the romantic, or to offer an aesthetic appraisal of individual buildings. Works of musical arts, for example, demand the sociological demystification as objects that have *a priori* aesthetic values. The aesthetic value of art cannot be the subject of sociological investigation since 'the application of a certain, even if most developed technique does not say the least about the aesthetic value of the work of art. . . . The creation of novel technical means at first signified only that there is a higher degree of differentiation, which has the potential of an increase in the quality of art – in the sense of *Wertsteigerung.* In reality it frequently leads to the opposite effect, the impoverishment of artistic sense of form' (1973:520–3).

While it is necessary for the sociologist to separate analytically an interest in technical dimensions of works of art, i.e., technical 'progress', from an evaluation of their intrinsic 'merit', Weber regards both these activities as essential to the art historian. This argument does not contradict Weber's claim that a developed personal sensitivity to intrinsic aspects of art appreciation was indeed essential for anyone interested in empirically studying the arts. Yet he suggests that unless this distinction is clearly drawn the scientific effect frequently will be that scholarly discussants will be talking past each other. In Weber's view the logical structures for empirical science and for the philosophical evaluating of aesthetics differ. Consequently, they must be kept apart in the analysis of art.

Weber's ethical quest for 'intellectual honesty' – knowing what you are doing and not pretending that you are doing something else – is a methodological consequence of his nominalistic approach to the study of social life. If one follows him, the reader will not find it difficult to conclude that rationalization in the arts may be exemplified by rather different specific referents and could be accomplished in different manifestations in different periods. In Weber's view it would be acceptable that, for example, the 'highest ideal of artistic perfection of the Renaissance was to be "rational" in the meaning of believing in a governing canon' (body of rational rules) – an ideal which was rationalistic in so far as it minimized traditional bonds and placed trust in the power, as well as the points of view, of natural reason in spite of some influences of platonizing mysticism (1920:266). Yet in his study of music, the meaning of rationalization would be the development of a sophisticated tuning system that accommodates simultaneous harmonic transpositions, i.e., the provision of a technical solution rather than the demand for normative–canonic compliance. What Weber says about the role of science in the study of religions may be extended to the sociology of the arts:

Fashion and the zeal of the *literati* would have us think that the specialist can today be spared, or degraded to a position subordinate to that of the seer. Almost all sciences owe something to dilettantes, often very valuable viewpoints. But dilettantism as a leading principle would be the end of science. He who yearns for seeing (showmanship) should go to the movies, though it will be offered to him copiously today in literary form in the present field of investigation also. Nothing is farther from the intent of these thoroughly serious studies than such an attitude. And I might add, whoever wants a sermon should go to a conventicle. The question of the relative value of the cultures which are compared here will not receive a single word (1930:29).

133

The sociologist, hence, will look for the *Sein* of art. In so applying rationalistic principles of empirical science to the study of art, speculations about the possible inner meaning (*Sinn*) of secular events are eliminated. For Weber there are enough questions raised by the empirical consequences of the arts to be made the focus of study. The intellectual gain will be the greater, the more the researcher resists the temptations of letting feelings and sentiments guide the analysis.

> Rejecting one's uninhibited surrender to the most intense – namely the artistic and erotic – forms of existential experience, is essentially a negative attitude. Yet it is obvious that it raises the power by which ethical and intellectual energies contribute to the course of rational accomplishments (1920:565).

It should be a significant clue for sociological studies of art that Weber on the basis of his comparative studies designates artistic along with erotic experiences as most (personally) intensive in history. His studies on religion make into a guiding theme the inquiry into the dialectic between the erotic and the religious, the intellectualization and rationalization of the erotic through the formalization of the religious realm (i.e., the *Askese der Religionsgemeinschaft*). Yet these studies also suggest to him that with increasing (empirical) rationalization there arises a dialectical return to heightened eroticism.

Regrettably there are few occasions in Weber's opus for systematic inquiry into the dialogue between religion and art. Weber's future studies might have led in this direction. Sporadic references in Marianne Weber indicate that Max was planning a series of systematic studies of this question. Numerous indications in his work suggest that Weber expected the interplay between religion and the arts to lead to a gradual emancipation of the arts from religion to a point at which the arts, with a full-fledged aesthetic and under the aegis of intellectualization, would take on quasi-ethical functions in social life. (Perhaps the contemporary interest in industrial societies in questions of the quality of life, the aesthetics of urban living, etc., rather than purely economic and rational considerations, would have been viewed by him as empirical evidence for his prediction?)

Max Weber and beyond

Weber did not live to elaborate these ideas about the historical processes in the arts into well-focused studies. But we can surmise what his chapters on these topics might have looked like. There

134

would have been inquiry into the conditions of artistic creativity under different economic systems. There would have been inquiry into the dependency of various art forms on the development of a cadre of artistic specialists (paralleling his interest in the religious virtuosi); there would have been inquiry into the relationships between the artistic priesthood and the congregation(s) of followers – as well as into the reciprocal impact of followers upon the creators of art. Methodological questions of what constitutes the boundaries of an artistic period, a style, would have been dealt with in his analyses. These and many other substantive topics would have been dominated by Weber's elaboration of methods for the study of the arts that would be self-consciously empirical, descriptive, non-evaluative, focused on the *Sein* rather than the *Sollen* of art.

The direct followers in these approaches are few and far between. Fewer still are those who specifically profess their indebtedness to Weber's precept. Most outstanding among those was Paul Honigsheim, who belonged to the circle of personal friends of the Webers in Heidelberg. He, too, was not alive long enough to complete his studies on the arts and music.

Elsewhere this author summarized some of these developments as they concern the sociology of music and came to the encouraging conclusion that – after a hiatus of half a century – renewed interest in the sociology of music is picking up where Weber left off with an effort at replacing the 'social problems' as well as the 'social indicator' approach to the sociology of art with a 'more directly sociological definition and study of music as musically defined social activity' (1920:40).

In conclusion, this author would like to offer a scheme for demystifying the arts which is consistent with Weber's concerns and proposed solutions.

For Weber, it would appear, studies of the arts would be essential for understanding the sweep of human history, on a level comparable to studies of religions and ethics. The arts are viewed as emanations primarily of civilizations with urban characteristics. Categorically he states at one point: 'The city and it alone has brought forth the phenomena of the history of art' (1927:316). But it can be assumed that Weber would have voiced similar reservations about the lack of historical and ethnographic data that forced him elsewhere to regard generalizations about religion as being of a tentative nature. It is Weber's thesis that artistic activities are linked to determined types of social development that interests us here, however, more so than the specific mention of the 'urban' characteristics of social life. This scheme built on

135

Weber would develop from the following demystifying considerations.

Art is of major significance in social history – on a level comparable to religion and ethics. Hence it can be empirically studied. The *empirical* mode of inquiry would need to differentiate between: 1) the *rationale* of art – within given contexts (theory and practice; but not ideology); 2) processes of *rationalization* within art.

1 The *rationale* of art can be established by the study of *intrinsic* determinants within the art community – such as the building materials available to architects, the musical tones and their relationships used by composers, the control of painting techniques and principles of perspective, etc., available to visual artists – and the relationship of the practitioners of these artistic occupations (their socialization, and the politics of control over intrinsic determinants) to other social institutions – religion, the state, the economic realm.

2 *Rationalization* within the arts can be established by focusing on:

  (a) rationalization of the *means* of artistic *activity*, which can be of two varieties:

    (1) *technical* means of art

    (2) *social organizational* means

  Appropriate examples would be:

    (1) the refinement of the tonal system through invention and perfection of musical instruments

    (2) the co-ordination of musical activities through the invention of the orchestra conductor; fund-raising schemes for the support of full-time musicians; theatre organizations; bureaucratization versus originality.

  (b) rationalization of the value system of the arts, as through the transformation of an implicit aesthetic into an extrinsic, intellectualized aesthetic with mandated ethical obligations.

The empirical study of the arts would examine the temporary, historically specific phenomenon through focusing on what is here called the *rationale* of the art (or elsewhere the sphere of artistic validity). Recently this author attempted to illustrate how the pluralistic dimensions of the musical lives of a major city could be brought under empirical control by using the tentative conceptualization of 'musical complexity'. The rationales of various musics would vary in their complexities within different musical communities (Etzkorn, 1976; 1973a).

The notion of *rationalization*, on the other hand, aims at defining these *empirical* elements that can be identified as being instrumentally related to artistic changes. Appropriate examples might be found in recent developments in avant-garde, mainly university-based, music. This music is sometimes viewed as breaking with the nineteenth- to early twentieth-century tradition of bourgeois, 'art for art's sake', music. This bourgeois quasi-absolute music had made its own break with prior traditions of functional music of a religious as well as secular (dance) nature. This break may be dated to the time of the development of the sonata form – or sociologically speaking, with the rise of organized middle-class audiences. These earlier as well as more recent musical changes can be empirically related changes within the *rationale* of music. Some contemporary composers (John Cage) explicate their views of the differences between the more traditional and the 'new' rationales. And, as Weber would have it, these rationales deal with intramusical dimensions (i.e., the rejection of well-tempered twelve-tone scales) as well as with relations between the performance situation and the music, i.e., multimedia involvement, or the break with traditional performance styles in the mannerisms of the performing artists. (There cannot be any extra musical situations in music since, unlike other arts, music requires a social situation to exist!)

The musical Dadaism of the present (Cage's anti-art) is posed as a total rejection of the traditional, bourgeois musical culture of the West. Cage postulates that the sounds must be unburdened from their traditions and the tones emancipated from structured music so as to be able to explore the true *nature* of sounds. Tonal relationships that are not found purely *in nature*, but are based on human constraints, should be rejected. Dahlhaus aptly named Cage's views 'musical Rousseauism' (1972:94–5). It can be demonstrated that this call for freedom from musical tradition and the thesis of 'back to the natural sound' is, indeed, nothing but an *Ersatz* (substitute) for traditional, bourgeois theory. It functions as a rationale for musical activity (or should it be for tonal soundings?). The mysticism of the search for natural music results in preventing music from negating its existence through an empty game of circular reasoning. With this new rationale came explorations of novel sounding techniques, of compositorial (notational) style, that remove musical decisions from the composer and assign them to performing artists (aleatoric music) – and again others that increase the composer's control over the sounds by making the composer the final controller over the computer-generated sound. Implied in the new rationale are specific relations between composers, performers, and audiences, new economic realities (the rejection of bourgeois musical traditions notwithstanding, the new composers insist on the econ-

137

omic support of bourgeois society), and electronic sound generating technologies (with associated costs that stagger one's imagination).

Weber's concept of rationalization of the arts easily provides an empirical handle for viewing these contemporary events. The rejection of the traditions of bourgeois music, as practiced by musical Dadaists, can be described and empirically analyzed by an examination of the means that are employed and that are considered appropriate for the given purpose. Such an analysis, of course, would extend Weber's very definition of 'rational action' to the sphere of artistic action. When this mode of analysis applied to Dada music, it can be shown that Dada musicians:

1 developed appropriate *technical means* for their un-form of artistic expression;
2 developed *social organizational means* for the support of these activities – if only by having maintained the bourgeois expectation that art must be supported for its own sake – note the U.S. government's support of contemporary music;
3 created a *'value system'* for the *'new art'* through making explicit the implicit aesthetic of artistic revolution.

These efforts among contemporary avant-garde movements have succeeded to various degrees among various splinter groups. One common characteristic would be, however, that they all utilize social mechanisms of 'workshops', conferences, symposia, festivals, New Music circles, composers' organizations, grants-man-ship committees, activities that lead toward the refinement and normative enforcement of the new aesthetic. It would appear that the New Music is perhaps more rationalized in this sense than almost any previous music, including the music of the bourgeoisie.

Perhaps it is prophetic that Weber responded to Ostwald's thesis that the balance of energy, not the diversity of phenomena, represented the perfection of life by saying, 'What a shame that what is art begins exactly where the point of view of the technician ends,' where, as it were, an evaluative and/or normative *Sollen* is superimposed on an empirically established *Sein* (1973:418). It is with this empirical generalization that the question of what is art, indeed, becomes a function of specific and determinable ingredients of social situations that add dimensions of *Sollen* (ethical obligations) to the *Sein* of existence. Claus Grimm (1979), without mentioning Weber's work once, appears to reach a similar conclusion when he argues that the concept 'art' as ordinarily used by art historians has analytic powers only for the most recent two centuries of the history of the West. Art as a separate form of social expression occurs only in certain historical circumstances. Current sociology appears to be catching up with Max Weber.

Part II

Historical-comparative case studies

7 Confucianism, Maoism, and Max Weber

David C. Yu

The purpose of this chapter is to apply Weber's typological concepts for the interpretation of Confucianism and Maoism. But before undertaking this task, we must ask this question: why do we discuss Confucianism and Maoism in relation to Weber? In order to answer this, it is necessary to give a brief review of some recent significant works on Confucianism and Maoism that are directly related to the problems which concerned Weber about China.

Some sinologists today, beneficiaries of the modern research on Chinese studies in the West, are challenging Weber's view that Confucianism lacks tension between categorical demands and empirical reality. As De Bary commented, 'to say that Neo-Confucianism [what Weber refers to as Confucianism of later dynasties, 960–1280, 1368–1644] either began or ended there ["adjustment to the world"] – as a polite obeisance to an authoritarian system – is what must be questioned'. He then introduces a contemporary Japanese sinologist's views on Neo-Confucianism and Weber.

> Shimada Kenji has adopted the Weberian critique to a reinterpretation of Wang Yang-ming [the dominant Neo-Confucianism thought of the Ming period] and its popular manifestations in the late Ming. . . . He has seen the 'innate knowledge' or 'good knowing' (*liang-chih*) of Wang Yang-ming as a potent concept and force for rationality in the Weberian sense, freeing the Chinese mind from the accepted doctrines and social conventions of Confucian tradition. . . . The spontaneous exercise of this 'innate knowledge' enhanced greatly the autonomy of the individual self, functioning much as Weber saw Puritan conscience doing in the process of volitional and ethical rationalization in the West (1975:3–5).

141

In referring to some Neo-Confucians in the Sung period (960–1280) who were uncompromising in their effort to institute educational innovations in the midst of national crises, De Bary said that their responses to social needs took the character of a religious mission. Hence, he argues, 'the rational adjustment of the Neo-Confucianism was conjoined, rather than juxtaposed, to the task of rational transformation in which Weber and others saw the Confucian as failing' (1975:7).

Raising the same issue as De Bary did, Metzger demonstrates that Weber, notwithstanding his unparalleled comparison between Confucianism and Puritanism, is simply mistaken in his understanding of the Confucian view about human nature and Confucian moral life. He argues that the crucial point which confronted the New-Confucianism was the 'elusiveness of the *tao*,' the divine force which they apprehended, although its meaning was too elusive to be put in words. These 'lapses in communication' created a 'predicament' which drove them to express their moral convictions in writing which has formed the Neo-Confucianism 'grammar'. For Metzger, it was precisely the 'elusiveness of the *tao*' experienced by the Neo-Confucians which generated moral tension between the ideal and the status quo. As he argues, 'it was just these lapses in communication which endowed ego with a charismatic mission of interpretation'. He then responds to Weber in these words

> [We] view the agonizing elusiveness of the *tao* not as an unfortunate condition but as an idea expressing some of the very 'tension' which Weber was looking for. Driven by a simultaneously egoistic and altruistic need to change the world, Neo-Confucians need a philosophy which made an unending need for change obvious and which glorified their 'efficacious moral efforts' as a process of salvation on which the whole world depended (1977:4, 200–1).

Concerning Maoism and its religious meaning, there are among the sinologists three major positions: Maoism is
1 a religion
2 a religionlike ideology
3 a doctrine embodying traditional Chinese features which have affinities with religion in the Chinese sense.
Needham is convinced that the Chinese doctrine today is nearer to the Hebraic vision of the Kingdom of God. This Chinese millennialist vision is rooted in her ancient literature under the concepts of Da Tong (the Great Togetherness) and Tai Ping (the Great Peace and Equality); both are strongly affiliated with Daoism. However, he cautions that the religious aspect of Maoism is para-

doxical; for the Chinese 'are implementing . . . the Second Commandment far better than has been done in Christendom at any period, and yet at the same time rejecting altogether the First One'. He adds 'China is the only truly Christian country in the world at the present day, in spite of its absolute rejection of all religions. But on the other hand there may also be a case to be made out for the view that the Chinese have never been really fundamentally gifted in the sphere of religion' (1974:15, 18–19).

Bauer traces the religious component of Maoism to the Chinese 'atavistic faith' rooted in the anti-Confucian, religious tradition of the secret societies which 'fed on Taoist, Buddhist and West-Asian thought [of theological dualism]'. He particularly points out that Maoist China's emphasis upon human will, courage, and fearlessness, the advantage of being 'poor and blank', and periodical calls for mass upheavals has its roots in the religious tradition of ancient China (1976:408). He recognizes the religious continuities of Maoism with traditional China.

> Indeed, the religious and even the magical are thus forms of expression which are almost inevitably associated with the idea of renewal, mobility and revolution. All anti-Confucian ideals which envisaged the replacement of the hierarchical social order based on a model of the family by absolute freedom and equality arose in a religious environment, as we have seen (1976:41).

Although Wakeman does not explicitly argue for a religious component in Maoism, he propounds that Maoism has spiritual roots in both China and the West, especially the Neo-Confucianism of Wang Yang-ming and Neo-Kantianism and Neo-Hegelianism (1973:338–73, 277–84). Munro observed: 'The unconscious historical legacy in Communist thought [Maoism] is made up of ideas about men or nature [e.g., Da Tong or the Great Togetherness] that were originally found in a philosophic setting but have, over the years, become unquestioned assumptions in the minds of educated Chinese (1969:162).

The foregoing review of the current literature on Confucianism and Maoism bespeaks at least three tasks that should be followed up:

1 it is necessary to update Weber's propositions on Confucianism in terms of the post-Weber research;
2 because there are continuities between Maoism and the traditional religion and philosophy of China, we can apply or modify Weber's constructed models to elucidate Maoism in the same manner as Weber did Confucianism; and
3 because Weber frequently applied his religious concepts to

interpret political or economic phenomena (Roth and Schluchter, 1979:145–6), we can do the same for Maoism even if it is to be understood as a political/economic belief system. This threefold task is the basic concern of this chapter. What this author intends to accomplish is

1 to demonstrate that Weber's typological concepts can be applied for the understanding of traditional and modern China;
2 to modify his concepts in terms of current literature on Confucianism and Maoism; and
3 to pursue the sociology of religion as a viable method for the understanding of contemporary China.

The same four concepts will be utilized for the interpretation of Confucianism and Maoism, although, as would be expected, the outcome of their application differs considerably between these two systems. These concepts are transcendence, prophecy, morality, and rationality.

Confucianism

Transcendence

Weber's concept of transcendence can be stated as follows: a monotheistic, personal God of creation who is the anchorage of man's actions and thought, who speaks through prophets for radical and moral actions capable of social transformations, and whose ultimate character, on which human salvation depends, is 'irrational'.

According to Weber, Heaven (Tian) is 'not a supra-mundane lord creator, but a supra-divine, impersonal, forever identical and eternal existence'. Also, 'the impersonal power of Heaven did not "speak" to man', it only manifests itself through nature, society, and man (1951:28). Heaven or Dao was not a 'cause' but, as Weber said, 'simply the embodiment of the binding, traditional ritual, and its command was not "action" but "emptiness" ' (1951:236). Thus in Confucianism 'all transcendental anchorage of ethics, all tension between the imperatives of a supra-mundane God and a creatural world, all orientation toward a goal in the beyond, and all conceptions of radical evil, were absent' (1951:228). These quotes and his many other references to the Confucianism concept of Heaven clearly show that for him Confucianism lacks a conception of transcendence. This resulted in Confucians' emphasis upon adjustment to the world. By contrast, the Puritans were compelled by their God of irrationality to change the world by mastering it.

Weber's proposition that Confucianism lacks transcendence is valid only if it is taken to mean that there is a lack of a theological concept of a creator-personal God. But to say that there is no such theological concept does not exclude the experience of sensing the deity *in practice*. Weber seems to have confused the absence of this concept of a personal God with the inability to sense him. In the book, *The Doctrine of Mean,* attributed to Confucius, there are clear indications that the Confucians in the act of worship do sense a personal God or spirits.

> The Master [Confucius] said 'How abundantly do spiritual beings display the powers that belong to them! We look for them; but do not see them; we listen to, but do not hear them; yet they enter into all things, and there is nothing without them. They cause all the people [in the kingdom] to fast and purify themselves, and array themselves in their best dresses in order to attend at their sacrifice. Then, like overflowing water, they seem to be over the heads, and on the right and left of their worshippers (Legge, 1950:397–8).

As Smith has said, in the act of worship by the Chinese gentry and peasants, 'sacrificial and ritualistic activities were carried for a sense of awe, wonder, and gratitude toward an unfathomable power which [could] never be explained simply in socio-economic and psychological terms' (1967:191).

Smith also argues that Confucius refrains from asserting a personal God because of his conviction that the proper object of religion (God or Heaven) cannot and should not be put into concise word-order: 'the impossibility of discussing objectively what can never be the object of such discussion' (1967:190). This can be seen in Confucius' comment on a well-known saying in the *Book of Odes,* 'The Mandate of Heaven, how beautiful and unceasing!' His comment is: 'It means this is what makes Heaven to be Heaven'. Here Confucius makes a tautological statement about Heaven similar to the biblical passage, 'I am who I am', in referring to God. He does not wish to conceptualize it. But his reticence to theologize Heaven does not mean that he is unable to sense it as a personal being (Chan, 1963:109–10). Confucius' experience of the numinous presence of Heaven certainly implies the theological meaning of transcendence.

Thus by giving exclusive attention to the impersonal character of Heaven, Weber neglected to look into the real significance of sacrifice and rituals in Confucianism, where transcendence is to be found. On the other hand, Weber's delineation of the impersonal character of Heaven is for him methodologically valid. It is largely through such an understanding that he was able to construct a Confucian world view that emphasizes adjustment to the world, living in harmony with man and nature, adherence to the attitude of rational resignation, and enjoyment of an ideal life of honor and scholarly cultivation. By and large, this does represent the Confucian way of life for the literati.

Prophecy

Weber's concept of prophecy presupposes his meaning of the transcendent. It contains at least three more elements:

(a) A prophet lives under the constant tension between God's demand and the empirical reality. Inasmuch as the demand is generally antithetic to the reality of the world, its proclamation entails the potentiality of world transformation. In this sense, the prophet is charismatic; his action disrupts the routinizaton of the world. Although a prophet does not derive his legitimacy from his calling or his followers, having a mission or being acclaimed by his followers would certainly testify to his charismatic authority. However, what distinguishes the ethical prophet from other types of prophets is that he considers himself as a 'tool' of God.

(b) A prophet has developed a systematic and coherent meaning to which, as Weber said, 'the conduct of mankind should be oriented' and only in relation to which 'does life obtain a unified and significant pattern'. And this coherent meaning is anchored in a transcendent God who serves as a leverage for his goal-directed action (1963:59). This system of coherent meaning is what Weber means by 'personality', which is a prerequisite of the ethical type of rationalism associated particularly with the Puritans (Roth and Schluchter, 1979:15). In this sense, a prophet combines charisma with rationality.

(c) An ethical prophet is anti-magical; he rejects a ritualistic, ceremonial, or 'piecemeal' approach to the solution of problems. Weber frequently associated magic with the traditional type of society which abhors social changes; but ethical prophecy implies the necessity for rational social changes. In this sense, magic and prophecy are ideally incompatible.

The students of Weber and sinologists under his influence are well aware that he did not think there is prophecy in Confucianism. Confucian scholar-officials lived without tension between categorical demand and the empirical reality; peaceful contemplation was for them far more important than tensions, as experienced by the inner-worldly ascetics. This is because the Confucians emphasized *li* (rites, ceremony, mores, propriety) as the norm of ethical conduct, which could not have produced the kind of inner drives and motivations necessary for radical changes. They were under the domination of a type of patrimonialism. Weber made many references to the Chinese patrimonialist administration, its patrimonialist bureaucracies or patrimonialist administrative staff (1951:56ff; 1968:462). Although Weber recognized the Confucian type of rationality (mostly in the sense of being an ethic of harmony), he also noted that the Confucian scholars tolerated magic, which was contrary to prophetic religion. It should be noted that in Weber's comparison of Confucian and Puritan rationalisms, he was using these two empirical phenomena to elucidate the differences between prophetic religion and contemplative religion as two ideal types.

Weber is right in his observation that the Confucian scholar-officials tolerated magic in the form of rites and ceremonies. But at this point his comparison between Confucian and Puritan rationalism becomes both revealing and problematic. Revealing, because Weber saw that magical rites were a major obstacle to the development of a rational economy in China. Thus, despite the fact that China did have the material potential to develop a capitalist system of her own, she never even reached certain aspects of development comparable to late-medieval Western Europe. By contrast, because of the Puritans' intolerance of magic, they resorted to ethical rationality and a 'matter-of-fact' attitude toward economic enterprises which contributed to the rise of Western capitalism (1951:115). Problematic, because according to Weber's constructed models, magic and ethical prophecy are antithetic. But post-Weber research has offered new insights into the meaning of rituals which were not available to him. In essence, rituals provide a sacred mode of existence that compensates and transcends the profane or daily life in the community. Fingarette noted that Confucius considered rites and ceremonies as the sacred dimension of human existence. Based on his study of the sayings of Confucius, he offered this interpretation of magic:

> By 'magic' I mean the power of a specific person to accomplish his will directly and effortlessly through ritual gesture and incantation. The user of magic does not work by strategies and devices as means toward an end; he does not use coercion or physical forces. . . . He simply wills the end in the proper ritual setting and with the proper ritual gesture and words; without further effort on his part, the deed is accomplished. Confucius' words at times strongly suggest some fundamental magical power as central to this way (1972:17, 3).

147

According to this view, magical rites are not interpreted as a human effort to control or manipulate the divine. Rituals are archetypal symbols which transport the participants momentarily to a more real or authentic existence unavailable in their daily life; they transcend the routinization of life. Understood in this way, magical rites can complement rational existence without obstructing it. Weber is right in affirming the mutual exclusiveness between magic and ethical prophecy as two ideal types. But in his application of them in historical experience, he exhibited a strong antipathy toward magic. This personal attitude seems to have prevented him from taking a more objective or ontological approach to the ritualistic behavior of the Confucians.

Perhaps Weber's view that there was never 'an ethical prophecy of a supra-mundane God' in Confucian China (1951:229-30) should be understood to mean that ethical prophecy was never a dominant Chinese religious phenomenon, as it was in the Hebraic religion. It can be anticipated that as we know more about Neo-Confucianism and Daoism, we shall be on a firmer ground to delineate the prophetic role in Chinese religion.

Although Weber took the view that prophecy is essentially anti-magical, he also said that prophets at times used magic to authenticate their charisma. He even went so far as to say that the legitimacy of Jesus' special relation to God is based upon the 'magical charisma he felt within himself' (1963:47). He certainly was aware that magical attitudes persist even in the secularized society of the modern West (Roth and Schluchter, 1979:51–2). In light of these observations by Weber, there may be room in his thought for a reinterpretation of the concept of magic as a complement to prophetic rationality.

Morality

Weber's notion of morality implies his concepts of transcendence and prophecy. He was thinking about the prophetic morality which disregards the differences between the 'insiders' and the 'outsiders'; it is universal and has no respect for particular persons or groups. Such universal morality is rational because it is impartial, impersonal, and calculative. Weber also ascribed the concept of autonomy to rational morality, that is, the moral agent has developed a core of values of his own toward which his entire life is oriented. This 'personality' is his image of the world. Because God is the leverage of his action and because he is compelled to do so, his action is supported by a great deal of psychic energy. When such persons act collectively, it produces social changes as in the case of the Puritans who brought forth radical economic transformations in post-medieval Western Europe.

According to Weber, Confucianist morality is natural, not based upon some agent beyond this world; it is a morality of harmony by emphasizing adjustment; it is formalistic, external, and personal, not derived from one's convictions but merely conforming to social prescriptions and is tied to 'blood and soil'. This type of morality, perpetuating a false sense of security and order, as manifested in the Chinese patrimonialist society, simply does not have the potential for radical social and economic changes. Weber's observations of the Confucianist morality were based primarily upon his understanding of the concept of *li*.

Li, whether as ceremonial words, acts, mores, or acts and words of propriety, was mainly understood by Weber as something which is 'ascribed' to the Confucian rather than something that is 'achieved' by him. It is something one does or says mechanically which really does not have 'meaning' for one. In this sense, *li* merely helps the Confucian to get along well in society; hence a well-adjusted Chinese 'does not constitute a systematic unity but rather a complex of useful and particular traits'. The mere observation of moral precepts due to external pressure, as Weber argued, does not 'allow men an inward aspiration toward a "unified personality", a striving which we associated with the idea of personality' (1951:235). Weber here probably had the lower-rank bureaucrats or Chinese traders in mind in his interpretation of the concept of *li*. He neglected to study *li* in relation to the religious virtuosi, the Confucians who were committed to Confucianism as a matter of life and death. Recently De Bary and Metzger focused their attention on virtuosi. *Li* is most certainly something these virtuosi have achieved internally, that is, they have shaped their personalities (in Weber's sense) through the nurture of *li*. More specifically, *li* is the ethos or medium through which these virtuosi ordered and molded their ideas, values, and mores to form their personalities. In disagreeing with Weber and in defending the view that the Confucian acts of propriety are inner-propelled, Yang said, 'there was a unified structure in the Confucian ethical principles that form the motivating core of the Confucian personality' (1968:xxxii). Fingarette (1972:7) implies that *li* is the primordial factor for the shaping of the Confucian personality:

Men become truly human as their raw impulse is shaped by *li*. And *li* is the fulfilment of human impulse, the civilized expression of it – not a formalistic dehumanization. *Li* is the

149

specially humanizing form of the dynamic relation of man-to-man.

Weber was certainly near the truth in perceiving *li* as the central factor which caused the Confucian morality to emphasize harmony. This whole issue is also closely related to his thesis that Confucians lacked tensions between deity and nature and to Schluchter's assertion that the difference between the Indian-Chinese world image and the Judeo-Christian world image is one between monism and dualistic theocentrism (Roth and Schluchter, 1979:22–32). The outcome of Weber's analysis – that the Confucians did not have moral tensions – was in part due to Weber's treatment of *li* in isolation from the Neo-Confucian concept of Dao or the Confucian concept of Tian (Heaven). Although *li* is normative, yet in the Neo-Confucian context Dao, being onto-logical, has the right to criticize *li*. When the Neo-Confucian was groping with the elusiveness of Dao, he was compelled to question the correctness of *li;* herein lies the tension between the ideal and the given in the historical situation. Yang said that because the theistic religion as an institution lost political power in early China, men of knowledge (Confucian virtuosi) often played the role of prophets in times of social political crises in the name of Dao. In Chinese history, 'there was pressure for transforming the given world in conformity to ideals which were often under the label of Tao or the "golden past".' Even on the mass level of Chinese religion, the observation of *li* was not absolute; for it was common, according to Yang, for a sectarian leader to be an emissary or ethical prophet under a deity in times of social or dynastic changes (1968:xxxvii–xxxviii).

Rationality

It has been pointed out that rationality in Weber's sociology is both a pervasive and an ambiguous concept; hence it is beyond the scope of this chapter to explore its many dimensions. However, in terms of Weber's historical understanding, Occidental rationality, until the most recent time, did imply the components of transcend-ence, prophecy, and morality which we discussed here. For the purpose of relating Weber's notion of rationality to Confucianism and Maoism, his two concerns are relevant. One is that Occidental rationality based upon scientific-technological calculation has resulted in the total disenchantment of the Western world (Roth and Schluchter, 1979:45–59). Another is Weber's analysis of the relation between bureaucratic routinization and personal charisma.

Weber's evaluation of Confucian rationality can be summarized as follows:

(a)   Although rationality can be observed in such Confucian institutions as humanistic education, the civil service examination, and bureaucracy, it was greatly handicapped by the domination of the clan system, which emphasized personalism and familialism in human relations. The clan system conditioned the Chinese formal law and moral principles and caused Chinese bureaucracy to be patrimonialist. As Weber said

> All social ethics in China merely transferred the organic relation of piety to other relations similar to them. Within the five natural social relations the duties to master, father, husband, old brother (including the teacher), and friend comprised the sum total of the ethically binding (1951:209).

In other words, the clan system prevailed within the patrimonialism of China. In referring to the conflicts between Confucian bureaucracy and the clan system, Weber observed, 'The rationalism of bureaucracy was confronted with a resolute and traditionalist power which, on the whole and in the long run, was stronger because it operated continuously and was supported by the most intimate associations' (1951:95). This is the reason, he suggested, why in China impersonal relations did not develop, whereas they were absolutely necessary for the legal-rational type of bureaucracy in the West.

(b)   Because the formal law and the rules of administration governing the bureaucracy in China contained particularism and personalism, they created protectionism and favoritism in economic matters. This hindered the Chinese from developing a free-market labor selection, which is essential for the development of a rational type of economic capitalism.

(c)   Confucian bureaucrats acquired their income primarily through the prebendary system, according to which their actual income depended upon the balance between the total collected revenues and what was left after the required amounts were delivered to the state. This prebendary system was irrational because it motivated the officeholders to view their districts as the source of their personal income rather than assigned domains for which they served; it drove them to view the economic interests as their primary function, thus preventing them from diverting time and energy to a more rational type of administration. Also, because the prebendary system could offer the incumbents many opportunities for pecuniary gains during their tenure, any attempts to change it were met with tenacious resistance. Hence the numerous attempts at political reform or innovation in history all

151

fell to the ground owing to the overwhelming vested interests of this special class of bureaucrats.

(d)   Confucianism promoted humanistic education as the qualification for office. Consequently, the scholar-officials were essentially generalists, gentlemen *(jun-zi)* who loathed specializations. Confucianism, like Islam and Catholicism, historically had a low estimation of merchants. The Confucians' self-conception as gentlemen together with their low opinion of the merchants could not have generated the kind of incentives required for the development of the Western type of capitalism. In summing up the foregoing evaluations, Weber concluded that capitalism in China 'has been handicapped not only by the lack of a formally guaranteed law, a rational administration and judiciary, and by the ramifications of a system of prebends, but also, basically, by the lack of a particular mentality' (1951:104).

As Sprenkel said, 'Weber deserves the highest praise for his recognition of lineage [clan system] as a main key to an understanding of rural China' (1964:366). His proposition that the continuing conflicts between the clan authorities and the local officials was a chief reason why China did not develop a legal-rational type of bureaucracy is certainly correct. There follow some qualifications to Weber's views of Confucianism rationalism:

(a)   According to Yang, Confucian bureaucracy had two structural components:

1   a national superstructure which stressed centralization, formalism, and impersonalism;

2   a substructure of local variations characterized by autonomy, informalism, and personalism (1959:135).

In light of this fact, Weber's judgment that personal relations prevailed in Confucian bureaucracy and that the clan system dominated Chinese society was more applicable to and characteristic of the local bureaucracy than the national scene. This also implies that national bureaucracy in China was more rational, in the Western sense, than the local organizations. Also, according to Sprenkel, the influence of the clan system upon the local bureaucrats was more dominant in the south than in the north because the southern rural districts were economically more productive than the northern ones (1964:367). Hence, Weber's judgment on clan domination and its ramifications was more applicable to South China than North China.

(b)   Weber recognized that there was formal law governing the Chinese officials, although it contained particularism and personalism. This was also verified by Yang, who said that Confucians 'clearly recognized the principle of formalistic impersonality as a requirement for the operation of the government' (1959:156).

152

He qualified this, however, by saying that whereas Confucian bureaucracy recognized both formal law and moral norms, in the normative sense formal law was supplementary to moral norms. This means that the Confucian formal law was inseparable from moral particularism; here Yang seemed to agree with Weber's position that the Chinese formal law was not pure. Weber seemed to define formal law strictly in the Western legal-rational sense. It was on this model that he judged the Confucian formal law as deficient in rationality. But there is no reason why 'formal law' must be understood in the Western sense. The Confucian law which contained moral norms can also be considered as formal; it can be called 'traditional formal law' in contrast to the 'juridic formal law' of the West. When Weber was deliberating about the deficiency in rationality in Chinese law, he was unaware that here was a fertile field to explore the possibility of moral tensions in Confucianism: the confrontation between the demand of the formal law and the demand of moral norms in decision-making by the Confucian officials. Such tension must have been experienced by the conscientious Confucian bureaucrats with religious virtuosity. Metzger (1977) has substantiated this point.

(c) In Confucianism it was the generalists who enjoyed the formal membership of bureaucracy; the high officials at the national level were, ideally, the most excellent generalists who had the broadest training in the humanistic education. The specialists (technicians), assigned 'to the ranks of the operatives and clerical workers,' were aides to the bureaucrats but not members of the privileged group (Yang, 1959:137). It may be said that the Confucian patrimonialist bureaucrats were qualified because of their general knowledge and moral character, not because of their professional and technological attainments, unlike their counterparts in the West.

Maoism

Transcendence

Like classical Marxists, Mao also rejected the belief in the existence of a transcendent creator-god. At the conscious level, Maoists are atheists. It is clear that for Mao Heaven has been replaced by the 'Chinese people' who were attempting to master the world. In a 1965 interview, Mao (MacInnes, 1972:17) told André Malraux:

When I said 'Chinese Marxism is the religion of the people',
. . . I meant that the communists express the Chinese people

153

in a real way if they remain faithful to the work upon which the whole of China has embarked as if on another Long March. When we say 'we are the Sons of the People', China understands it as she understood the phrase 'son of Heaven'. The People has taken the place of ancestors.

Then, in telling an ancient Chinese fable about the Old Foolish Man who was determined to remove the two mountains which were obstructing his view from his house and how God out of compassion dispatched two divinities to help him remove the mountains, Mao said that God is 'none other than the masses of the Chinese'. In 1935, at the end of his now famous Long March with his Red Army, when he finally reached the cave capital in northwest China, Mao wrote a poem about Kunlun, the greatest mountain range in China where, according to legends, sacred plants grew and divinities lived:

Now I say to Kunlun:
don't be so high,
don't have so much snow.
Leaning against the sky,
could I draw a sword
and cut you into three pieces?

In this stanza, Mao wants to cut apart Mount Kunlun, the center of the cosmos in Chinese mythology (1973:74). Here he seems to imagine himself as another 'Old Foolish Man'. Men, like himself, collectively and with determination can change nature and society; they have replaced God in revolutionary China.

This author proposes that Maoism, viewed as a doctrine, implies a godlike transcendence in the sense that there is something on the fringe of reality that is always changing and unpredictable to which man must conform for his salvation. This transcendence can be detected in Mao's epistemology and dialectical materialism. Knowledge for Mao is derived from practice. He assumed that there is an objective reality, but how one knows it depends upon how one experiments with it. One begins to have some knowledge by formulating a certain concept or theory based on perceptions derived from practical experience in the physical or communal environment. Then one returns to it to put one's theory into practice. The effectiveness of its outcome determines the extent of its correctness. Thus, through practice one discovers that one's theory needs modification or correction. This modified version or the 'reconstructed theory' is then tested in practice for its adequacy, which is called 'revolutionary practice'. This cyclical process goes on 'over and over again in an endless spiral, with the ideas becoming more correct, more vital and richer each time' (Mao, 1967, 3:119). The reciprocal relation between theory and practice in fact is endless; it is a 'becoming' with no absolute end in view. Knowledge understood in this way is relative and uncertain because one's theory is always at least a step behind the objective reality. This kind of epistemology implies that there is something in the objective reality which man cannot foreknow because it forever changes. As Mao said, 'the process of change in the world of objective reality is never-ending, and so is man's cognitive truth through practice. Marxism-Leninism has no way exhausted truth but ceaselessly opens up roads to the knowledge of truth in the course of practice' (1975, 1:307-8). Thus there is indeterminism in Mao's theory of practice; change is ultimate and contains its own law of explanation.

In Mao's dialectical materialism, there are two inseparable aspects, whose relation he called the principle of contradiction: one is the opposites in mutual complementarity and the other is the opposites in conflict. It must be noted that these two aspects actually refer to the same process viewed from different perspectives: complementary and conflicting. Complementary means that the two opposites need each other for existence. As Mao said, 'without life there would be no death; without death there would be no life'; or 'without the bourgeoisie, there would be no proletariat; without the proletariat, there would be no bourgeoisie' (1975, 1:338). Mao here probably had the complementarity of *yin yang* in mind. He was certainly aware that this aspect of thought is embodied in the *Lao Zi* and the *Book of Changes*. He quoted the *Lao Zi:* 'Good fortune lies within bad, bad fortune lurketh within good'. But for a political application of the opposites in complementarity, there is a classic passage in the *Book of Changes*

> He who keeps danger in mind will rest safe in his seat; he who keeps ruin in mind will preserve his interests secure; he who sets the danger of disorder before him will maintain good order. Therefore the Superior Man, resting in safety, does not forget danger; resting in security, does not forget disaster; and when having good government, does not forget disorder. Thus his person is kept safe and his country is preserved (Fung, 1952:392):

But for Mao the complementarity of the opposites – also called the union of the opposites – is relative because it depends on certain external conditions; for example, at certain stages in history, because of the concurrence of certain conditions, the proletarians were able to absorb the bourgeoisie and form one larger class. On the other hand, the conflict in the opposites is

155

absolute because it is internal within existence; for example, there is the conflict between the will to continue to be proletarian and the desire to be bourgeois within the individual or group. The conflict in the opposites is absolute also because it is universal: no sooner does the union take place than it as the new pole is in conflict with its opposite; a new struggle ensues. Mao's notion of conflict in the opposites was derived from classical Marxism for it was not a prevalent idea in Chinese thought.

Mao's principle of contradiction, particularly the idea of struggle between the opposites, implies that the objective reality changes. It is change that disrupts the stability of order (the union of the opposites) and causes struggle. Here Mao's dialectical materialism coincides with this epistemology in regard to the notion of change: it is change which necessitates the correction of theory by forcing it to conform to new reality; and it is change which underlies dialectical materialism.

As a dialectician, but not as a metaphysician, Mao had no wish to develop the idea of change as the transcendence. However, unlike the classical Marxists, Mao in his later years seemed to be increasingly leaning toward indeterminism regarding the future; he was uncertain about the future of Chinese socialism. In 1956, he said that there are two points in history that we must know. The first is that nothing in the world is not brought forth in history. 'The second is that anything which has been brought forth in history must also disappear in history. The Communist Party has been brought forth in history, and because of this, it is bound to disappear one day' (Wakeman, 1973:321). In speaking about the transition of one stage to another in history, Mao said: 'In the communist period too, there will also be uninterrupted development. Communism may well go through many different phases, can it be said that after communist society is reached there will be no changes in anything anymore?' In commenting on this passage, Schram said that Mao was convinced that 'socialism and communism, however they might be achieved, were not the last word in mankind's experience, which was in any case only a passing phase in the development of the universe' (1977:61, 62). Mao's feeling of uncertainty toward the future was certainly predicated upon the inevitability of changes in history.

Although there is a transcendence in Mao's thought, it is nevertheless immanent because his dialectics purports to be naturalistic and materialistic. This transcendence is something evolving from the world rather than presiding over it; hence it is different from the transcendent God in Puritanism. It is also different from the transcendent in Confucianism: the Confucian Heaven is conscious and was an object of worship, whereas change in Maoism is impersonal and not an object of worship even though it is closely associated with political celebrations of the glory of the Revolution. But because Mao's transcendence is godlike, it is worthy of being recognized. Even if Maoism is purely political, we can still argue that it has certain religious implications which have made it a surrogate of the traditional Chinese religion.

Prophecy

We shall apply the concept of prophetic religion for the interpretation of the Maoist revolution. Within this general theme, we shall also discuss Mao himself as a prophet. While adhering to the typological method, we also attempt to modify Weber's concepts in order not to distort the reality of contemporary China.

According to Weber, when the Puritans' religiosity was joined with the ascetic ethic, a new dynamism ensued, which produced a revolutionary impact on Western morality and economy:

> The religious virtuoso can be placed in the world as the instrument of a God and cut off from all magical means of salvation. At the same time, it is imperative for the virtuoso that he 'prove' himself before God, as being called *solely* through the ethical quality of his conduct in this world. . . . No matter how much the 'world' as such is religiously devalued . . . yet psychologically the world is all the more affirmed as the theatre of God-willed activity in one's worldly 'calling' (1946:290–1).

The above statement can also be understood as a description of 'active asceticism' which embodies religious virtuosity and ascetic ethics. How were these two elements present in the Maoist Revolution?

Mao and his close associates in the early 1920s were the heirs of Confucianism, which emphasized the primacy of moral will. But this will or virtuosity was then seeking a new rationalization in order to change China from national submission to national mastery. This they found in Marxism–Leninism. Thus by combining virtuosity (Confucian moral will) with an ascetic ethic (Marxism-Leninism), they were able to generate a kind of active asceticism which both rejected and affirmed the world: they rejected the old Confucian world of adjustment and its clan social system as well as the bourgeois values shared by contemporary Western-influenced Confucian intellectuals; but they affirmed the existing impoverished conditions of China by transforming them into new and positive ones. Maoist Revolution may be viewed as

157

a variant of 'a religion-like revolutionary messianism' for it contains all the necessary characteristics (Murvar, 1972:188–91).

Now to focus more specifically on Mao as a prophet. He can be considered as an ethical prophet because he was an instrument of an ideal which revealed certain imperatives and for which he was the spokesman. Mao certainly lived in constant tension between that ideal and the empirical reality of China, between the demand for social and institutional changes and the different forms of human resistance, between his genuine wish to serve the public and his desire to serve himself. His calls for periodic national campaigns (Rectification Movement, the Five-Antis, the Great Leap, the Cultural Revolution) to sustain the revolution, apart from being politically motivated and from conflicts between himself and other factions, perhaps reflected his own tension between the determination to fulfil the ideal goals and temptations for temporary security and ease. Underlying his own principle of contradiction is the view that conflict is the essence of life, and tension between the ideal and the given is perhaps the most intense type of conflict in which prophecy may occur. According to Weber, the ethical prophet has an autonomous personality anchored in God. Mao certainly possessed it in this sense; for his own blend of Marxism, derived from many years of revolutionary experience and based on his theory of practice, is the best testimony of what an autonomous personality means. It was anchored in the authority of the Revolution.

Weber said that a prophet does not derive his authority from his followers but from God. As indicated above, for Mao the Chinese people have replaced God and they gave the communist party the legitimacy to rule China.

> Our [party's] power – who gives it to us? The working class gives it to us and the masses of laboring people who comprise over ninety percent of population give it to us. We represent the proletariat and the masses, and have overthrown the enemies of the people. The people therefore support us (Chen 1970:156).

Critics of Mao would certainly disagree with his claim that the Chinese people voluntarily supported the communist party. But in view of the improved living conditions, there is some truth in it. Assuming that most of the Chinese peasants supported Mao, this means that they gave him the legitimacy to rule over them as long as they continued to approve of him. Thus the claim that Mao derived his power to rule China (via the party) from the people has nearly the same effect as the claim that he was chosen by God.

158

For Weber a prophet is not primarily interested in economic matters for the execution of God's will. This appears to be a contradiction to Marxism, which viewed the economy as the over-riding explanation of history. However, Maoism in this respect differs from classical Marxism by not emphasizing economic deter-minism. As Oksenberg said, 'At no point did Mao stress wealth or material abundance as a major source of power' (1977:81). Indeed, the two major enemies of modern China, according to Mao, were landlordism which exploited the peasants and foreign imperialism which dominated China then; neither one was a purely economic phenomenon. Mao's revolution was initially motivated by a genuine concern for the well-being of the Chinese people in their total existence – the removal of their moral degra-dation and of foreign domination; the importance of self-suffi-ciency and the inculcation of political consciousness; the actualiz-ation of their power as human beings through will and persever-ance. Although economy was certainly a major factor in the Maoist Revolution, its central core was moral and political. In the last two decades of his life, Mao was quite worried that economism might overtake China and in 1958 warned the cadres:

> Those who pay no attention to ideology and politics, and are busy with their work all day long, will become economists or technicians who have lost their sense of direction, and this is very dangerous. Ideological work and political work are the guarantee that economic and technical work will be carried through, they serve as the economic basis. Ideology and politics are the supreme commander; they are the soul. Whenever we are even slightly lax in our ideological and political work, our economic and technical work will certainly take a false direction (Schram, 1971:228).

Because Mao's primary concern for man is morality and politics and because in Confucianism these two also were inseparable, Weber's idea that the prophet is not immediately concerned with economic matters is quite revealing for the understanding of Maoism.

Once the attitudes of the Chinese populace toward Mao are observed, especially in the 1950s and 1960s, Mao loomed larger than being a prophet; he conveyed the image of God. To the Chinese masses (not to his close associates, nor to the Chinese intellectuals) who knew him only normatively, he was the spiritual symbol of China. He was an object of reverence and adoration, particularly at mass rallies and public ceremonies. Being an astute student of Chinese history and politics, Mao was aware that he was the heir of the Chinese emperors who were semidivine in the

159

eyes of the masses. Mao therefore manipulated the people's desire for worship and permitted himself to be worshipped mainly for his own political advantages. He wanted to rally the Chinese masses behind him, especially during the Cultural Revolution of 1966–9, when he was immersed in the battle against his political opponents.

Because the deification of Mao in the 1960s was primarily an organized strategy instigated by Mao's alleged 'successor', Lin Piao, it was a temporary and unspontaneous phenomenon. And because the post-Mao party leaders today have officially said that some of his policies and actions were wrong in this period, the deitylike image of Mao is now broken. However, the present party leaders have also affirmed that Maoism, despite the fact that it has made some gross errors, is still the guide of Chinese socialism. This means that Mao's legacy has nevertheless become the 'charisma of office', that is, whoever they are in control of China today or in the near future still have to derive at least a part of their legitimacy from his heritage. This also means that whether Mao is a godlike universal Father or not is not a foreclosed question.

Morality

In discussing the Maoist morality, our main concern is whether or not it was moving toward ethical universalism and was based on autonomy; both requirements are essential for Weber's type of prophetic morality. We also believe that the Maoist morality is perhaps the most important aspect of Maoism; for most of Mao's ideas on human nature, education, and self-reform are in fact an explication of this ideal. It should be kept in mind that morality – the striving for virtue and self-perfection – was a perennial concern for the Confucians.

The Maoist Revolution in both the normative and empirical sense was breaking up the deep-rooted clan system in rural China, the citadel of the Confucian particularist ethic. The proletarian ethic was replacing the Confucian morality of familialism by emphasizing the importance of 'public-mindedness' *(wei-gong)* against the attitude of 'selfish-mindedness' *(wei-si)*, that is, people's self-interests should be contingent upon the interests of the society in their workaday ethic. Although 'public-mindedness' was also advocated in Confucianist China, its practice was confined to the literati as a norm for their administration. Thus it was a bureaucratic concept. This concept was now universalized and was given a new meaning: the working for the well-being of the proletariat – peasants and workers. According to Mao in 1957

160

this class constituted ninety percent of the Chinese population (1977, 5:501). Thus its morality is close to universalism in contemporary China. Even empirically there is some truth in this assertion, for in both rural and urban China some of the basic functions of the family have been taken over by other agencies: in rural China it is the agricultural communes which control many of the social, economic, and educational activities formerly initiated by the families; in urban China it is the plants, workers' neighborhoods, and schools which perform many of the activities formerly exclusively confined to the families. Certain social forces are at work today which induce the Chinese to embrace a more socialist and universalist morality. But the present trend toward universalism certainly does not mean that the ethic of particularism will soon disappear. It is well known that the basic units of the agricultural commune are the families located in the villages which were the traditional bases of clanism. Because of the geographical proximity of these families which were related by blood, there is a natural tendency for them to practice the ethic of particularism in the commune even though it is against the norm of their socialist morality. Furthermore, within the proletarian hierarchy there are powerful status groups whose members in order to maintain their vested interests and privileges are violating the egalitarian ethic. This is the major moral problem in the post-Mao era.

The other question is whether or not the Maoist morality is autonomous. At the outset, it is recognized that the proletarian ethic in contemporary China is under the control of the state: it is the state agencies (communities, plants, workers' neighborhoods, schools) which inculcate it. Under this educational system, morality is prescribed for the individual rather than being the autonomous product of the individual himself; thus it appears to be incapable of producing the kind of personality which Weber emphasized. But in order to see the full force of the state education, it is imperative to explain the relationship between the concepts of thought-reform and human nature.

Maoism recognizes the fact that human beings are inclined to be selfish and profit-motivated, which must be curbed. Thus, thought-reform *(si-xiang gai-zao)* as an educational device involves essentially the struggle between the temptations to be 'selfish-minded' and the demand to be 'public-minded'. Through self-study, individually or in a group, the person may develop a personality befitting the society. This self-study, in terms of the Maoist jargon, involves 'self-struggle', 'self-criticism', and 'self-reform'. It can be seen that this type of learning does require a process of internalization: the assimilation of the socialist values

161

and the comprehension of their meaning. Although this morality is state-prescribed, its meaning is nevertheless personally *acquired* through the active process of 'struggle-criticism-reform'. This thought-reform is analogous to the phenomenon of regeneration in the religious sense. It is also analogous to the Confucian concept of self-renewal *(zi-xin)* in its psychological sense.

In Maoist China human nature does not refer to the biological or physical nature of man, nor does it refer to the innate nature of man. According to Munro (1977), human nature refers to the social nature of man *(she-hui-xing)*, that is, the dominant attitudes, interests, values, and ideas of the society which each member has inherited and assimilated. Because one's human nature (thought) is derived from one's society, it is paramountly important that society have the right kind of ideas and values. This means that it must ceaselessly examine its prevailing ideas and values, and see that they are worthy of being inculcated (1977:16–17). This also means that society is obligated to educate its citizens in such a way that they can both sustain and innovate it. The reciprocal relation between human nature and thought-reform is crucial: human nature means the possession of the right kind of social attitudes, values, and ideas by individuals and thought-reform means self-struggle in order to rectify one's attitudes, values, and ideas to conform to the prevalent norms of the society.

One more question need be raised: how do we know that the proletarian attitudes, values, and ideas in society are right since society is bound to change? Mao's answer is that the cadres must live close to the masses and be aware of their needs and desires; this he called the principle of 'from the masses, to the masses':

> This means: take the ideas of the masses (scattered and unsystematic ideas) and concentrate them (through study turn them into concentrated and systematic ideas), then go to the masses and propagate and explain these ideas until the masses embrace them as their own, hold fast to them and translate them into action, and test the correctness of these ideas in such action. Then once again concentrate ideas from the masses and once again go to the masses so that the ideas are preserved and carried through. And so on, over and over again in an endless spiral, with the ideas becoming more correct, more vital and richer each time (1967:3:119).

The criterion of what is 'right' is the relevance of the social attitudes, values, and ideas to the needs and desires of the people. Thus when their needs and desires change, there should be a corresponding change of the existing social norms. Mao (Starr,

162

1979:149) said that whenever any party leader is alienated from the masses, he ceases to have an insight into the affairs of the nation. The party must continuously consult the various people's organizations in order to learn what are the needs of people, which in turn affect the norms of society.

As noted earlier, there is an autonomous personality in the Maoist type of morality. But this autonomy is obviously not the same kind as Weber had in mind. Weber's analysis of society is based upon the atomistic concept of the individual which is irreducible to social terms (1946:55). This conception of the self is probably derived from the philosophical tradition of Descartes, Locke, and Hume. On the other hand, the Maoist concept of the self is ultimately inseparable from society; it has its roots in the Neo-Confucian view of self as a social organism and the Marxian view of self as a mirror of social/economic history.

Rationality

It appears that Maoism is typologically nearer to Weber's concept of rationality than is Confucian rationalism, at least in the following aspects: (a) It is moving toward ethical universalism by eliminating the clan system. (b) It embodies a prophetic morality by transforming the lives of the Chinese people in the last three decades from degradation and dehumanization to simple dignity and self-reliance. (c) It emphasizes the necessity of change and conflict by instilling in the Chinese people a moral will for self-transformation and social changes. However, at the empirical level the Maoist rationalization reveals notable differences from the legal type of rationality which Weber associated with Western rationalism in modern times. Both Weber and Mao had an ambivalence about bureaucracy, though for different reasons.

It is worth noting that the word 'bureaucracy' in Chinese conveys the idea of a type of administration prevalent among Confucian officials. This word (*guan-liao zhu-yi*) as used by Mao often implies a historical reference to the evils of Confucian officialdom. However, there the word is used to mean any type of organization which requires the distribution of authority among its officials and the communication and implementation of group strategies by its members. Bureaucracy in this sense is essential for Mao because he was fully aware that there could be no revolution without organizations. In this regard, bureaucracy as an institution in Maoist China is a means to achieve certain ends; it is not an autonomous, self-propelling organization which carries out its specific functions judicially independent of politics, as Weber conceived it to be in referring to Western legal-rational bureaucracy. Any organization in Maoism is subservient to the Revolution; it is an instrument for social change, and its internal structure is also subject to change when the situation calls for it. It is precisely for this reason that Mao felt that any organization, once established and regulated, wants to maintain its own status quo. Thus the strength of bureaucracy is also its weakness – its rigidity and its resistance to change. This is one of the reasons why Mao personally launched the Cultural Revolution through mass accusations and mass criticisms, which were the organized strategies among the youth groups and lower-rank cadres *vis-à-vis* the high- and mid-rank officials and professionals; its purpose was to interrupt the routinization of bureaucracy and force the incumbents to undergo personal and institutional changes.

Weber was also fearful of the effect of routinization in bureaucracy. But his chief concern in this regard was the inner conflict of the incumbent as a functionary who follows objective demands and the same person as an individual who wants to follow his personal wishes – bureaucracy cannot allow individual freedom. On the other hand, Mao's fear for bureaucracy has to do with the rigidity of the bureaucratic structure and operation which prevents the possibilities of change (Starr, 1979:133).

Mao believed that general political knowledge is essential for the continuation of revolution, which must be possessed by the leaders of the party and state as qualifications for office. As for the professionals and technicians, they are required to have both general knowledge and technological expertise in order to hold office. Assuming that this is the level where most of the bureaucrats in China are, then Maoist bureaucracy differs from that of Weber, who viewed specializations as the primary criterion for office. In this regard, the Maoist bureaucracy has some strong affinities with its Confucian counterpart which also emphasized general knowledge, although there is a distinction in content: for the former it is political knowledge of Maoism and for the latter it was the humanistic knowledge of Confucianism.

For Weber, efficiency is a basic attribute of bureaucracy; in order to facilitate it the official must be impersonal and objective in executing his or her duties. Although Mao recognized the importance of efficiency for an organization, this was not its primary requisite, because he was convinced that an organization must be flexible in the Chinese social situation. Hence, he said that there are times when efficiency must be sacrificed; for example, he felt that because of the scarcity of resources in China, it was more important to be frugal in office expenditure than to be efficient in management. Following the same line of argument, in order to meet certain existing conditions, efficiency should be put aside in exchange for local support for the accomplishment of a project. Maoist bureaucracy, according to Starr, is situation-oriented rather than goal-oriented; pragmatic considerations may necessitate modifications of the goals. This means that it is sometimes imperative to change or interrupt the internal structure or operation of an organization. As for the attribute of impersonalism, Mao's concept of organization requires both impersonalism and personalism: the former refers to unselfishness and honesty in executing office functions and the latter refers to empathy and friendliness in relation to the clients, who are the Chinese masses with whom the bureaucrat comes into contact (Starr, 1979:174, 183, 167–72). It can be seen that the exercise of personalism may at times necessitate the sacrifice of efficiency in bureaucracy.

What remains to be considered is the juridic aspect of the Maoist bureaucracy. During Mao's rule there was the absence of a formal law and an objective judicial system in China. What were called the laws and rules of administration were based upon the proletarian morality; they changed constantly. This certainly affected bureaucracy in modern China. Because the laws and rules of administration governing the various organizations were not clearly defined and were changing from time to time, due to the impact of the Revolution, the incumbents were perpetually facing the uncertainty of their own jurisdictions; they were in an *ad hoc* atmosphere indefinitely. In this regard, the Maoist organizations certainly did not reflect the legal type of rationality as seen in the bureaucracy of the modern West. However, in contemporary post-Mao China there has been a great discussion going on among the leaders and intellectuals on the importance of government by law. At the same time, a series of legal codes, which were drafted during Mao's era, has been finalized and have been in operation since the early 1980s. The law schools are now reopened and the surviving legal experts and lawyers, trained three decades ago, are once again busy with legal research and writings. All these signs seem to indicate that there has been a concerted governmental effort to move the nation toward a consciousness of law as a means of modernization. But the present Chinese law is controlled by the party; it is not independent of politics. It can be said that, in the foreseeable future, the characteristics of Chinese bureaucracy will continue to be dominated by a patrimonialist type of rationality based upon the combined authority of the ruling party and the Chinese populace.

Conclusion

This chapter analyzed many affinities between Maoism and Confucianism. This should strengthen the proposition that Chinese Marxism is a combination of Western Marxism and Confucianism, Daoism, and other elements of the Chinese cultural heritage. On the other hand, Maoism has definitely departed from Confucianism; it is more dynamic and more changing. If religion is defined as the power to change society or that which is capable of bringing forth a breakthrough in society, then Maoism is more religious than Confucianism.

It has been demonstrated how Weber's constructed models are equally applicable to Confucianism and Maoism. But his concepts need to be significantly modified for the interpretation of both systems: in Confucianism we have emphasized that there is prophetic morality in reference to tension between the ideal and the given, and in Maoism the emphasis is that Weber's ideals of morality and rationality, when applied to contemporary China, show notable differences between the Western and Chinese varieties of morality and rationality.

It was repeatedly emphasized that there are affinities between Maoism and Puritanism. These affinities may be a source of temptation to think that Maoism could be a stimulant to the rise of capitalism in China as Puritanism was in the West. But this is most unlikely both in terms of the Chinese mentality and of the empirical reality: there is a lack of rationalization in the three major systems of Confucianism, Daoism, and Buddhism on the importance of private ownership. Indeed, equal distribution of land or the elimination of private property is a dominant ideal in the Chinese tradition (Bauer, 1976:81, 86, 303). Also, empirically in Maoist and post-Maoist China, there are no signs which can assure us that there will be a comparable configuration of cultural and historical events in China in the foreseeable future. On the other hand, the continuities between Maoism and Confucianism which were documented here point to those aspects of Chinese culture which are more in harmony with a type of socialist economy and politics.

The post-Mao China will most probably continue to utilize the principal ideas of Maoism as the basis of her national life. It will promote active asceticism and socialist morality and will instill a kind of rationalization which stresses a balance between public interests and self-interest.

In post-Mao China today traditional religions no longer play an important publicly conscious role, and proletarian ideology has allegedly replaced the traditional Chinese religions. However, there are differences in the manner in which the West and China are facing the problem of disenchantment: in the modern West many counterculture movements and ritual-like activities have become the expressions of religion, whereas in China it is mainly the political ideology and political actions that are the expression of religion.

8 Weber and sultanism in the light of historical data*

Susan K. Croutwater

In his analysis of traditionalist rulership, Max Weber develops a constructed subtype of patrimonialism. He extends the two subtypes of traditionalist domination – tradition-based rule and arbitrary will – to explain the development of patrimonial bureaucracy. As an extension of the sphere of arbitrary will, Weber presents the concept of Near-Eastern sultanism characterized by extreme arbitrary will and grace. Sultanism seems to reflect a misconception of Islamic religio-political organization, which stems from Weber's analysis of the historical development of Islamic statescraft and religious law. The arguments presented herein suggest that however logical the progression from patrimonialism to sultanism, the historical record does not support Weber's use of the latter.

The purpose of this chapter is to examine Weber's concept of sultanism, rather than to provide a general critique of his understanding of Islam, as Turner (1974) has done. However, the assertion that Weber misconceptualized Islamic government requires examination of Weber's general analysis of Islam, as well as his specific concept of sultanism. The argument put forth is that Weber's treatment of Islamic patrimonialism led him to a logical, but non-evidenced, concept of sultanism.

Weber did not exhaustively describe sultanism and often treats it as an afterthought of some other topic. He develops sultanism most extensively as a subtype of traditionalist rule. Among the three types of legitimate rulership, Weber distinguishes traditionalist rule as 'resting on an established belief in the sanctity of immemorial traditions and the legitimacy of those exercising authority under them' (Weber, 1968:215).

In this definition, the chief who exercises domination receives the right to dominate through traditionally transmitted rules.

168

Obedience to rulership is owed, not to a set of enacted rules, but 'to the person who occupies a position of authority by tradition or who has been chosen for it by the traditional master' (1968:341).

Weber presents traditionalist domination as a conglomerate of traits which he separates into two broad categories, one of action bound to specific traditions and the other of action free from specific rules. These two categories, or the 'double sphere' of traditionalist rule, legitimize the commands of the chief in two ways. Tradition determines the content of command and imposes limits on the chief that cannot be overstepped without endangering his traditionalist status. The prerogative of free action by the chief is also traditional, in that obedience to the chief tends to be essentially unlimited (1968:227).

Although Weber attributes the existence of both 'spheres' of traditionalist rule to all forms of traditionalist domination, he distinguishes among gerontocracy, patriarchalism, and patrimonialism according to the strength of a particular 'sphere' in each pure type. In both gerontocracy and patriarchalism, the group obeys the chief primarily because of his traditionalist status. In the case of gerontocracy, obedience is given to the elders of the group 'who are most familiar with the sacred traditions' (1968:231). Patriarchalism occurs where the group is ruled by an individual who is selected on a hereditary basis: Weber specifically cites the example of the 'Arabian sheik' in relation to patriarchal domination. In neither case does the chief have a personal administrative staff, and therefore he must rely on the group's recognition of his right to rule; nor can the chief appropriate the right to dominate in matters beyond the bounds set by tradition, which limits the extent to which arbitrary will may be exercised. Weber cites the lack of an administrative staff and tradition as factors that constrain the free action of the chief. The chief must rely on the compliance of the group because it consists of members who are not really subjects (1968:231).

Patrimonialist domination differs from gerontocracy and patriarchalism precisely because the chief's personal administrative staff allows him to assert his personal right to rulership over and above the 'pre-eminent group right' afforded him by tradition. The patrimonialist chief is then free to exercise a broad range of arbitrary power because his control of the administration and the army has changed the status of the group from members to subjects (1968:231–2). The distinction between patrimonialism and sultanism is made according to the degree to which arbitrary discretion becomes the basis of rule: 'Where domination is primarily traditional, even though it is exercised by virtue of the ruler's personal autonomy, it will be called *patrimonial authority;*

where it indeed operates primarily on the basis of discretion, it will be called *sultanism'* (1968:232). Sultanism thus represents a form of traditionalist domination in which the sphere of 'arbitrary will and grace' is exaggerated at the expense of traditional limitations on the chief's power, although Weber admits that sultanism is never absolutely free of tradition (1968:232).

The greater possibility for discretion that occurs in patrimonialism depends on the development of an 'administrative and military force which are purely personal instruments of the master' (1968:231). Patrimonialist recruitment includes those individuals who are 'already related to the chief by traditional ties of loyalty', such as kinsmen, slaves, clients, coloni, etc. (1968:228). Weber clearly regards patrimonialist recruitment of the army as the most common mode in the Near East and relates the use of a purely patrimonialist army as one of the major sources of power in sultanism. The more completely the army is dependent upon the ruler's economic support, the greater control the chief has over his subjects (1968:1019–20). Thus, the method by which sultanism arises is clearly outlined by Weber: the ruler can go well beyond the limits of tradition only if his troops are independent of the subjects' influence and support (Turner, 1974:123).

Weber also regarded excessive dependence upon the patrimonial troops as a major weakness for the ruler:

> Scarcely anywhere does the political authority of the patrimonial prince rest exclusively upon the fear of his patrimonial military power. Wherever this fear is very real, it meant in effect that the ruler himself became so dependent on his army that in the event of his death or ill-fated wars and similar cases, the soldiers simply dispersed, went on strike, deposed and installed dynasties, or they had to be newly won through donations and promises of higher pay. . . . To an extreme extent, this was the fate of the ruler in the classic locale of patrimonial armies, the Near East, which was also the classic location of 'sultanism' (1968:1020).

This condition, which Weber referred to as the paradox of sultanism, clearly shows the dangers of excessive 'personal despotism'.[1] The more dependent the ruler is on his patrimonialist army to control the subject population, the more he relies on the army to maintain his position of power (Bendix, 1960:344; Turner, 1974:80–1).

In Weber's development of the constructed subtype of sultanism, his most persistent concern was the role of the army. The issues raised center around the ruler's acquisition of complete personal control over the army. Several sources of troops are conducive to the sultanic regime. Weber's first example is drawn from the 'Abbasi caliphate (750–850) in which Turkish slaves were used to replace the Arab 'theocratic levy'. The major advantage, according to Weber, of 'Abbasi use of Turkish military slaves was their independence from agricultural production and tribal ties. The 'Abbasi caliphs did not have to disrupt agricultural production in times of war and freed themselves of the tribal alliances among the troops which had plagued earlier caliphs.[2]

Contrast is drawn between the 'Abbasi caliphate and the Mamluks (literally slaves) of Egypt (1250–1517), who became the actual rulers of Egypt after they were assigned land grants, or benefices (1968:1015–16). Weber asserted that slave armies may either develop into well-disciplined instruments of the ruler or usurp the ruler's position through the process of feudalization (Turner, 1974:241).

The ruler might counteract the independence of a patrimonialist army if his position is strong enough. Such measures could include the limitation of the status independence of the troops combined with a sufficient monetary reward to insure loyalty to the sultan. Weber cites the *Yeni Čeri* of the Ottoman empire, which originated from the *devširme* (child levy) (1968:1016–17). These *Yeni Čeri* were a standing, professional army of the sultan's court. Other recruits formed the infantry and were stationed at the palace in Istanbul.

Clearly Weber conceptualized sultanism as a recurring form of Islamic socio-political organization. Because of different military recruitment and maintenance methods, the sultanic state might have different fates. If the troops became feudally entrenched, as Weber saw the Mamluks, the ruler could lose control at the hands of the army. For centuries, the *Yeni Čeri* were strictly under the sultans' control. Eventually, the corps became so powerful as a class that it could, and did, depose sultans.

In this review of Weber's constructed subtype of sultanism, an important item has been neglected – the role of the patrimonialist official. Weber outlines the official's position in patrimonialist bureaucracies extensively, but leaves unclear whether the official's position is substantially different in the sultanic state. It can be inferred from Weber's argument that patrimonialist rulers attempt to prevent the monopolization of offices by a status group (1968:1027) that this tendency would essentially be more pronounced in the sultanic state. In other words, the view of sultanism as an extreme form of personal despotism would seem to include extreme control over officeholding and officials.

Weber identifies maintenance and recruitment practices as the key to control of the administrative staff, as he has done for the army. Most of Weber's examples from the Near East attribute the development of the administrative staff to patrimonialist sources. The prevalence of slaves and freedmen was noted by Weber, who remarked that, 'It has not been rare for Grand Viziers to have been at one time slaves' (1968:228). Household officers, such as the head eunuch of the harem and the executioner, often were assigned duties other than those associated with their titles and became part of the administrative staff.

One group of Islamic officials, the *'ulama* (religious scholars), was given particular attention by Weber in relation to the *Shari'ah* (holy law) and as a set of patrimonialist officials. Weber recognized the development of the sultan's own law, alongside the *Shari'ah*, but unfortunately he does not relate the rise of customary law to sultanism *per se*; he is really concerned with the way in which intervention of sacred norms prevents 'systematization of even the secular law' (1968:882; Turner, 1974:107–21). One may again infer that the development of secular law in the sultanic state would be marked, as a method of strengthening the sultan's control over his subjects and as a hedge against the restrictions of the sacred law. However, Weber does not say so and the matter must remain moot.

Weber's comments on the *'ulama* as officials deal primarily with (1) their monopolization of the offices of *qadi* (judge), *mufti* (jurisconsult), and *imam* (prayer leader) (1968:1028) and (2) the benefices that supported the *'ulama* (1968:1037). Neither of these two passages addresses what connection, if any, Weber saw between the *'ulama* and the sultanic state, except that as a group they could monopolize offices. This control of legal offices would seem to be contradictory to the subtype of sultanism as proposed by Weber within his traditionalist type of rulership.

In sum, Weber's argument about sultanism is most extensively presented in his discussion of traditionalist domination. The sultanic state arises when the patrimonialist chief uses his personal army to extend the sphere of his discretion at the expense of traditional rulers. Although the army may be recruited from either patrimonialist or extra-patrimonialist sources, the most frequent pattern in the Near East is patrimonialist recruitment.

Weber's position on the development of arbitrary will in the sultanic state presupposes, in effect, the analytical distinction between sacred and secular authority in traditional Islamic political organization. This is a risky assumption at best, because the *Shari'ah* may be regarded as both a body of doctrine over individual belief and as a legal code defining membership and practice for the Islamic community (*ummah*). Shari'ah has historically held a primary position in the determination of Islamic conceptualization of proper societal order. Weber's distinction between tradition and arbitrary will may therefore indicate a separation of offices and norms that actually form a continuum. It is, however, useful, in order to distinguish between religious and secular aspects of Islamic political organization, to examine Weber's dichotomy between the two spheres of traditionalist domination. Religious authority will mean here the status and power of legitimation exercised by those in the Islamic community who are (by education and consensus among scholars) considered to be knowledgeable about the religious law and by those who occupy a role which is sanctioned in the religious system (caliph, *qadi, mufti*, etc.). Political power will mean the status and power exercised by officials who occupy positions of military leadership and decision-making at the community level.

Weber's distinction between the two spheres of traditionalist domination operates on two levels in relation to Islamic states-craft. Weber recognized that the traditional religious rules of the *ummah* were binding on the caliph or sultan as head of the Islamic community. But Weber also noted the development of secular sultanic institutions alongside the traditional legal system associated with the *Shari'ah*. Weber saw in the sultanic decrees the potential for the ruler to exercise arbitrary will, although the potential for such action was limited by the ruler's relative control of the patrimonialist army. When Weber examined contemporary Islamic statescraft, he found evidence of absolutism in the existence of sultanic law and a patrimonialist army. On another level, primarily in his work on the sociology of religion, Weber recognized that the *'ulama* were the perpetuators of the traditional rules, i.e., *Shari'ah*, and monopolized the sacred religious offices. Even so, Weber's analysis of the *Shari'ah* as a body of law was kept separate from his consideration of the *'ulama* as a group of scholars and government officials. This separation of the *'ulama* as a body of scholars and legalists from the development of Islamic law and statescraft does not permit Weber to explain the role of tradition in Islamic patrimonialism.

The force of the ideal presented by Muhammad and his Medina community is represented, within the *Sunni* tradition, in the concepts of *sunnah* and *ijma'*. *Sunnah*, the 'established practice' of the Prophet and his early community came to be a standard against which the *ummah*'s political and social organization could be measured. *Sunni* adherence to the principle of *sunnah* crystallized as the doctrine of *ijma'*. *Ijma'* became a principle of *Sunni* jurisprudence, holding that whatever was generally accepted by the *ummah* was to be regarded as sanctioned by God (Hodgson, 1975, I:324).

Weber was familiar with this consensual aspect of Sunnite law, and he recognized the conservative effect of *ijma'* on Islamic doctrine when he noted that consensus precluded 'any possibility of the proliferation of dogma' (1963:74). In contrast to this relatively static view of the *Shari'ah*, Weber explicitly states that a system of secular courts existed outside the *Shari'ah* courts. Because Weber contends that Islam, as a 'religion of salvation', tends to develop stereotyped legal institutions and social conventions that do not distinguish between secular and sacred law, it may seem difficult to reconcile his apparently dual conception of Islamic law.

Weber's two views of Islamic law are tied to his analysis of the relationship between religion and economic change. Weber found that the stereotyping effect of religion on law and society is strongest in the stage where 'a religion of salvation has been systematized and internalized in the direction of an ethic based on an inner religious state' (1963:207). Weber does not clearly identify when this stage occurred in Islam, although he does seem to link the stereotyping effect of religion to the classical religious texts of several religions (1963:207).

Weber explains the existence of non-religious courts in Islamic society (presumably in a later stage), as well as similar developments in the Catholic church, to the limitations that religion puts on the 'rationalization of the legal order and hence also on the rationalization of the economy' (1963:208). Religion cannot generally eliminate economic conditions, and religious commandments must either be reinterpreted or by-passed to meet economic 'needs' (1963:208). Weber stresses that it is impossible to state a general formula for the interaction of economic need and religion. In relation to the specific case of Islam, however,

> The frequent ambivalence or silence of religious norms with respect to new problems and practices . . . results in the unmediated juxtaposition of the stereotypes' absolute unalterableness with the extraordinary capriciousness and utter unpredictability of the same stereotypes' validity in any particular application. Thus, in dealing with the Islamic *shari'ah* it is virtually impossible to assert what is the practice today in regard to any particular matter (1963:208).

In effect, as economic conditions changed, the religious law of Islam became more and more unworkable and yet remained unalterable because of its sacred origins.

The argument that *Shari'ah* became immutable in connection with the appearance of sacred texts is incomplete because Weber does not define what he means by 'sacred texts'. It may be that

Weber was referring to the *Qur'an*, which took on a relatively fixed form at an early date. But the same argument cannot be made for other elements of the *Shari'ah*, such as the *hadith* literature. Even if one accepts the idea that the body of 'inquiry' (*usul al-fiqh*) utilized by *Sunni* legalists, i.e., the *Qur'an, hadith, ijma'*, and *qiyas*, was fixed, it is difficult to explain the development of opposing 'schools' (*madhahib*) of law in Islam. The process of personal interpretation (*ijtihad*) was an important element of the religious law and never totally ceased either within a particular legal school or among the *Sunni madhahib* (Makdisi, 1979:2). Weber's evaluation of the stereotyping effect of religion on law in Islam is, then, somewhat overestimated.

Although Weber discussed the *Shari'ah* throughout his analysis of religion, he says very little about the *'ulama*. Weber's comments about the *'ulama* as part of a 'passive ecclesiastical association' (1963:64) are unclear because Islam did not produce an ecclesiastical body like that of the Christian church. Rather, it produced a group of scholars and jurists who were at once the perpetuators of the sacred law, yet dependent on some temporal authority for enforcement of it.

Weber also refers to the *'ulama* as 'the official bearers of the ecclesiastical teaching organization, who were primarily theologians or priests as the case might be' (1963:74). Of course, he was incorrect in using the term 'priest' instead of 'prayer leader', because there were no priests and no clergy in Islam. Weber mentions the *'ulama* as officeholders (1968:1037). However, it is not clear whether Weber recognized that both of these groups consisted of religious scholars trained in *usul al-fiqh*. Weber did not fully describe the role of the *'ulama* in the administration of religious law, especially in the various patrimonialist states which he examined in his work on traditionalist domination in the Near East.

The early Islamic state was commanded by a *Khalifah* (caliph), or 'successor', of the Prophet Muhammad. The caliph was originally to be the temporal head of the *ummah*. The caliphate was a position legitimized within the religious law, and as Abu Usuf wrote to the caliph Harun al-Rashid (r.786–809)

> The illumination of the light of the holders of authority consists of enforcing the penalties for offences as laid down in the holy law and the rendering of what is due to those to whom it is due. . . . The maintenance of the traditional practices (*sunan*) established by worthy men is of the greatest importance, for the maintenance of traditions is one of the good deeds which lives and does not die (Lewis 1974, I:155).

Al-Ahkam al-Sultaniyyah, written by Al-Mawardi, also contains a list of ten conditions for holding the imamate. Among these are religious prescriptions for the maintenance of Islam according to tradition, execution of judgments between litigants, and personal trusteeship of the community as *Khalifah*. The *imam* was also responsible for the defense of Islamic lands and *jihad*, or holy war, as the supreme commander (*amir al-mu'minin*). These two aspects of the caliphate put responsibility for enforcement of the *Shari'ah* on the caliph's court, and specifically on the *'ulama* who filled the positions of *qadi* and *mufti*.

Because of the caliph's dual status as a religious figure and a political leader, the position of the *'ulama* was both strengthened and weakened. The office of *qadi*, for example, was filled by caliphal appointment. The *qadi* was theoretically free from government interference, but was dependent upon the caliph's power for enforcement of legal decisions. The ambiguous relationship of religious authority to political power was a very early feature of the Islamic state. The *'ulama* could neither be excluded from the political process because of their legitimating role nor usurp the position of the caliph as the leader of the *ummah*.

The dependency of the *'ulama* upon the state along with the ascendancy of the traditionalist (or *hadith*-oriented) *madhahib* (Makdisi, 1979:8) undoubtedly contributed to the relative rigidity of the *Shari'ah* after the 'Abbasi collapse. By 900, the right of *ijtihad* had been restricted and was even considered closed among some *Sunni* scholars.[3] Watt (1968:73–4) points out that this protected judges against pressure from rulers for favorable decisions; the *qadi* could cite precedent and deny competence to review prior decisions.

The effect of the self-containment of the *Shari'ah* on the legal institutions of the state can be seen even in 'Abbasi times. Recognition of the *'ulama* prevented modification of the religious law, but also allowed rulers to extend the areas covered by personal administrative decrees (Watt, 1968:75). Often these decrees addressed areas of administration about which the *Shari'ah* was vague or silent. The 'Abbasi caliphs developed judicial and quasi-judicial institutions such as the 'court of complaints' (*al-nazar fi'l-mazalim*) – this practice seems to have started under the Umayyads – and the office of 'inspector of the market' (*muhtasib*), which operated concurrently with the *qadi* courts (Schacht, 1970:556).

Another important element in the relationship between the caliphal court and the *'ulama* was the *fatwa*. *Fatwa* consists of a legal opinion rendered by a *mufti*, usually upon request, on a controversial or ambiguous point of law. The *fatwa* in theory enforced the autonomy of the religious law because they could only be issued by the *'ulama*. *Fatwa* more often served as a cohesive element for the sacred law, adapting it to local conditions and customs and allowing for a legal flexibility not to be found in the basic legal texts (Hodgson, 1975, II:123). *Fatwa* was also a means by which a caliph or sultan might get religious validation of a new administrative decree that might otherwise be interpreted as *bid'ah*, unlawful innovation contrary to *ijma'*. Although Weber recognized that the sultanic decrees allowed a place for the arbitrary will of the ruler within the Islamic legal system, he did not address the issue of the legitimizing effect of the *'ulama* through the vehicle of the *fatwa*.

If the *'ulama* had possessed only religious prestige, their influence on political matters would probably have disappeared altogether. But the *'ulama* were always able to command the support of pious Muslims. Public acceptance of many administrative decrees depended upon the opinion of the *'ulama*. Probably the most important factor in the preservation of their influence, however, was economic and educational independence from the state.

In the 'Abbasi era, the practice of *waqf*, or mortain, was expanded. These religious foundations are generally landed property (sometimes urban) whose income is set aside for some pious purpose. *Waqf* land as such is a distinct legal category of land, inalienable and not subject to governmental control. Often *waqf* property was set aside to support public services, such as schools, mosques, and hospitals, but could also serve as a means of personal support. Many *waqfs* were set up to be administered by the court and were assigned to a *qadi* who received a portion of its income (Hodgson, 1975, I:51; Schacht, 1970:561, 565). Many of the *'ulama* came to be supported by *waqf*, and as a group they became extremely wealthy.

Often the Islamic schools of law, *madrasahs*, were supported by *waqf*. By the twelfth century nearly all the major *madhahib* operated *madrasahs* that supplied room and board for students, as well as salaries for instructors through *waqf* income (Makdisi, 1979:8). Ibn Tashköpdrüzade relates, in *Al-Shaqa' iq al-Nu 'maniyyah*, the story of how Molla al-Fanari, a *mufti* during the reign of the Ottoman Sultan Bayezid, became very wealthy in the sultan's service. Molla al-Fanari later left the court after a disagreement with the sultan and took a well-paid teaching post in Karaman (Lewis, 1974, II:49).

The great Seljuk Vizier Nizam ul-Mulk also gave impetus to the development of the *madrasahs* in the eleventh century. Nizam ul-Mulk's concern with the development of a centralized bureaucracy had a lasting effect on the *'ulama* that extended into the Ottoman period. To staff the bureaucracy, Nizam ul-Mulk conceived of a corps of well-educated, loyal, *Sunni* scholars to fill posts in governmental bureaus. To this effect, he established a system of *madrasahs*. Although the *madrasahs* ultimately did not provide a pool of administrators, they had the effect of creating independent standards of expertise for the *'ulama* as a group. After the development of the *madrasahs* in the eleventh and twelfth centuries, the *'ulama* stood socially and politically apart from the military class in training and outlook. Even though it was recognized that a *qadi* must be appointed by a political authority, it was also accepted that he must have achieved the authority to do so in the *madrasahs* (Lewis, 1973:47–8).

The role of the *'ulama* in Islamic government even at the time of the Seljuk empire is clearly more complex than recognized by Weber when he referred to them as members of the ecclesiastical teaching organization (1963:74). The teaching system of the *madrasahs* did constitute a major factor in the organized structure of the *'ulama* and perpetuated the traditional standards of religious law. But the *madrasahs* also provided a standard of education for scholars who filled court-appointed positions as *qadi* or *mufti*.

Progress through the *madrasahs* was achieved through certification (*ijazah*), or license to teach or practice law. *Ijazah* was conferred on the student by the master for a particular work, or works. The certification was a personal matter between master and pupil, and state officials could not grant license or interfere with the process of certification even if the sultan or caliph happened to be the founder of the *madrasah* (Makdisi, 1970:260,262).

The *'ulama* were raised to high administrative positions in the Ottoman empire, forming one large division of the ruling class. On one hand, there were the *'askeri*, which included the *Yeni Čeri*, the *sipahi* cavalry, the sultan's personal retainers, and the *Kalmiye* who served as scribes and secretaries. (The *Kalmiye* eventually became a distinct branch of Ottoman administration.) At the top of this military-administrative system was the Grand Vizier to whom the sultan granted the authority to supervise this large bureaucracy. Most of the members of the *'askeri* were recruited from the *devširme*, and therefore were the sultan's slaves. Outside this hierarchy of officials were the *'Ilmiye* (*'ulama*), headed by the *Šeyk ul-Islam*.

The *'Ilmiye* included the *qadis* (judges) who enforced the *Shari'ah* (Turkish *Šeriat*) and the sultan's legislation (*örf-i sultani*) in the judicial districts (*qazas*) assigned to them. The *qadis* had numerous other responsibilities in their jurisdiction, including certification of tax assessment lists and dismissal of officials who violated the law. In this respect, the *qadis* were as much representatives of the sultan as of the *Šeriat*. However, the *qadi* was respected and trusted in his district because of the conviction among the people that the *Šeriat* guaranteed certain rights that no official of the sultan could remove (Shaw, 1976:135). *Qadis* also had the right to appoint teachers of the local *madrasahs*, representing the traditional right of the *'ulama* to control the standards of their profession.

Another group included in the *'Ilmiye* were the *muftis*, who acted as legal consultants on points of law and issued *fetvas* *(fatwa)*. Suleyman the Magnificent (r.1520–66) established the office of *Šeyk ul-Islam* for the general purpose of providing a grand *mufti* for the empire, who would issue *fetvas* on the administrative decrees *(qanun)* of the state. He is well known for his *qanun*, an extension of the old practice of allowing the sultan to legislate in areas where *Šeriat* was inadequate. Suleyman's *Šeyk ul-Islam*, Ebu us-Suud, made a collection of applications of the *Šeriat* in the empire, along with the law codes *(qanun-name)* previously issued on the administrative, financial, and military affairs of the state. This process culminated in the *qanunname-i Al-i Osman* (Law Code of the House of Osman) which reconciled the *kanun* with the *Šeriat* through a series of *fetvas* (Shaw, 1976:103). Although the *Šeyk ul-Islam* was appointed from the *'ulama* by the sultan, his office gave him control over the *muftis* and *qadis* selected for the major cities and *qazas*. The selection was often made on the basis of which *madrasahs* the *'alim* had studied in, since positions and salaries were graduated according to the rank of various *madrasahs* in the empire (Faroghi, 1973:211–12).

In view of the professional standards achieved in the *madrasahs* system, Weber's treatment of the *'ulama* as benefice officeholders in a patrimonialist state (1968:1037) is only a partial explanation of the role of religious law in Ottoman rulership. The offices of *mufti*, *qadi*, and *Šeyk ul-Islam* represent the formal governmental positions occupied by the *'ulama*, but do not on the surface show the operation of the elaborate educational system or the operation of professional standards among the *'ulama*.

Weber's constructed subtype of sultanism indicates that the sultan never completely escapes the dictates of traditional rules. He does not explain why this occurs or what form the restraint of tradition might take. Traditional restraints or conditions applied to political leadership could take the form of qualification for rulership, such as the requirement that the caliph uphold the religious law. Islamic traditions of leadership placed other require-

179

ments on the ruler, and over time a set of religiously sanctioned roles grew up around the office of sultan. The definition of valid leadership for the *ummah* changed, as well as the conception of the office of rulership.

The gradual disintegration of the 'Abbasi caliphate from ca. 850 onward was followed' by a period of political fluctuation in the Islamic East. By the time of the Ghaznavi empire (944–1040), the caliphate had lost most of its political authority and much of its military capability.[4] Although the Ghaznavi sultans sought the caliph's support and aggressively claimed religious legitimacy, they did not themselves claim to be caliphs (Bosworth, 1963:47).

During the period of Seljuk domination of the East, the sultan's exalted position gave him the responsibility to institute God's orderly plan by the formal establishment of Islam. In earlier times, the caliph had performed this duty, but by this time he had lost most of his political authority and had been replaced by the sultan as 'The Shadow of God on Earth'.

In the four and a half centuries between the death of Muhammad and the Seljuk empire, Islamic conceptions of government had changed a good deal. At first, the actual administration of the empire had been in the hands of the caliph and his ministers. As we have seen above, the classical *Sunni* theorists had regarded the caliphate as simply a delegation of authority for preservation of the *ummah* in its pristine Medinian form (Lambton, 1954:126). The *'ulama* had been opposed to the encroachment of absolutism in subsequent caliphates. With the decline of the 'Abbasi, however, the religious scholars gradually reconciled the increasing absolutism of the sultans with the *Shari'ah*.

The jurist Ghazali, who was contemporary with the Seljuks, worked out a compromise through which the sultan's position was legitimized by his oath of allegiance to the caliph and the caliph's appointment by the sultan. This amounted to the sultan's recognition of the caliphate's institutional authority which rested on the functional authority of the *Shari'ah* itself (Lambton, 1956:129fn). Ghazali, like Nizam ul-Mulk, recommends complete obedience to the sultan even when the rule is unjust; for Ghazali, the preservation of order is more desirable than the religiosity of the sultan.

This concern for stability and order in the empire probably reflects the political turbulence of the era. The caliphate was often used to strengthen the claims of the sultans against political rivals. Lambton (1954:49–50) has written about such use of legitimation of the sultanate after the reign of Malikshah, through the device of caliphal diplomas.

It was the Seljuk prince Tughrul-Beg (1050) who was first officially recognized as sultan by the caliph (Cahen, 1968:24). This official recognition and later expansion of the *madrasahs* tended to increase the equation of orthodoxy with the state, and hence accentuate the sultan's power. The conflict between the caliph and sultan surfaced during the reign of Malikshah (1072–1092) over the idea that the sultanate derived legitimacy from itself. Cahen remarks that Malikshah may have died by 'an intervention of Allah at the hands of the Caliph' (1968:42). In Weber's terms, the sphere of the sultan's arbitrary will had not become complete. The caliph could still offer legitimacy to the sultan, and the *'ulama* had by now gained some independence through the *waqf-madrasah-system*.

Whatever authority that had remained to the caliphate began to collapse after the Mongol invasions of 1258. After Baghdad fell, the 'Abbasi caliphate was reinstated in Cairo by the Mamluk Sultan Baybars. Between the rise of the Mongols and the adoption of the caliphal title by the Ottoman sultans, *Sunni* jurists made the final concessions to political authority. There were many formulations of the relationship between military leaders who seized power and the historic caliphate. Of particular interest here are the *Aklaq-i Jalal* of Jalal ud-Din Dawwani and the *Muqaddimah* of Ibn Khaldun, which relegate the caliphate to the first thirty years after the Prophet's death. After that, there was only an *imam* (spiritual guide) to whom caliphal titles were given as a matter of courtesy (Gibb, 1962:144–5). Both authors clearly specify that only the ruler who is just and enforces the *Shari'ah* may be considered caliph or *imam*.

An Ottoman tradition relates that the last 'Abbasi caliph, al-Mutawakkil, transferred the caliphate to Sultan Selim I (r.1512–20) and his heirs after the Ottoman conquest of Egypt. The assumption of the title of caliph had already been practised from the time of Murad I (r.1360–89) in the style of Dawwani and Ibn Khaldun, but now it changed form. The Ottoman sultans henceforth assumed the title of 'Caliph of all Muslims,' and claimed to succeed the Prophet and the patrimonialist caliphs as 'the best of the ghazis and of fighters in the Holy War (*afdal al-ghuzat wa'l-mujahidin*)' (Inalcik, 1970:320).

Ghazi, 'warrior of the faithful,' had always been a title of the Ottoman sultans, relating to the Ottoman heritage as march-warriors on the Byzantine-Seljuk frontier in Anatolia. As late as 1353, the caliph retained the title 'commander of the faithful' (*amir al-mu'minin*), but the Ghaznavid, Seljuk, and Ottoman sultans all referred to themselves as *ghazis*. The fact that war against the unbelievers was an important source of legitimization can be seen in this adoption of *ghazi* as a title of the rule. *Jihad*

had changed in form over time from a religious duty into an act of legitimation (Busse, 1973:67–8).

Among the other titles assumed by the Ottoman sultans was 'Servitor of the Two Holy Sanctuaries' (*Khadim al-Haramayn al-Sharifayn*), which referred to the sultan's protection and patronage of Mecca and Medina, as well as the pilgrimage routes into the Hijaz. In adopting this title, Selim I claimed that the Mamluks had been incapable of assuring the pilgrimage and therefore God had entrusted him with the duty of restoring order to the laws of Islam (Inalcik, 1970:321).

In one respect, the sultan had ended the struggle between the historic caliphate and the sultanate by incorporation of the former into the office of sultan. However, the power of the sultan's religious role as a legitimating device can be seen in the steady adoption of various religious roles and titles. These roles and titles symbolized the Ottoman sultans' increasingly strong claims to legitimate leadership of the Muslim community. The Ottoman sultans performed the vital task of maintaining the *Šeriat* in the absence of a legitimate caliph; military force alone would never sustain the legitimacy of the sultanate (Lambton, 1956; Hodgson, 1975, II:42ff). This supportive role of traditional rules in the Ottoman sultanate does not, then, meet Weber's specification that the ruler's arbitrary will must virtually displace the power of tradition.

The area of law also shows an example of the apparent rise of absolutism. By the late fifteenth century, sultans often initiated legislation and administrative law. The prerogative of administrative decrees had been recognized since at least the 'Abbasi era, but in the Ottoman empire it took on a special relationship to the *Šeriat* through the *Šeyk ul-Islam*. The sultan's *qanun* always contained a formulaic statement of agreement with the *Šeriat*, usually in the form of the *Šeyk ul-Islam's fetva* (Inalcik, 1973:70–1). The *qadis*, of course, enforced both the *qanun* and *Šeriat*, but as members of the *'Ilmiye* were subject to non-state regulated licensing procedures in the *madrasahs*. The *qadis* retained substantial power in law enforcement; although the beys had the sole right to enforce the *qadis'* sentence, without that sentence 'they could not exact even the smallest money fine' (Inalcik, 1973:75).

The *'Ilmiye*, under the leadership of the *Šeyk ul-Islam*, represented the most powerful body of officials in the empire outside the *'askeri*. The *Šeyk ul-Islam's* control of *qadi* appointments, the force of public disapproval when the sultan failed to enforce the *Šeriat*, and the sultan's religious roles all served as checks upon his absolute power. The general pattern which emerges from this overview of Islamic statescraft is that tradition never completely gave way to the arbitrary will of the sultan-caliphs. The presence of despots and patrimonial armies cannot be overlooked in various Islamic states, but even those who ruled by force sought religious legitimation (Busse, 1973:47). Neither the 'Abbasi, the Ghaznavi, the Seljuks, nor the Ottomans ever achieved the advanced state of sultanism.

Weber explicitly states that 'the ideal type and historical reality should not be confused with each other' (1949:107), because '[I]n its conceptual purity, this mental construct (*Gedankenbild*) cannot be found anywhere in reality' (1949:90). The historian must adopt the task 'of determining in each individual case, the extent to which the ideal-construct approximates to or diverges from reality' (1949:90).

These considerations, along with Weber's assertion that 'an ideal type has nothing to do with any type of perfection other than a purely logical one' (1949:98–9), have shaped the content of this chapter so that we go no further than Weber would have the historian go. Weber's concept of sultanism derives quite logically from his treatment of traditionalist domination, but fails to incorporate an adequate explanation of the religious bases of authority in Islam.

The emphasis that Weber places on patrimonialist military domination and a dearth of information on the *'ulama* as a force in Islamic government skew the elements of sultanism toward an extreme view of arbitrary will and grace. For this reason, the concept of sultanism as a recurrent type of Islamic government diverges so significantly from the historical record that it is virtually useless as a heuristic device.

Notes

* Many thanks are due to Helen Helwig, David Orenstein, and Marilyn Waldman. Their individual and collective support made this chapter possible.

1 This term was used by Bendix, but seems to be an appropriate substitution for 'sultanism'.

2 Weber was only partially correct in his assessment of 'Abbasi military organization. The 'Abbasi imperial army never completely controlled the provincial armies. This was certainly the case during the reign of al-Mansur (774–5), who sought to eliminate 'Alid loyalists in Khurasan and insure that revenue came to the central treasury rather than be distributed in the province. Despite al-Mansur's own troops he had to be careful not to cause revolt among the troops of al-Jabbar, his commander in Khurasan. Eventually, it

was the army of al-Taliqani which defeated al-Jabbar, not the imperial army.

3 Hodgson (1975, II:406) sees this restriction as a response to the fall of the caliphal empire and as a partial accommodation of Turkish dynastic organization.

4 The disintegration of the 'Abbasi caliphate and subsequent events in Khurasan are complex and must be omitted here. This era is described in a general way in the *Cambridge History of Islam*, vol. I (Cambridge University Press, 1970).

9 Patrimonialism in China and the Islamic world*

Vatro Murvar

Introduction

The perdurable Chinese power structure and its pervasive religious legitimation is one of the best-documented cultural case studies of a long-lasting, well-functioning patrimonialism. In his (1951) work on Confucianism and Taoism as well as elsewhere, Weber (1968) discusses not only religion but the entire society and culture of China, in which the political power structure and religion are inseparable. Among several propositions Weber suggested that an apt understanding of the Chinese doctrines of celestial harmony and celestial kingdom legitimizing the power structure, an exciting intellectual venture in itself, is in pragmatic terms crucial for evaluating the present and future of this great civilization. And today, after Mao, this appears much more substantiated than in Weber's era.

Weber's projected volume on Islam never materialized; his poignant observations of the Islamic unity of power structure remain diffused over several segments of his opus. Islamicists point out that there was only one Islam before the tenth century and many Islams thereafter. Still, for many centuries, patrimonialist rulership and legitimacy represent the common political experience shared by all Islamic nations.

However, before the living forces of cultural heritage and their differential impact on modern societies can be fairly presented and analyzed, it is mandatory to examine past power experiences and their respective sources of legitimation in order to recognize any present-day similarities that might otherwise escape us. Without the often celebrated, but rarely practiced, 'comparison of things in time', we would remain innocent in our admiration for the novelty, originality, and 'revolutionary' success of some modern patrimonialist rulerships.

The main purpose here then, is to suggest a rationale for an analysis of the impact of the specific cultural heritage on the present-day power structures and legitimizing ideologies in China and the Islamic world by evaluating Weber's early and unfinished efforts in the light of modern research.

There was always a general consensus among sinologists and islamicists that the unity of power structure in Chinese and many Islamic societies of various periods was indisputable and that there was ideologically no need and structurally no room for any differentiation between political and religious, temporal and spiritual. This typically Western dichotomy, based on past Western experience, if applied to China or Islam, has almost unanimously been criticized and rejected by sinologists and islamicists.

Western scholarship, in the past, has debated how to classify this unity/identity of power structure in the sense of attempting to decide which features were predominant, the political or the religious. The most frequently chosen label for the Chinese and Islamic power structures was theocracy. Weber argued explicitly against it and postulated that the evidence in both Islam and China indicated political use of religion and the economy for the political rulership's purposes.

The patterns of unity of all power in the Chinese and Islamic civilizations are not of 'theocratic' or even hierocratic monistic rulership, in spite of lofty religious doctrines calling for and legitimizing various myths of the deity's rule through his presence at the top or through the executants of the deity's messenger. The only possible exceptions were those instances when a power vacuum existed between two dynasties or before a new ruler stabilized his patrimonialist structure, and the religious structures were expected to fill the vacuum only temporarily.

Finally, there were in the Chinese or Islamic legitimizing doctrines certain similarities with the Byzantine or Eastern Christian doctrines, and also with Western Christendom's first thousand years of vividly demonstrated inability to give up universal political monism or at least to esteem the need for emergence of a differentiated religious power structure from the totality of monistic power. In spite of claims to 'theocracy' made by the Western European kings and emperors, their power structures were not theocratic: they were purely political. Claims of royal and imperial 'theocracy' legitimized their dynasties and their absolute power. Only in the eleventh century when Pope Gregory VII firmly challenged the political monism of the Western European rulers with his own blueprints of hierocratic monism, did the theocratic, divine, sacred claims of the Western European political rulers cease.

Patrimonialism in China

Modern Maoism and traditionalist Confucianism

The magnificent cultural heritage of China appears still an essential part and perhaps even the central core of the Maoist and post-Maoist power structure and ideology. While the similarity of both power structures is unquestionable, the Chinese doctrines of the past are to some scholars very much alive today in one form or another. Although in post-Weber literature there are, for example, many elaborate comparisons of the Confucianist and Calvinist systems of ethics, Meisner (1968) compared the Maoist code of virtues with the 'more utopian pronouncements of Karl Marx' concerning the future classless society's ethics and added:

> Divested of their particular ideological jargon, the ethical commentaries and biographical sketches of model 'red and expert' which appear in *Chung-kuo ch'ing-nien* (China Youth), for example, might easily be mistaken for Calvinist-inspired moral tracts rather than products of the 'Marxist-Leninist' thoughts of Mao Tse-tung (1968:106, 107).

But what seems imperative here is a comparison of the Confucianist and Maoist codes of ethics, especially of the virtues which are glorified and recommended to the respective bodies of faithful followers as essential for the realization of the good society. Some, if not many, of the Confucianist beliefs were easily adapted and integrated into the Maoist ideological programs; some Maoist teachings are so similar to Confucianist ones that they hardly seem new to the Chinese people.

If found correct, this set of propositions also seems to support, at least in part, the Russian accusations that what is going on in China today is not Marxism, but something else marked by fundamental deviations from Marx's doctrinal blueprints. And not so paradoxically, the Chinese, Titoist, Dubčekian, and others' arguments that Soviet Russia has deviated from whatever the original Marxism is supposed to be into something else are also valid. Like the Chinese, the Russian cultural heritage has a great deal to offer in building, maintaining, and legitimizing the Soviet Union power structure, perhaps much more than Marxism offers.

In any event, whatever future research will determine, there are some striking, definitive similarities in China's past and present political power structure as well as in her historical and modern legitimizing ideologies. Only some aspects are suggested here:

1 Central to both Confucianism and Maoism are the core-attributes of patrimonialism. Confucianism legitimizes the ruler (the emperor) as the Supreme Father of the universe. The entire society was his family: all the land, all the riches, and all the people. As will be shown, the test of the ruler's success was to keep harmony between the human society and the universe, which are considered one. Maoism presented the same Supreme Father–Supreme Ruler in the person of Mao and his successors with some minor, if not slight, modifications in the contents of charisma as a test of the ruler's success to suit modern needs.

2 Both Maoism and Confucianism are universalist doctrines, destined for all humankind. Confucianism predicts a totally voluntary acceptance of Chinese ways after the rest of humankind recognized its superiority; the voluntary aspect of the universal acceptance of Chinese domination in Maoism is debatable.

3 Maoism and Confucianism share the main propositions that the supreme goal of the Father and his children (people) is to build a good life here on this earth, and not to make preparations for the hereafter.

4 This supreme goal of a good life could be achieved only by exactly practicing an elaborate code of social-ethical behavior which calls for great personal sacrifice. The Maoist and Confucianist codes of behavior as expected from the faithful are very similar, if not identical in many of their contents: honesty, honor, sincerity, diligence, self-discipline, frugality, hard work, unselfishness, self-denial, duty, loyalty, obedience, especially filial piety, public self-criticism of unacceptable thought, action, or mistakes, guilt-feeling for the betrayal of the goals as prescribed, etc. In both systems these virtues are defined alike; the only variations are in the emphasis, traditional or modern, and in its applicability.

5 Both Confucianism and Maoism share absolute convictions concerning collective responsibility. In practicing the Confucianist/Maoist virtues, the individual is always subordinated to the collectivity; the correct attitudes are mandatory and they must be acquired through the process of learning. It includes frequent soul-searching to maintain the correct attitude toward the supremacy of the collectivity. If this is not achieved, the collectivity is betrayed. Neither Mao nor his great teacher, Stalin, invented the elaborate procedures of soul-searching, self-induced guilt-complex, and public self-

criticism. It is a significant aspect of the Confucianist heritage which immensely benefited modern patrimonialism.

6 The extended families as basic collectivities blended with all other families into the Emperor's national family to form a supreme collectivity; the Maoist and post-Maoist farming and industrial collectivities are natural extensions of the traditional extended-family collectivities. Thus, Maoism, with help from the modern state-owned and managed media, successfully transferred or revived loyalty, honor, filial piety, and other virtues from the traditional collectivities to the highest national collectivity of the entire modern Chinese society. The same virtues of hard work, sacrifice, and national pride are utilized to transfer the traditional family self-sufficiency to national self-sufficiency, in principle at least, if not always in practice.

7 The totality of control which regulates every aspect of life simply continued and only intensified from Confucianism to Maoism. The common people do not find the totality of Maoist control unusual; it is natural to them for it is continuous with the past.

Celestial mandate and celestial harmony

As suggested by Weber, the impact of the Chinese traditional doctrines, both celestial harmony and celestial mandate of the central kingdom, on the future which is now Maoism and post-Maoism will be examined to support the main propositions here. Contrary to many Western misinterpretations, these two doctrines are *not* mutually exclusive, but complementary. The core of this complex configuration is a monistic value-system.

The universe and human society are one, inseparable, identical existence. In this order of unity there is no choice, only one set of proper actions to meticulously observe the norms of the celestial mandate in order to maintain societal (political) legitimacy of the ruler and celestial harmony at the same time. Political legitimacy and cosmic harmony being *one and the same* is tested by and manifested through the well-being and general prosperity of the entire society for which the successful ruler is glorified because in accordance with *Dao* he observed *li*.

Dao is not bound by limits of any polis or national state; it operates limitlessly as far as the earth is populated. *Dao* does not function through the use of force by the power-holders, but through the silent example of *li* which assures order and justice, which in turn would secure the true happiness of the peoples of the world. To Weber, the laws of nature and of rites were fused into the unity of *Dao* (1951:28).

Li in its root meaning is close to 'holy ritual', 'sacred ceremony', but Fingarette says that 'one has to labor long and hard to learn *li'* and he adds that *li* is a 'medium within which to talk about the entire body of mores, or more precisely, of the authentic tradition and reasonable conventions of society' (1972:6). *Li* is based on the effects of ethical sentiments, and these ethical sentiments, leading to ethical action, must radiate into unlimited space from the perfect personality of the *One* who stands in the midpoint of earth and heaven; then the nations bow of their free will in humility because they see that here is peace.

The well-known advice of Confucius to the supreme ruler is: 'Let your own volition be good and the people will be good. The actions of the ruler are like the wind and the nature of the subjects is like the grass: as the wind blows over, the grass will bow'. Under the true rule, the nearby living subjects are happy and the distant people will eventually come to him to subordinate themselves. The *One* guarantees with his own person to heaven for such effects: if he proves himself unable to secure the happiness of the nations, heaven will reject him; he will lose his mandate; and a *Superior One* will replace him. However, in actual everyday experience, *li* frequently meant mostly etiquette and correct ceremonial observance, but its ethical aspects should not be minimized. Weber suggested a plausible sequence, namely, that 'personal qualities which are necessary to the charismatic image of the emperor were turned into ritualism and then into ethics by the ritualists and philosophers' (1951:31).

Non-observance of *li* by a ruler (or official below him) automatically means spectacular cosmic consequences: changes in the rotation of the stars and earthly seasons that, in turn, impose major calamities and suffering on large numbers of people. The list of proofs for a ruler's failure is long: floods, droughts, epidemics, famines, lost wars, invasions of grasshoppers, lack of mulberry leaves to feed the silkworms, etc. Here, Weber uses his concept of traditional magical charisma:

> the Chinese emperor ruled in the old genuine sense of charismatic authority. He had to prove himself as the 'son of heaven' and as the lord approved by heaven insofar as the people fared well under him. If he failed, he simply lacked charisma . . . it was evidence – such was expressly taught – that the emperor did not have the charismatic qualities demanded by heaven (1951:31).

Public confession of failure and public penitence by the emperor were expected but if these were of no avail, the emperor was to abdicate or even to contemplate suicide.

However, there is a typically patrimonialist solution to this unpleasantness and the historical evidence is plentiful. The officialdom under the emperor shared in the office charisma and, needless to say, shared in the penalties for failure to maintain the cosmic-societal identity. It was not only anticipated by the power relationship and vast spaces of land but is also amply supported by evidence that an emperor was able much more frequently to pin the blame on his subordinates, especially the provincial governors, rather than the other way around. After all, the calamities usually did not hit the whole empire at once, but hit individual regions.

How much of this magnificent legitimizing doctrine was put into the daily living experience of the people with the monistic power structure during that long period of time? Certainly, there were many changes in persons, dynasties, elites, conquerors from all sides but Weber recognized the crucial aspect of the power's stability and durability contributed by the doctrines of celestial harmony and celestial kingdom's mandate which were well integrated into one

> Above all, such matters of fate were not the business of the common people. Successful usurpation of the throne or successful invasion simply meant a different tax receiver, not an altered social order.
>   Thus, the unshaken order of internal political and social life, with thousands of years behind it, was placed under divine tutelage and then considered as the revelation of divine. . . . For the heavenly powers of China, however, the ancient social order was the one and only one (1951:27).

In actuality, then, the legitimacy was clear and simple. While the person in charge was successfully maintaining himself on top and for as long as he was successful in doing so, his legitimacy was never questioned. Once he failed to maintain himself on top, he not only lost his legitimacy, but perhaps never had it in the first place. As a consequence of failure, his existence, past and present, was frequently obliterated. Weber uses 'the charismatic principle of success' in this context:

> the retention of religious belief was politically even more important than was the concern for food . . . the imperial power was the supreme and religiously consecrated structure; in a sense it stood above the crowd of popular deities. The emperor's personal position . . . was based exclusively on his

charisma as the plenipotentiary ('Son') of Heaven where his ancestors resided. But the veneration and significance of the individual deities were still subject to the charismatic principle of success. . . . This charismatic character of religion suited officialdom's interest in self-preservation (1951:143).

Otto Franke, who influenced Weber, actually compared the Chinese durable rulership and legitimacy with the blueprints for the papal world monarchy, which never really made a lasting entry in history. Remarkably strong humanist values, Franke argued, were shared by the Chinese and papal ideologies and by none other – neither the Babylonians, nor the Persians, nor the Macedonians, nor the Romans.

Outside China in all other Asian world-states the naked concept of power was . . . absolutely dominant. . . . The Chinese doctrine saw in all mankind the cosmically ordered unity; in their spiritual make-up the segments of mankind are quite different, but these differences are to be equalized and the heavenly mandate given to the [divinely] selected ruler, the most wise among men, is exactly this equation. He and his environment must live in perfect harmony and unity with *Dao* (1930:121, translation by this author).

Commenting on the elaborate casuistry employed from the eleventh century on by papal curialists to defend the doctrine of papal monism which, in being a revolutionary novelty, greatly needed philosophical and scriptural justification, Franke said that such documentation was never needed in China. In the Chinese cultural context the undivided worldly political power structure was without question and without alternative and 'in the Chinese spirit the conception of the indivisible unity of the highest earthly summit held strongest'. To Franke, the Chinese political structure is the core of the entire Chinese value-system (1930:125, 162). However, Weber cautiously limited the scope of Franke's comparison by contrasting the religiously sanctified *claims* to such a political power structure of just one pope, to be sure the most worldly and power-hungry ('caesaropapist') incumbent of that office, Boniface VIII (1951:126).

While meticulously accounting for the religious, charismatic, and magical foundations of the Chinese rulership, including the emperor's pontifical titles and claims, Weber staunchly classified the Chinese monistic power experience of over two millennia as a basically political and not religious power structure. Recently, C. K. Yang agreed with Weber's and Franke's positions. Indeed, Daoism and Buddhism attempted religious resistance, but in the

192

final analysis after these religious movements were spent and routinized, the political monistic rulership re-established traditional control over religion. Some new values of the religious movements were mixed with the old, but the unity/identity of power under the political patrimonialist rulership was again total. According to Yang, from the eleventh century to contemporary times there has been even more dramatic stabilization of political control over religious (1967:105).

Western misinterpretations of celestial harmony and celestial mandate

Is this the right to rebel, as some Western writers, influenced by Western doctrines of tyrannicide and regicide, from Manegold of Lautenbach in the eleventh century to Juan Mariana (1599), automatically assumed, or only affirmation that the *Superior One* will inevitably replace the unworthy one? Weber suggested 'that this idea – a quasi-superstitious Magna Charta – was the only available and gravely feared weapon the subject could use against the privileged, the officials and the rich' (1951:25). In general, however, Western scholarship has not recognized the complementary nature of celestial harmony and celestial mandate and the basic oneness of patrimonialist power and legitimacy in China. Those anxious to discover Marx's evolutionary stages in Chinese history pictured patrimonialist society as an old game of dialectical trinity and came up with a class struggle and two totally conflicting class ideologies. The others ascribed to Confucianism some populist attributes. In addition to those in the West, historians and philosophers in the People's Republic of China, especially during the 'Cultural Revolution' in 1966–8 and again in the early 1970s, argued for the continuous existence of two irreconcilable class ideologies emanating from the alleged doctrinal contradictions of celestial harmony and celestial mandate.

Consequently, the doctrine of the celestial (central) kingdom, with its mandate of heaven, was popularized as the ideology of rulership and the ruling elite, exclusively necessary for justifying their continuous warfare to expand the celestial kingdom to the ends of the earth. A hardly evidenced 'positivist-legalist school' was ascribed the unnecessary job of selling to the masses of peasants the sacredness of the ruler and his absolute rulership and ownership of the globe. This is absurd because the allegedly contradictory school of Confucianism was doing that more successfully all along; the Confucianist scholars were the permanent patrimonialist bureaucracy. (See the section *The Literati*, pp. 199–203)

Celestial (great) harmony was misinterpreted as the exclusive class ideology of the peasant multitudes over the centuries who were looking for the happiness and peace that only celestial harmony could guarantee. Then the Confucianist school was charged with this contradictory and unlikely task of promoting the peasant class's exclusive right to rebel and to limit the ruler's absolute power in order to actualize the promise of celestial harmony. As suggested earlier, the Confucianists are not a school of thought contrasted to another school, much less a school identified with the alleged class ideology of the peasants.

The modern proponents of these views ascribe to Hsün Tzu (ca. 315/298–238 BC) or two of his immediate students the creation of a 'positivist-legalist school' in total contradiction to Confucianism. When the historical evidence is examined, considering especially the short duration of a few decades and the Confucianist origin of that 'school', this entire assertion appears highly exaggerated. It only seems to project into early Chinese history the Western dichotomy of two conflicting doctrines, positivist legalism versus natural-law jurisprudence, that raged for centuries in Western Europe.

Hsün Tzu, Ch'in Shih Huang Ti, and Mao

Hsün Tzu considered himself Confucianist and was generally accepted by his contemporaries and posterity as a great disciple of Confucius and one of the most influential interpreters of Confucianism. He raised, however, some pragmatic, skeptical questions. He doubted that the natural calamities were a consequence of the ruler's failure to observe *li* and that his tenure was dependent on heaven, etc., but he was willing to defend the Confucianist doctrines on the grounds that through long experience they had proved themselves useful. In general, he said that *li* and other beliefs are clever devices instituted by the ancient sages to control man's greed and selfishness. He argued that natural events follow their own course and are not directed by spiritual forces for the purpose of rewarding the good and punishing the bad performance of the ruler. The primary purpose of the rulership is to achieve constant regularity among men by establishing social order and eliminating conflict, which are caused by human evils.

Reacting in part to an interpretation of the celestial mandate by Mencius (ca. 372–288 BC), Hsün Tzu disagreed with his teaching on human nature. Hsün Tzu argued that goodness can only be acquired through education, ceremonies, music, art, and especially through good, efficient, and successful political rulership. In this most important task of ruling and being ruled, Hsün Tzu agreed with Mencius' teaching. Humankind should

194

follow the great sages, especially Confucius, who explained how personal perfection and social order could be integrated and how universal peace could be achieved by using the means recommended by Confucius.

The intellectual development of Hsün Tzu is an excellent case study in the sociology of knowledge, because his reinterpretation of certain aspects of Confucianism reflected the radically changing conditions of political life surrounding him. He witnessed the growth of a powerful unifying empire: through terrible bloodshed, approximately fifty-five 'warring kingdoms' were swallowed up by about ten surviving kingdoms which would soon be annexed by the clearly emerging new Chinese empire of the first emperor, Ch'in Shih Huang Ti. Disturbed by the endless violence in direct contradiction to the values of Confucianism, Hsün Tzu offered typically intellectual *post facto* rationalization to reconcile the brutal reality of his era with the lofty universalist humanist goals of Confucianism.

The first emperor, Ch'in Shih Huang Ti, started his rule in 246 BC as a thirteen-year-old king of Ch'in, a major surviving kingdom, and after considerable success in destroying his competitors, he became emperor in 221 BC until his death in 206 BC. At the expense of millions of lives in conscript labor, he far overshadowed the Egyptian pharaohs in building not only the Great Wall but also his tomb, which is enclosed in 500 acres of architectural and sculptural wonders. His underground tomb is now being excavated and, thus far, it includes 6,000 life-size sculptures of soldiers with individual features and thousands of horses and other sculptures outfitted with actual weapons and chariots. (This represents about one-tenth of the entire structure.) Also, he is the one who buried alive 460 Confucianist scholars because, most likely, they questioned his celestial mandate.

Not too surprisingly, Mao hailed the first emperor to unify China as a man whose 'positive efforts hastened the progress of history'. The official hosts for the foreign archaeologists recite Mao's words. According to Topping, the official scholarship reflects 'not only the attitude of the Ch'in dynasty but also of China today' (1978:452–3). Indeed, as Loewe and others have documented, the historians in China today glorify the first emperor with most exalted images and frequently compare Mao favorably with him (1975:56–60). This is, however, in sharp contrast to the traditional historians who, deeply chagrined with the first emperor's brutality, were portraying him in a negative light.

The ideological legitimizing implications of both glorifications and comparisons are unquestionable. One of several perceptive observers, Schram, said, 'There are also clear echoes of traditional emperor worship in the current image of Mao as mediator between the Chinese people and its historic destiny' (1967:387). 'The Red Sun in the hearts of the peoples of the world', 'the greatest figure in Chinese history', 'the highest theoretical attainment of the Chinese people', and numerous other exaltations of Mao cannot, however, be dismissed simply as 'recent pathological tendencies'.

But this is not the entire configuration of Mao's uses of historical heritage. He also skilfully blended the heritage – 'real or imagined' – of the Chinese popular and messianic movements, including peasant rebellions, with that of the successful emperors. In this, too, as Wakeman pointed out, Mao made the past to serve the present (*yi gu wei jin yong*). 'The "proletarian" spirit of self-sacrifice which Mao Tse-tung encouraged in his people certainly did not arise from cooperative production, as Marx would have expected' (1977:225).

Mao not only benefited by the impressive legitimizing heritage and achievements of the first emperor and all subsequently successful emperors, but he, indeed, heavily utilized the traditionalist doctrines and philosophical interpretations of the same, such as those of Hsün Tzu, including the doctrine of the central kingdom's celestial mandate to rule China and to continue the expansion of China's power in the economically underdeveloped Third World. As is well known, Mao claimed that he was the one to finally establish the peace, tranquility, and true happiness that celestial harmony had promised for so many centuries. In Mao's actual interpretation of the Chinese heritage, these doctrines were not contradictory but complementary, and this is a correct interpretation. Mao was also celebrated as allegedly the first Chinese ruler who successfully combined both 'contradictory' doctrines, while in reality he had been preceded by many successful emperors who also employed both doctrines rather efficiently for their legitimation.

Continuity of the patrimonialist legitimacy

When those who overthrew the first emperor's dynasty attempted to return to the old ways, it was impossible because the old pre-patrimonialist Chinese society had been permanently destroyed. Hsün Tzu with his interpretation had offered his vision of the future before the first empire was actually created. His experience with the extraordinary conditions of immense suffering and brutality had forced him to re-examine certain current teachings with the purpose of finding a solution, namely, to re-establish the peace, tranquility, and justice that Confucianism calls for. His concentration on crimes of violence and their punishment led him to recommend a differential distribution of irresistible rewards for those who respected peace and justice and harsh treatment for those who did not.

To stop the constant horrors of destruction and to prevent future ruin, this unlimited source of power should be placed only in the hands of one successful, all-powerful ruler. Confucius, Mencius, and Hsün Tzu did not share the same beliefs concerning the origin of goodness in human nature and other philosophical issues; however, the legitimizing doctrine of the unity/identity of all power in the hands of one remained practically unchanged. Hsün Tzu and his disciples made it much stronger by adding some efficient practical means of enforcement to the old spiritual but, at times, unenforceable methods.

The two immediate disciples of Hsün Tzu, Han Fei Tzu (ca. 280–233 BC), a prince and emissary from the Han kingdom to Ch'in Shih Huang Ti, and Li Ssu, his prime minister, developed an all-embracing system of a single, formalized imperial law in which an elaborate distribution of penalties for disobedience and privileges for those who served the ruler was the central core. Han Fei Tzu was deeply disturbed by the breakdown of his kingdom of Han and in his writings he seeks the best means to safeguard a durable, successful and efficient rulership to prevent any future breakdowns. He compared the tiger's advantages over the dog to illustrate his point:

> If the tiger abandons its claws and fangs and lets the dog use them, it will be subdued by the dog. Similarly, the ruler controls his ministers through punishment and kindness (i.e., the 'advantages' of 'congratulations and rewards').

Commenting on the above, Fingarette concluded that to these apologists of the new empire 'reliance on anything but the stick or the carrot was sentimental self-deception' (1972:28). This is an early documentation for the differential distribution of rewards and penalties which is one of the major structural characteristics of patrimonialism.

This, however, is all there is in the Chinese intellectual 'school' or 'movement' of the so-called legalists in terms of challenge to the original teachings: it was a successful adaptation of some new elements within the traditional legitimizing doctrine. If it was a challenge, it certainly did not last long, for the 'school of legalists', if the name is warranted, passed from the scene as soon as the Han dynasty (202 BC–AD 220) was firmly established.[1] After that period, no group or structure of legal scholars or legalists has ever been evidenced in the Chinese past; without such a structure, it is not possible that a challenge could be kept alive.

As noted earlier, in spite of intense longing for the old ways, the overthrow of the first emperor's dynasty did not restore the old society. The several years of political anarchy and civil war that followed the Ch'in dynasty's downfall supply additional evidence of the soundness of the reinterpretations of Hsün Tzu and his followers. The establishment of the Han dynasty was legitimized with the same doctrine, although a blending of both the old and new is evidenced. 'The martial emperor', Wu Ti (141–87 BC), of the Han empire with his actions represents proof of the accomplished synthesis, its finality. It does not matter whether he contributed significantly to it or just symbolized an already achieved fusion. Officially, he embraced the Confucianists by condemning the supporters of Hsün Tzu and Han Fei Tzu, while he eclectically chose from them, perhaps – as some scholars claim – more than he accepted from the old. What he took from them all were those elements that meshed well with his own patrimonialist power structure, a seemingly new imperial order, but one remarkably similar to any typical patrimonialism. Revitalized and reconciled with the political reality, the Confucianist value-system continued to perform a major durable role for the legitimation of the future patrimonialist rulerships.

In summary, the one heavenly rulership in China was established for the well-being of all. In principle, equality for all, including the patrimonial administrative staff, was guaranteed by the sacred rulership. Of course, the reality was different from what the ideological blueprints called for, though the longing of the common people for the peace and justice of celestial harmony was real indeed. Most emphatically, celestial harmony and the celestial kingdom were not class ideologies. Also, most emphatically, they were not contradictory to each other because to push the celestial kingdom to the ends of the earth was to strive for the actualization of celestial harmony. Both were well-integrated, essential elements of the same religious-philosophical doctrine that helped to balance out the total ideology in relation to the reality of power and surely they contributed to the longevity of the power structure and its legitimacy. After proof from heaven was delivered that the celestial order was disturbed by the non-observance of *li* by the ruler, it was evident that he lost his power to rule – not a right to power, but a magical sort of power. Finally, more so than the peasants and the common people, the members of the ruling elite were concerned with the question of succession, for it could be personally more beneficial or detrimental to them. For the masses of peasants, the imperial succession or a dynasty change made little difference.

The literati

The famous Chinese literati, the patrimonial administrative staff *par excellence*, cannot be construed to be opposed to the Confucianists as some Westerners have assumed; simply they *were* the Confucianist scholars. Yang reiterates how deeply Confucianism was committed to the sanctification of the doctrine of the ruler's celestial kingdom (1968:xxix). 'But, above all,' he said, 'the Confucianists fully endorsed the divine character of political power by supporting the concept of the mandate of heaven' (1967:108).

Weber's proposition on 'the two greatest powers of religious rationalism in history, the Roman church in the Occident and Confucianism in China' (1968:537) was ignored until recently. Very popular notions still identify rationality with Western development only and thus misrepresent the legal-rational bureaucracy as the only type of bureaucracy. After saying that 'rationalism can mean very different things' and pleading for a long-overdue recognition of 'a particular kind of rationalization' in China, namely, the Confucianist rationalism of the literati, Roth concluded:

Rationalization in the form of Confucian ideology and administration thus contributed to the very persistence of the Chinese imperial system. In the West, however, rationalization of a different kind destroyed the *ancien régime* and created a new world (Roth and Schluchter, 1979, 188–91).

However, some argue that to Weber each of the great world religions, especially Islam, in addition to 'the Roman church in the Occident and Confucianism in China', developed major attributes of a particular kind of rationalization of its own in relation to the political/economic reality of its age.

Today, quite appropriately, the sinologists including Molloy (1980), Zingerle (1972), Sprenkel (1964:353, fn.14), and others are less concerned 'with Weber's account of Chinese religion than with the relevance of Weber's concept of a patrimonialist state for the analysis of modern China'. However, some major misinterpretations of Weber's purpose here are still dominant.

For Parsons and Yang, Weber's account of the history of China's social and religious institutions is often seen as a rather tiresome prolegomenon to a characterization of their distinctive features at the relevant stage of development. In

199

fact, Weber was concerned, not with a Chinese social system analogous to the social system of pre-capitalist Europe, but with a unique and immensely lengthy historical process: the rationalization of Chinese culture (Molloy 1980, 398, 395).

Molloy continued to say that the 'interpretive equation offered by Parsons and Yang, where Confucianism is conceptualized as a coherent value-system, concretely existing at the vital pre-capitalist stage' in fact 'does not accord with the way in which Weber conceptualized Confucianism and its role as a factor inhibiting the development of capitalism.' The significance of Weber's (1951) work on China is in his

> offering an historically sensitive account of the process within which the metaphysical assumptions of Confucianism, and the interests of the Literati, led to a progressive reconstitution of practical ethics. At various points . . . [Weber] discusses: the basic religious conceptions of the Chinese which were drawn upon, and modified, by the group of princelings' advisers which eventually produced Confucius himself; the way in which these beliefs were synthesized by Confucius and his near contemporaries; the later utilization of Confucianism as the basis of a state ideology when the literati had come to adopt the role of an imperial bureaucracy; and the subsequent successive modifications as the literati strove to establish and maintain a Confucian orthodoxy which had to survive even in those periods when the Empire was ruled by a non-Chinese dynasty, or when the emperor favored the Buddhists or Taoists (Molloy 1980:394–5).

The literati were the patrimonial administrative staff who for over two thousand years displayed most typically the basic attributes of a patrimonialist bureaucracy. 'The educated stratum of China', Weber said, in contrast to some misconceptions dominant today, 'simply has never been an autonomous status group of scholars, as were the Brahmans, but rather a stratum of officials and aspirants to office' (1951:122). The stratum of literati even in the earliest times was neither hereditary nor exclusive, as were the Brahmans. He emphasized that this leading stratum never had the characteristics of the Christian clergy, Jewish rabbis, or ancient Egyptian priests (1951:108).

The only difference between the literati and all other patrimonialist bureaucratic servants was their highly competitive, and for the patrimonial ruler very convenient, method of selection: the celebrated examination system. Only a small number of those who qualified by passing the examination were given a patrimonial office; therefore, the ruler had at his pleasure a large group of aspirants who, having qualified by passing the examination, did not receive an office. To be sure, these aspirants were anxious to please the ruler. In Russian patrimonialism, the ruler had, without the examination system, the same opportunity to exact absolute slave-like dependence of the office-holders on him by the ever-present threat to use and actual use of a large pool of aspirants. Zingerle noticed that Weber stressed the enormous efficacy of the 'characteristic or even typical punishment for political bad behavior in China': cancellation of the examinations for the entire province(s) or temporary, indefinite exclusion from the examination of various strata, especially the intellectuals (1972:84).

After comparing the Russian *mjestničestvo* (the patrimonialist bureaucracy without the examination system, staffed by the Russian servant notables), with the Chinese literati, Weber pointed out that both systems, by maintaining a large pool of aspirants for a limited number of positions, 'facilitated a competitive struggle for prebends and offices among the candidates,' which, in turn, prevented them 'from joining together into a feudal office nobility' as happened in the West (1951:119).

Almost identical punitive measures are used in modern patrimonialist societies when entire regions or classes of people are denied, as a punishment for their lack of enthusiasm in co-operating with the rulership, the right to apply for the candidacy (a form of novitiate) for the one-party membership.

Zingerle (1972:78–97) extensively and Yang (1968:xxii, xxvii, xlff) also reported that there is a great deal of support in recent research both in the United States and abroad for the assertion that the literati were a typical patrimonial administrative staff unable and unwilling to challenge a successful ruler.

The celestial kingdom pushing to the ends of the earth to establish celestial harmony was always in need of money; consequently, in certain periods it had to sell some offices to 'capitalist purchasers of office' irrespective of their qualifications and without examinations. To Weber this was a 'natural result of the leveling of status groups and of the fiscal money economy'. The literati were sucessful, though, in not letting this situation become permanent. The greatest enemies of the literati, however, were the ever-present eunuchs, a group of the ruler's servants at his court who were even more dependent on him than the literati were. In addition to being in charge of the ruler's harem, the eunuchs were frequently military and secret police chiefs and other crucially important staff members of the celestial court. The literati had to bribe them constantly in order to maintain the emperor's favor. But the whole context of the struggle between the two groups of

201

ruler's servants did not involve in any way the sacredness of the monistic power of the emperor; his power was not the subject of the controversy.

The ceremonial and symbolic assumption of certain religious functions by the Chinese emperor excluded the need for the role of a hierarchy that might have challenged the patrimonialist power structure. In this context, Zingerle rightly objected to Weber's too-frequent usage of the Western church's terminology, such as prebendal, pontifical, canonical, orthodox, etc., when discussing the emperor's religious ceremonies (1972:93ff). These terms could imply some hierarchic or church-state *(kirchenstaatlichen)* attributes of Chinese patrimonialism, but it is clear from the context of the entire analysis that this was not Weber's intent (see pp. 186–93 of this chapter). With the limited exception of Daoism, no priesthood ever existed. The Daoist religious movement, Yang said, 'historically . . . performed no such revolutionary function for the social order . . . the long unrelenting domination of Confucian traditionalism had choked off any Daoist potentiality for innovation' (1968:xxvff). The Buddhist religious movement, faithful to its own way of life which rejected a hierarchy or any structure, did not create any power base to make a lasting impact, even though it did inspire several political rebellions. The cults of the great deities of heaven and earth, of various special spirits, of deified popular heroes, and of some magically qualified high mandarins were all strictly affairs of the patrimonialist ruler's power structure; in modern terms they were political or state affairs. These cults were managed not by religious elders, priests, monks, or virtuosi, but by members of the patrimonialist bureaucracy.

There is a consensus that Weber's analysis of the Chinese city represents one of the best-documented case studies of the non-free, non-Western, so-called 'oriental' or patrimonialist city, as proposed by this author (Chapter 3 in this volume; also, see Charts 3.2 to 3.4). The long-awaited Skinner (1977) symposium, which had been in the publishing mill for almost a decade, was anticipated to become an articulate challenge to Weber's and others' constructs of the Eastern and Western city, but it did not, mainly because it focused on some urban changes of later imperial China only, which, to say the least, is a recent and only a small fraction of the durable existence of the Chinese city as conceptualized by Weber. Skinner was also criticized for multiple inadequacies, some arbitrary methodological choices, and an anti-scientific pro-historical bias in general (Samuels, 1978). The German sinologist Herbert Franke said that in his judgment Weber offers most fruitful insights leading to a recognition of the specific characteristics of the Chinese city and interrelated with it, the particular qualities of the Chinese patrimonialist rulership. He seems to wonder why this has not made the impact that it so richly deserves (1966:118ff).

In summary, in China the absence of an independent or autonomous hierarchy is correlated with the absence of free cities and the absence of feudal diffusion of power. No autonomous religious, economic, political, or other forces to challenge the existing power structure or to introduce radical change were ever able to develop in China. The literati were precisely the efficient Confucianist patrimonialist bureaucracy who actually prevented growth of any autonomous religious or political sources of power. This has prompted some historians to speak of the Chinese emperor as the Roman pope and the Holy Roman emperor rolled into one.

Patrimonialism in the Islamic world

Caliphate and sultanate

The Islamic power structure carried by the Arabs after the death of the founder in the seventh century was the caliphate. It continued through 'the Persian renaissance [which] forms a kind of overlapping interlude between the decline of the Arabs and the rise of the Turks' (Lewis, 1974, I:xiv). When, in the sixteenth century, the Turks emerged as the chief protagonists of Islam, the sultanate became the dominant power structure of Islamic patrimonialism. Both the caliphate and the sultanate represent the same unity of power. Those who profess the Islamic values would prefer to have them classified as theocracies, though this is difficult to accept even for the early caliphate. Because egalitarianism, equality of all under the exalted ruler, was a much-practiced Islamic virtue and because there was no clergy in Islam, it is easy to appreciate Massignon's labeling the Islamic power structure *une théocratie laïque égalitaire*. This seems to express a cherished religious goal, an ideal pattern for the Islamic community, but it does not reflect the actual Islamic experience. The prestige of the caliph, Weber said, grew immensely from the start in such a way that there was no serious attempt made to subordinate him hierocratically (1956:708). While cognizant of the Shiites' sectarian minority rejection of the caliphate, he still firmly located the caliphate within the unity/identity of power structure under political rulership (1956:697).

The most recent research seems to support this position. Islamicists vehemently object to the projection of Western conceptual tools (church, state, separation of religion and politics, hierarchy, secularization, etc.) made on the basis of the Western experience into Islamic cultures without such an experience (Abu-Lughod, 1966; Berkes, 1963). Calverley speaks of the difficulty confronting Western scholars who do not realize that the 'separation of ecclesiastical and civil authority is a comparatively modern minority movement in Christendom and is practically unknown to Islam and the other world religions' (1951:106–7). Binder concurs, saying that 'Islamic theology cannot accept the idea of tension between religion and politics. Islam is at once a religion and a nation . . .'. He also recognized that the Islamic unity of power structure was dominated by political and not hierocratic attributes: 'there is much in the literature on the caliphate which insists on its essentially political nature' (1964:51, 54). Strayer says that 'the caliph was more like the Roman combination of emperor and pontifex maximus than he was like the Christian pope. And when the power of the caliph declined, it was lost to new political leaders and not to religious authorities' (1958:41). To Newman, even the early caliphate was an absolutist monarchy and not a theocracy (1963:20). From AD 622 on, Islam was a political power structure and it did not have separate terms for religion and state.

From tribal egalitarianism to sacred universal monarchy

An older proposition was that from the death of Muhammad in 632 up to the rise of the persianizing 'Abbasid dynasty in 749, the early Islamic power structures should be sharply distinguished from all those that followed. According to Spuler, in early Islam there were no patterns of oriental despotism because the caliph was *primus inter pares* – a strong reference to the ideals of tribal equality. Only after the ascendancy of the 'Abbasid dynasty in 749 did a far-reaching synthesis of the Islamic Arab and the pre-Islamic Persian cultures take place, orientalizing the caliphate, and only then did the caliph become the absolute, sacred, and unapproachable patrimonialist lord – the monarch of the universe (1967:167, 173). This proposition appears untenable today.

Originally, the term 'caliph' meant a successor exercising the Messenger's authority. The earliest caliphs took the title of *Khalifat rasul Allah*, caliph of the Messenger of God, but only thirty years after the death of Muhammad, the title changed to the caliph of God. A significant change it was. The 'Abbasids' chosen title 'Shadow of God on earth' and other titles all suggest divine appointment and commission.

The replacement of tribal egalitarianism by a sacred rulership of universal monarchy was a gradual process that was almost completed before the 'Abbasids. It was achieved under the impact of the Hellenistic and especially the Byzantine cultural heritages. Indeed, it would have been strange had the caliphate resisted the influences of these two powerful civilizations surrounding it, the implication being that the caliphate had developed in a 'primitive', almost illiterate vacuum, deprived of intellectual curiosity.

Nothing could be further from the truth. The Islamic intellectuals wrote impressively in the early periods and showed sophisticated familiarity with the doctrines, ideologies, and concepts, as well as with the existing power structures, in the Hellenistic states and especially in the Byzantine empire. Rejection of a congenial cultural heritage is not frequently found in history, especially when that cultural heritage could be beneficially used by a nascent rulership such as was the caliphate. Emphasizing the impact of Hellenism on the early Islamic theologians and philosophers, Calverley said: 'They accepted the Hellenistic description of the universe, and then made Allah the Creator and Ruler of that system' (1951:108).

It is proposed here that even the early caliphate was a patrimonialist power structure, modeled closely on numerous successful and durable Hellenistic and especially Byzantine patrimonialist experiences. The attributes of patrimonialism in the caliphate grew in strength as the caliphate developed. The rise of the 'Abbasid dynasty in 749 and its impact on Islam only solidified, magnified, glorified with new ideological values that which had already been achieved. Even if there had not been intellectual interaction, the many Arab military victories established contact with their neighbors that led to imitation of their desirable patterns of power structure.

The original Islamic community inspired by Prophet Muhammad (570–632) was not patrimonialist, in spite of some strong appearances. There is agreement by islamicists on the quality of Islam as being a political and religious movement at the same time. When Muhammad, with his discipleship, moved to a city which was renamed Al-Madinah, the City of the Prophet, he, the religious virtuoso of a large and successful movement, also became the ruler of that city. The structure he ruled was a political and religious one at the same time, the distinction being nonexistent. Muhammad was the ruler who held in his own person for the rest of his life all the spheres of power: he was the imam who led the prayers of the faithful; he was the supreme judge: he was the creator of the constitution; he was the military and administrative chief.

It was a monistic power structure that did not need artificial differentiation into religious, economic, and political spheres. And it was a charismatically sanctified power designed for the extra-ordinary times. Whatever the charismatic gifts Muhammad possessed, the fact is that he was accepted as the Messenger of God by a large and ever-increasing number of enthusiastic followers. This extraordinary religious calling, together with his military victories, enhanced the respect and enthusiasm for his cause. But, in spite of these extraordinary achievements, Muhammad's rule did not disrupt the traditional pattern of tribal egali-tarianism. He was reluctant to accept the calling to be the Mess-enger of God in the first place for he did not wish to be superior to the other tribal chiefs: he claimed to be their equal.

Patrimonialism before AD 749

All evidence points out that the first caliph discussed with the other tribal chiefs the choice of his own successor. Allegedly they agreed on the person of the second caliph, who then received formal approval by ceremonial and festive acclamation of the whole community. Formal only because the choice made by the first caliph and the tribal chiefs was for all practical purposes an irrevocable decision. To select his successor, the second caliph appointed six men, presumably the most likely candidates for the caliphate, as an electoral council. Under the impact of the traditional values of equality, the caliph limited their task by requesting that they exclude his sons. Of course, islamicists agree that this was an instance of successful resistance to strong monarchical tendencies creeping into the earliest caliphate, but it was perhaps the last major instance of such resistance.

Even these constitutional proceedings surrounding the first and second caliphs show remarkable similarity to the old Roman and Byzantine imperial patterns of succession. The choice already made by the actual power-holders would then be formally 'approved' by the masses of people in the capital city and even more frequently by the army. In no instance did 'the people' – a cherished myth from the days of the Roman republic, now reduced to mobs in the capital city or armies in the field – have a chance to reverse that informal decision short of outright rebellion. The crucial element of succession in the early caliphate, as well as in the Roman and Byzantine imperial structures, in spite of the formal traditional arrangements of selection and acclamation, was the actual informal power of decision-making by the successful ruler or ruler-to-be.

The growth of patrimonialism in the early caliphate was bitterly resented by many pious followers of Muhammad who became appalled as gradually certain religious qualities of Muhammad's original power structure were displaced by the worldly, power-, glory-, and luxury-seeking attitudes of succeeding caliphs. Also, sentiment over the loss of tribal egalitarianism (real or already mythical at that time) is significant here and can be considered to be at least in part a religious attribute rooted in the religious doctrine of equality of all believers.

When several candidates competed for the caliphate, the issue of succession was eventually resolved by the exercise of greater political strength through military supremacy, with territorial and economic considerations playing roles also. But the political factors were dominant over the religious as well as all other factors: political power, undifferentiated from religion, was crucial. To speak as some Western students do of the 'secular', in this context, replacing religious qualities is pure nonsense.

Twenty-eight years after the death of Muhammad and after only four *Rashidun* caliphs, 'those who walk in the right path', the new caliph who was ceremoniously acclaimed in Jerusalem in 660 was more markedly patrimonialist in all the basic attributes of his rulership than his predecessors. He claimed a distant kinship to the third caliph, of course; however, he was politically the most powerful in Islam anyway and as governor of Syria he commanded the largest Islamic army. In direct contradiction to religiously sanctified, traditional egalitarianism, he designated his son as his successor, thereby founding the first Islamic hereditary monarchy, the Umayyads. His task at this point was to justify religiously this change which formally may appear significant, particularly to a constitutional scholar, but which in actuality went practically unnoticed by the masses of supporters. Commencing with the rule of the caliph in 660, the caliphate clearly became a political power structure – a monistic patrimonialist rulership.

It is proposed here that the *'ulama*, which emerged at this point, performed very well, in general, the assigned task of religious legitimation for the new caliphate in the same way that the literati did for Chinese patrimonialism, although there are some interesting differences between the *'ulama* and the literati.

Patrimonialism after AD 749

With the ascendancy of the 'Abbasid dynasty from 749 on in Baghdad, the traditional Islamic heritage of egalitarianism and other religious virtues was increasingly exposed to the powerful impact of the ancient and much glorified civilization of the Sassanids that lasted from the third until the seventh century. This far-reaching synthesis took place as it universally does when two powerful cultures meet through a durable political conquest. Technologically (a celebrated irrigation system, architecture, roads, etc.), the conquered country was superior and the conquerors were quick to benefit. Ideologically and intellectually also, the ancient civilization of Persia was able to offer a great deal to Islam, particularly in the area of strengthening the unity/identity of rulership and religion. These new elements adopted in the post-749 caliphate, however, were very congenial to the experience of the earlier caliphate, especially after 660. The 'Abbasid caliphate was glorified with some new, more sophisticated, but still basically the same religious and ideological beliefs on eternal harmony, unity, and the inevitability of the sacred universal rulership under the deity. In utilizing the heritage of the Sassanids' sacred rulership, the caliphate's claim to divine authority and absolute imperial autocracy was legitimized most effectively. The new elaboration of patrimonialist power unity behind the caliphate was logically more complete and more appealing to the masses, as well as to the intellectuals and staff members, than the older one. However, the caliphs had already assumed, much earlier, many of the patrimonialist attributes from the Hellenistic and Byzantine civilizations; so the removal of any restrictions was just a natural extension in the development of a successful, divinely approved rulership.

Among other aspects of visible political change reflected in the post-749 caliphate and supportive of patrimonialism, was that mercenary armies almost completely replaced the traditional Arab armies based on tribal and religious loyalty. The mercenaries were religiously loyal, and totally dependent on the caliph. As discussed in Chapter 3, the use of mercenaries represents a typical prerequisite for a full-fledged patrimonialism. When the earlier caliphs were militarily or politically unable to reject the demand of the provincial governors to make their offices hereditary, the caliphs would pretend that they had made the original appointments of their sons to succeed them. Now, with the presence of mercenaries, the caliphs were freed of this handicap. This, in turn, facilitated the acceptance of mercenaries as a legitimate means of perpetuating the total independence of the patrimonialist structure of the caliphate from any regional or tribal pressures.

Egypt's restoration of the caliphate, after the destruction of Baghdad's caliphate by the Mongols in 1258, was only a formality designed to increase the legitimacy of the Egyptian patrimonialist rulership; and the re-establishment of the caliphate by the Turkish sultans in 1517 only continued the process of perpetuating the subordination of religion to the political rulership. In these later periods of Islamic expansion under the Turks, the caliphate was not a ruling institution, but it did enjoy some traditional prestige cherished by the believers. Weber said that the *Sheik-ul-Islam* was formally or *de iure* above the sultan but the sultan appointed him and therefore enjoyed an expandable measure of religious authority over him, including the title of defender of the faith. Of course, the *de facto* power, undifferentiated, is permanently 'delegated' to the sultan (1956:721).

Islam preserved the commitment to equality of all believers with the one exception of the ruler, to be sure. Conversion to Islam automatically opened the door for members of various national groups to occupy highest positions in the patrimonialist structure. This was especially dramatized during the early Turkish sultanate when two dozen Croats occupied the office of First Vizier (equivalent of prime minister). The voluntary mass conversion of Croats to Islam in 1463 as a final act of protest against the Roman papacy, after centuries of struggle for political and religious freedom, may have been a reason for their pre-eminence in the Turkish empire. But, also, the Croat Western-oriented administration and literary skills were welcomed during that period of Turkish imperial growth. In the sixteenth century, the Croat language became a diplomatic language at the Sublime Porte second to Turkish. In subsequent centuries, Greeks, Armenians, and others occupied top positions in the Turkish patrimonialist bureaucracy. The equality of all under the exalted patrimonialist ruler who is far above everyone, including his patrimonialist staff, is not contradictory: it is one of the most powerful integrative and supportive attributes of patrimonialism.

Much earlier than is generally assumed, the caliphate merged with the almost universal human experience of sacred patrimonialist rulership in the hands of God's substitute on earth – naturally, there can only be one worthy of this divine vicegerency. All the sacred doctrines or ideologies legitimizing patrimonialism are remarkable in their similarity, if not identity, of basic features.

The specific details of the legitimizing doctrines may be different when taking into account the particularities of the power structure under a basileus, caliph, tsar, sultan, Chinese emperor, khan, Inca king, or any other patrimonialist ruler. For example, the sultan's official titles ceremoniously proclaimed at the Turkish equivalent of coronation (girding the sword that originally supported the House of Osman, inherited from his predecessors and performed by the head of a religious brotherhood) are similar to the titles of the tsar, khan, basileus, or caliph: the sultan of sultans, the ruler of rulers, the shadow of God, the dispenser of crowns upon the earth, lord of the two worlds, etc. 'The shadow of God' implied more than headship of religion and, as long as the ruler was successful, it was not interpreted in any other way.

209

Sacred tradition called for a perfect society, willed by God, that would achieve a perpetual order of harmony, tranquility, and equilibrium with the divine forces in the universe. Almost identically with the Chinese, Byzantine, Russian, and other patrimonialist politico-religious doctrines, the fall of a particular ruler in Islam did not contradict the eternal order of patrimonialist rulership as willed by God. The sacred power structure remains the same; the person of the ruler only changes because of his unworthiness, i.e., his unsuccessfulness. As Berkes (1974:297) said for the Turkish sultanate, the same applies precisely to all other patrimonialist power structures:

> In none of the rebellions or uprisings was the idea of establishing a new order to replace the one against which they had revolted ever envisaged. The rebels, like their adversaries, believed in the immutability of the traditional order. Their leaders envisaged neither the subjugation of the sovereignty to the will of the ruled nor the abolition of the existing political order. Returning to the starting point, the restoration of the original, which was believed to be corrupted merely because of the non-observance of eternally valid rules, was still dominant in their outlook.

Newman raised an interesting question on the relationship of the theological doctrine of monotheism and the doctrine on the unity of power in Christendom and Islam (1963:19). And Binder, unaware of Newman's work, offered this statement: 'Monotheism and monism do not necessarily go together, but they happened to be found together in Islam' (1964:52). Persia and China are two great civilizations in which the monistic power structures are not disturbed by the absence of monotheism. Patrimonialism has co-existed harmoniously with various non-monotheistic religious doctrines for centuries and for millennia in the case of China. Newman, however, recognized the impact of monotheism on the very durable monistic power structures and doctrines that are dominant in Christianity and Islam. The images of the One God are heavily used to legitimize the monistic power structure of the patrimonialist vicegerent of God on this earth, not only in Islam, but very much so in Christianity as well. The cherished myth of the automatic separation of religion from rulership with the emergence of Christianity was taking an awfully long time to pass away.

The 'ulama

The guardians of sacred tradition, the much respected scholar-jurists, the 'ulama, trained in Islamic theology and law (Shari'ah), have no priestly or pastoral functions. In no way can they be interpreted as a hierocracy, for they never monopolized the administration of sacred or religious values. When comparing Islamic politico-religious structures with Western ones, several islamicists recognized one, a few, or several hierocratic characteristics that are absent from Islamic but present in the Western structures (Arnold, 1924; Berger, 1962; Cahen, 1967; Duchesne-Guillemin, 1967; Rosenthal, 1958; Watt, 1968).

A methodological note is in order here: if all these comparative statements concerning the missing characteristics in one or other culture case study were put together, the need for the conceptual tool of hierocracy becomes evident. This typological construct is a configuration of all the basic attributes found to be common to most, if not all, instances of independent or autonomous religious structures. Absence of these attributes from the culture case studies under scrutiny clearly demonstrates that a hierocracy did not develop simply because all or some crucial attributes which are constitutive of it are lacking. This heuristic device, if commonly used, would eliminate a great deal of bona fide confusion and embarrassment to those who overlook the total configuration by overemphasizing one or more attributes. Even though a statement may cover most of the attributes, the need for the concept of independent or autonomous hierocracy remains.[2]

Weber clearly recognized that the 'ulama's failure concerning the establishment of specific rights for their own structure was the inability to create a legal configuration equivalent to the Western logical formalism of procedural law. In the West the natural-law theories were originally conceived in Roman juristic, Stoic, and early Christian thought. The specific product of Western culture, the full rationalization of procedural law, or in Weber's terms, the 'logically formed rationality' in law, was made possible through the reception of Roman jurisprudence first by the Italian legal professionals (notaries) and later in the North by the learned judges. This logical formalism of legal procedure cannot be found in the legal system of any other culture of the time: in Weber's words, 'there is no analogy to this on the whole earth'. The rudiments of rational juristic thought in certain periods of Hindu and Islamic legal scholarship were smothered, Weber said, by their theological forms of thought (1956:836).

Perhaps the crux of the matter is that a separation of law from theology never took place in Islam. The 'ulama responsible for

211

the indistinguishable sacred doctrine of oneness was unable to differentiate and eventually separate them. The next step would have been separation of the *'ulama*'s structure into two specific segments: the theologians and the jurists. This never happened because the *'ulama* operated in a totally different context, that of patrimonialism. In the West, the separation of canon law from theology was supported by several autonomous, if not independent, power structures.

Apparently, in Weber's time, the absence of feudalism in Islamic societies was somewhat questionable and, of course, this is reflected in his writings. Sifting through post-Weber research, Hintze modified some of Weber's tentative propositions by documenting that the land grants were originally rewards for the Arabs' outstanding military services and that later the land grants became a substitute for monetary payments to the Turkish military (1962:169). But, in both Arab and Turkish land grant systems, there were no substructures – feudal lords, vassals, subvassals, or knights – and no personal mutual relationships between them as in Western feudalism. Instead, there was a uniformly shared religious obligation to the ruler to fight for the global advancement of Islam. The Spahi were a privileged class of mounted warriors who enjoyed an aristocratic style of life and luxury comparable to that of the Western feudal aristocracy, but they were unable to achieve the same political significance of actually participating in sharing the power as did even the Western knights at the bottom of the feudal structure. Again, the reason is that their class solidarity was never anything more than an additional and not-too-effective aspect of the much stronger feeling of joint responsibility and solidarity that permeated the entire Islamic society and bound them, Spahi and all, in solid religious loyalty to the patrimonialist ruler. The Islamic power structure was, above all, a religiously inspired political community and this precluded the development of what Hintze labeled 'the dualistic spirit' of the three Western *Stände*. Not only the hierocracy, the feudal structures, and the free cities as major power structures, but also the various revolutionary religious movements and, especially, the free universities aided in separating canon law from theology. Such autonomous structures were absent from the cultural context in which the *'ulama* functioned. Also, because an Islamic equivalent of the Western legal experts never developed, their enormous impact in the West was entirely missing from Islamic society.

As late as the turn of the twentieth century, some attempts by the *'ulama* in Iran to achieve a degree of lasting power structure of their own independently of the ruler which, in turn, could have challenged the ruler were unsuccessful. The Shiites' religious deviation, due to its doctrinal images of the Occult Imam, was perhaps more conducive to the role of questioning the actions of the ruler than anywhere else in Islam. Still, Algar documented that the *'ulama*'s

> essential lack of hierarchic organization would have been an obstacle to any active reshaping of the political structure. . . . Intervention in political affairs to gain permanent control thereof never appears to have been even a distant aim of the ulama. The continued occultation of the Imam meant, inescapably, the absence of all legitimizing authority from worldly affairs, so that the political attitudes of the ulama could, in the final analysis, be only quietism or opposition. Any wish to reshape definitively the norms of political life and the bases of the state was foreign to the ulama in Qajar Iran (1969:259–60).

During the complete collapse of a political structure, the *'ulama* exercised some degree of political decision-making for a brief time, only to lose their gains as soon as a political rulership was in control again. Similar phenomena are visible in the development of some early Islamic cities in which the city's initial achievement toward some rudimentary autonomy would be annihilated as soon as a new political structure ended the power vacuum. (See Murvar, 1966:384–5.)

In the historical reality, according to Rosenthal, 'Islam knows no distinction between a spiritual and a temporal realm, between religious and secular activities' (1958:8). While the *shari'a* was designed to limit the government's power in certain instances in the name of religion, the actual situation according to Newman, Cahen, and Grunebaum was a far cry from its constitutional prescription, partly because of the *'ulama*'s vested interest in close association with the political rulership. This basis of orientation of the *'ulama* fairly well typifies most of the Islamic historical experience. Strayer said that 'while there could be conflicts between religious principles and political expediency, it was much harder – in fact, almost impossible – to have conflicts between religious *institutions* and political institutions (1958:41ff). And Watt emphasized that 'the scholar-jurists became largely subservient to the ruling institution'. Practically all the rulers in their successful attempts to manipulate religious ideas had come to some sort of understanding with the *'ulama* who were allowed complete control of theological dogma and the legal foundations of the social structure

> provided they gave the ruler a free hand elsewhere and in

213

general supported him. While this looks like a bargain between equals, it was not in fact so. The ruler appointed men to the judgeships and other official positions . . . and thus they were almost entirely at his mercy. Their only strength was in their ability to rouse the populace, but where there were several rival groups of scholar-jurists, this was not easy, since they opposed one another (1961:173, 180).

The *shari'a* includes all the prescriptions of the different orthodox legal schools–four of them surviving today. To be sure, this was a splendid opportunity for the ruler to choose only the interpretation he wished and, at the same time, that particular school as the most willing tool to promote it for him. Only the presence of some autonomous and/or autocephalous centers of power able to support the various schools could have made the diverse interpretations of the *shari'a* have an impact. Consequently, the four remaining orthodox legal schools only serve to strengthen the legitimacy of the patrimonialist rulership in general and of a successful ruler in particular; they have in no way served to open the way toward pluralism.

In addition to the absence of material or economic independence, the judges were unable to make their decisions accepted by the rulership. The judges, Cahen said, were 'tied directly to the wielders of public power, who lent their effectiveness to its decisions' (1967:141–2). And Grunebaum emphasized that the 'political absolutism parallels the theological absolutism of God's relation to His creatures' (1955:135).

The entire structure of the *'ulama* with its numerous divisions and gradations, Hintze said, was a privileged class though more in fact than in law. Yet, it could not exercise the political function of representing the people or the country, because the *'ulama* itself was an essential and important part of the machinery of the state government. According to him, religion and state formed a complete unity governed by a patriarchal spirit and prevented the dualistic principle of the *Stände* to arise as happened in the West (1962:169).

In the historical periods of political crisis, the *'ulama* could grow to fill the vacuum; but when power was again safely in the hands of a strong ruler, the learned opinion, Cahen said, was that 'any power being better than anarchy, it is legal to respect a power sprung from force'. Finally, it was believed that 'the caliphate falls by right to the effective holder of power', and thus 'the union of the temporal and the spiritual for which the believers had felt a nostalgia since the beginning of the caliphate' is reconstituted (1967:154, 157).

214

Conclusion

Today, certain Islamic religious movements – particularly those labeled 'fundamentalist' rightly or wrongly by Western observers – are precisely calling for the restoration of power unity/identity through reaffirmation of the traditionally total religious legitimacy. Even to some reformist Islamic movements, as well as to several Islamic governments searching for programs and reforms, the unity/identity of all power remains very attractive, at least as a means to attain the desired goals.

Notes

* The author is grateful to Roland Ye-lin Cheng, Abbas Hamdani, and David C. Yu for useful suggestions and criticisms. However, they are not responsible for final formulations.

1 Waley, quoted by Sprenkel, preferred the label 'realists' instead of 'legalists' and Sprenkel added that their 'teachings . . . were naturally attractive to the ruler' (1964:357).

2 Such a statement was offered by Strayer who, without using the concept, eloquently described the absence of a hierocracy in the Islamic world (1958:42):

> There was nothing like the church in Islam, no separate organization devoted to the presentation of the faith and the salvation of the individual. There were preachers and teachers, there were doctors of law and theology who headed rival schools of interpretation of the Koran and Sunna. These men might have great influence and moral authority, but they had almost no power of their own. They did not control the 'divine mysteries'; they did not stand between the individual and God. They were not even presiding officers of congregations of the faithful; they could not inflict penalties like the Christian excommunication. Without the support of the . . . power, their decisions could not harm a private citizen. Much less could they contradict the authority of the state, short of joining a political revolution. They did not have the independence, the authority, the organization or the autonomy which enabled the Christian church to stand in open opposition to . . . rulers for decades at a time.

10   Max Weber's human ecology of historical societies*

Patrick C. West

This chapter discusses Max Weber's important but little-recognized ecological analysis of society-environment relations.[1] By 'ecological analysis' this author is referring to the casual interactions between social structures and the full range of their non-human environments. Weber's ecological analysis emphasized the interactive role of geography, climate, natural resources, and the material aspects of technology[2] in the structure and change in historical social structures.

Weber did not self-consciously develop an explicit human ecology theory or perspective. But a comprehensive analysis of the role of ecological factors is implicit in historical and comparative studies. These ecological relations are treated within the context of his comparative sociological perspective and thus provide rich contributions to a sociological human ecology.

Weber treated ecological interactions with society in a wide diversity of historical settings. He dealt with such topics as:

1 the natural habitat and social structures of the stockbreeders, agriculturalists, and Bedouins of ancient Palestine around 1000 BC;
2 the environmental and technological context of the great hydraulic empires of Egypt, Mesopotamia, and China:
3 ecological conditions and the creation of the Indian caste system;
4 the role of technology and environment in the development of feudalism in Europe;
5 the role of geographical conditions, frontiers, technological change, and material and energy resources in the birth and development of capitalism; and
6 the role of geographical conditions and demographic factors in the decline of the Roman Empire.[3]

As a basis for the analysis of Weber's implicit perspective on human ecology let us begin with a detailed example from these historical studies. Using this and other examples, we will then explore Weber's use and critique of causal models, functional analysis, evolutionary theory, and the role of culture and ideas in his implicit human ecology of historical societies.

The ecological context of feudalism and patrimonialism

Weber describes the basic contrasts in ecological contexts of environment and technology that differentially favored feudalism in Europe and state patrimonialism in Egypt, Mesopotamia, and China (1968:1090; 1976:351).

Weber does *not* suggest that the ecological context *determined* these contrasts in social structures. But he (1968:1090) does assert that changes in the productive and military technologies played an important role in the *origin* of feudal manorial domination, and that the environmental conditions of the clearing of the European forests favored its *expansion* and *triumph*. In contrast, the ecological conditions of river flood and recurrent drought stimulated the development of elaborate flood control and irrigation works that favored the development of patrimonial bureaucratic forms of centralized state domination.

In the social changes that produced European feudalism, a distinction must be made between the ecological factors important in the *origin* and in the *expansion* of feudalism. The development of the manorial (seigneurial) form of agrarian economic organization was important in the development of feudalism. Key changes in productive and military technologies played an important causal role that transformed an agricultural society of independent freemen into a highly stratified system of feudal domination based on ascriptive status contract.

Weber (1968:1090) ascribes very little causal weight to 'hand-mill' technology. 'The hand-mill has lived through all conceivable economic structures and political "superstructures".' However, changes in agricultural and military technologies were crucially important in the *origins* of feudal manorial domination. The intensification of agriculture, brought about by technological changes, necessitated that men take over heavier work formerly done by women. This tied them to the land and 'diminished their familiarity with military tasks and the opportunities for military training.' At the same time, this intensification of agriculture produced differentiation of wealth; and changes in military technology produced an inability of the former army of freemen to equip themselves. These technological changes, involving the diffusion

217

of the stirrup and other military changes, made knightly cavalry the basic military force (Weber, 1968:1077).

Certain environmental conditions favored the *expansion and survival* of this form of social and economic organization over the former structure of independent free peasants. The main environmental condition was the great European hardwood forest that underwent massive clearing during feudal times (Darby, 1956). The task of clearing the extensive woodland of the continental frontier was managed more easily by the social organization of manorial domination. Thus, as the clearing of the woodland progressed, the manorial system expanded and triumphed. Weber (1968:1090–1) observes that this situation created a process of selective survival that favored feudalism. 'The acquisition of new land through the clearing of forests in Northern Europe *favored* the manorial system and therefore feudalism.'[4] Note that this environmental effect played a greater role in the *expansion* of feudalism than in the initial origins of *manorial* domination.

These technological and environmental conditions also played a key role in the equalization of the status of slaves and freemen in the feudal social structure. Particularly from the eighth to the twelfth century the slaves began acquiring rights to improved conditions. As a result of the drying up of the slave trade, and the concomitant need for labor to clear the forests, the lord was forced to improve their conditions of life (Weber, 1927:66). Elsewhere, Weber (1978:302) notes that the difficulty of farming in the sandy soils of the East contributed to this development. Conversely, changes in military technology brought the freemen under feudal domination of a lord (Weber, 1927:66).

These ecological interactions stand in contrast to those in the development of patrimonialist domination in Egypt, Mesopotamia, and China. For Weber (1968:1261; 1976:38), the necessity of irrigation in arid climates and river regulation to control flooding played a key role in the development of royal bureaucracies. 'The necessity of river regulation and irrigation policy in the near East and in Egypt, and to a lesser degree also in China, caused the development of royal bureaucracies. . .'. That this royal bureaucracy should take the form of patrimonial domination, however, depended more on interaction with its preexisting social *origins*, in Weber's view. The irrigation technology favored the development of patrimonialist domination that had its origins in other historical causes (Weber, 1968:1091). Thus, environmental and technological conditions and the beginnings of political forms of patrimonialism interacted in the multiple causation of centralized patrimonialist states.[5]

A special variant of patrimonialist bureaucracy was favored and held in place in China, in part due to the special ecological context of Chinese civilization that favored a status group of literati over monarch absolutism and other competing strata such as military elites and eunuchs within the patrimonialist bureaucratic state.

In comparison to Egypt, China had a different form of patrimonialist bureaucratic rule. The difference was rooted in the nature of the religious status group of highly cultured literati; the religious system of ideas they produced; and their peculiar position of power. In Egypt, kingly power dominated much more completely than in China. In China, the bureaucratic structure and political power were variably but firmly in the control of the literati (1951:108).

A number of environmental conditions were important in creating and maintaining the power position of the literati. Weber (1951:111) asserts that the close relation of the literati to princely service came about during the struggle of the prince with the feudal powers. The development of centralized patrimonialist bureaucracies placed them in a situation of great power. This structure of domination was conditioned by the need for river regulation. But, in addition, the unique and extreme conditions of ecological instability and natural depredation played a key role in the extension, entrenchment, and persistence of literati power, in Weber's interpretation. Chinese civilization existed on an ecological stage that periodically created massive catastrophes despite the elaborate water works for flood control and irrigation (Whitney, 1925:207–8).

The fact that the elaborate water works were not sufficient to prevent these extremely severe natural depredations had two significant consequences for domination by the Chinese literati. First, the recurrence of natural disaster placed the literati in a unique position of power because natural disasters of flood, drought, and famine were highly conducive to peasant unrest and the possibility of peasant revolt (Weber, 1951:203). The literati were, *par excellence*, in a position to suppress such possibilities due to the power of religion and religious ideas in pacifying the masses (1951:109–10). Second, each inundation and drought put power into the hands of the literati in another related sense. Each disaster was symbolically interpreted in religious mythology as social transgression against the traditional Confucian way. This provided a powerful ideological leverage for the continual reassertion of their dominance (1951:138–9). From this we can make three basic observations about the structure of causal models in Weber's ecological analysis.

First, environmental factors are neither all-pervasive nor deterministic causes of social phenomena. But at certain junctures in

219

the histories of societies they can impinge on social relations, and where they do, they become important elements in Weber's causal analysis of social stability and change. In Weber's view, ecological factors rarely, if ever, totally determine social phenomena. They are, however, very frequently necessary or 'contingently sufficient' conditions. (A 'contingently sufficient' condition is a sufficient contributing cause in combination with other factors.) Where Weber argues that an ecological factor does not 'determine' a given social structure, he is not arguing that the factor does not play an important causal role. It may be a necessary or a contingently sufficient condition that he treats as an important causal element within a complex causal network.

Second, in demonstrating how ecological and social factors combine to cause a social structural phenomenon, Weber most often employs *interaction* causal models in which the effect of one factor varies for different categories or degrees of other interacting causal variables. The effect of an ecological factor cannot be fully determined without examining how that factor interacts with other social factors in the multiple causation of a social phenomenon. The effect of the hardwood forests on the European economic and social structure, or the impact of drought and flooding on Chinese society, would have been markedly different under different interacting social and economic pre-conditions.

Third, in this contingent, interaction causation, environmental conditions, or changes therein, often operate by favoring the 'selective survival' of one or several social strata or institutional forms over others, thus contributing to the emergence, persistence, or change of a particular balance of forces and forms of social organization. This is clearly seen in the above case and is common in much of Weber's ecological analysis. This selective survival causal model represents a specific form of 'conflict functionalism.' The key theoretical aspect requires a more detailed analysis.

In the broadest sense, as Davis (1959) argues, all sociological analysis can be seen as functional analysis, and thus the notion of a special functional analysis is a myth. Nevertheless, within this broader view, a number of dubious assumptions have been virtually identified with functional analysis. With respect to these specific assumptions Weber can be seen as a functional analyst only in a highly restricted sense. Weber (1968:15) did recognize the functional frame of reference as a valid 'provisional orientation.' But he is quick to warn that functional metaphors of the 'parts to the whole organism' can be reified and infused with hidden value judgments. 'If its cognitive value is overestimated and its concepts illegitimately "reified" it can be highly dangerous.'

In relation to Weber's human ecology, his selective survival causal models are essentially functional causal models in this provisional restrictive sense. This complex form of selective survival functional analysis follows from a true Darwinian (as opposed to social Darwinist) orientation and is inseparable from his central focus on tragic, irreconcilable conflict in society.

For Weber it is the broad conditions of selective survival that form the basis of his statements concerning functionalism as a necessary provisional orientation. Weber uses this form of analysis to analyze the triumph and persistence of specific strata and/or institutions as the unit of analysis in his generally mosaic view of society. Structures must also be seen to selectively survive (or not survive) over historical time. There is no valid way of making a-historical functional causal statements in the analysis of selective survival processes.

Weber's (1968:39) selective survival functional analysis is also inseparable from his 'conflict theory.' Conflict and competition are inherent in Weber's selective survival functionalism; for persistence is often bought in the arena of conflict and competition with other groups or structural forms, and it is conflict that produces one of the strongest selective survival pressures.

Nor does functional analysis, in the restricted sense of selective survival, pertain solely to stability and persistence. It can also account for development, expansion, contraction, and structural change of social structures. Indeed, selective survival processes are central causes of social change (1968:39–40).

Weber emphasizes that a mere positing of selective survival as a concept does not in itself explain anything. Mere labels that are vague and can be confused with other non-scientific meanings often lead to dangerous misinterpretations and value judgments. In particular, Weber strongly objects to any social-Darwinist misuses of these selective survival concepts:

> In every case it is necessary to inquire into the reasons which have led to a change in the chances of survival of one or another form of social action or social relationship, which has broken up a social relationship or which has permitted it to continue at the expense of other competing forms. The explanation of these processes involves so many factors that it does not seem expedient to employ a single term for them. When this is done, there is always a danger of introducing uncritical value-judgments into empirical investigation. There is, above all, a danger of being primarily concerned with

justifying the success of an individual case. . . . The fact that a given specific social relationship has been eliminated for reasons peculiar to a particular situation, proves nothing whatever about its 'fitness to survive' in general terms (1968:40)

Selective survival was a very important theoretical causal structure in Weber's ecological propositions about specific environmental effects on historical social structures. Ecological factors of environment and technology, or changes in these factors, enter into this form of functional analysis as objective elements of a social situation favoring the selective survival of one or another social form due to the different consequences of those social forms.

In European feudalism, the environmental conditions of the European hardwood forest created an external selective pressure that favored the manorial system over the independent class of freemen. Similarly, patrimonialism and the particular status of the literati were conditioned by selective survival processes. We see this repeatedly in Weber's ecological analysis.

In the case of ancient Judaic social structure a variety of environmental conditions (drought, soil erosion, insect pests, etc.) produced instability in political structures of charismatic sib leadership. These environmental conditions acted on the array of herder groups as a selective survival pressure. Some tribes adopted the religious ideas and political forms of the covenant, which had *latent* consequences that counteracted the environmentally induced instabilities and thus caused the selective survival and expansion of that institutional form at the expense of other competing forms. This institutional form was adopted out of religious interests. The consequences of these institutional forms in counteracting environmental tensions were initially unrecognized (i.e., they were latent consequences). However, once they began to have their selective effect in counteracting environmental tensions, these consequences became recognized and thus manifestly functional to the interests of tribal bands (1952:8–42, 80).

Notions of 'adaptation' to the social or physical environment often accompany functional theories of 'selective survival.' Weber (1949:25) expresses a number of reservations with respect to the unqualified use of the term 'adaptation.' The ambiguity of the term 'adaptation' leads to imprecise usages, does not in itself explain anything, and often masks hidden value judgments. 'It is entirely ambiguous as a scientific term, although it perpetually recurs both as an "explanation" and as an "evaluation." ' To say that a society or group 'adapts' or must 'adapt' to social or natural conditions does not, for Weber, really explain anything. Nor can one structure among several be said to be 'better adapted' to an ecological context where either could survive. Weber cites an example of the 'adaptation' of Indians and Mormons to the harsh ecological conditions of the Salt Lake Desert:

> The few Indians who lived in the Salt Lake area before the Mormon migration were in the biological sense – as well as in all other of its many conceivable empirical meanings – just as well or poorly 'adapted' as the later populous Mormon settlements. *This term adds absolutely nothing to our empirical understanding, although we easily delude ourselves that it does* (1949:26 emphasis added).

The term 'adaptation' also has rhetorical potential for misuse due to its susceptibility to value judgments that have no place in a scientific theory. Referring to the Salt Lake example again, Weber observes:

> one person may assert that the greater numbers and the material and other accomplishments and characteristics which the Mormons brought there and developed, are proof of the superiority of the Mormons over the Indians, while another person who abominates the means and subsidiary efforts involved in the Mormon ethics which are responsible at least in part for those achievements, may prefer the desert and the romantic existence of the Indians (1949:26)

With these restrictions in mind, Weber does employ the term in his empirical works, strictly in a value-neutral sense as a provisional orientation to analyses of just how groups and institutions have historically adapted and selectively survived in relation to various ecological conditions and changes. Closely related to selective survival causal models is the relation of ecological analysis to evolutionary theories of social change.

Ecological analysis and evolutionary theory

This section considers
1 the common assumptions of social evolutionary theory;
2 the use of social evolutionary theories in human ecological analysis;
3 a Weberian critique of social evolutionary human ecology; and
4 an alternative Weberian approach to the ecological analysis of social change.

Nisbet isolates the key assumptions in social evolutionary theory and argues that neo-evolutionary theory is really based on ident-

223

ical assumptions in a more subtle form. The basic assumptions of social evolutionary theory are derived from the basic metaphorical imagery of organismic growth. Nisbet traces the development of this basic notion in Western thought and describes its widespread, subtle tyranny over social theories of historical change.

The basic assumptions that permeate social evolutionary theory, stemming from this organic growth metaphor, are:

1 Change is *natural* – 'Change in time is natural, is normal, and . . . when fixity is encountered it is either to be categorized as abnormal . . . or else it is fixity of appearance only, with reality to be understood in terms of underlying forces of change which required only further time for their manifestation.' (Nisbet 1969:166).

2 Change is *directional* – This assumption makes a metaphorical leap perceiving directionality in change; diversity and complexity of the myriad of disconnected historical changes are bound into a single ongoing process. The metaphorical leap further presents the image 'that this single, ongoing process has a beginning, middle, and end – that is, direction in time' (Nisbet, 1969:168)

3 Change is *immanent* – Change derives from the *internal* structure and processes in the development of the social organism itself.

4 Change is *continuous* – Change is seen as continuous in the sense of 'logical gradation of steps within a single series.' It metaphorically denotes 'gradations of growth, cumulative, genetic . . . the very opposite of the broken or discontinuous' (Nisbet, 1969:174).

5 Change is *necessary* – Social developments are assumed to be necessary outgrowths of previous evolutionary conditions. A given change is *ex post facto* deemed to be inevitable.

6 Change has *uniform causes* – This refers to uniformity of the fundamental mechanisms or causes of evolutionary change processes.

These organismic growth-based assumptions were applied through the use of a so-called 'comparative method.' This was not a comparative method at all, as we ordinarily think of one; rather, it was a classification of 'stages,' linearly ranked in a hierarchy from lower to higher 'stages' that purportedly explained social change. The contortions created in force fitting the complexity of history into these 'comparative stages' was ludicrous. Where historical data were employed, diverse societies bearing no actual historical relation to one another were seen to be hierarchically evolved from one to the other, from lower to higher forms. More often, history was simply ignored. As Nisbet ((1969) and Teggart

(1960:77) point out, social evolution was studied in an historical vacuum; astonishingly, the study of evolution and the study of history were thus conducted in totally different worlds.

Social evolutionary theory was thought to be analogous to Darwinian biological evolution. Yet, as Nisbet points out Darwin's theory of biological evolution had little in common with social evolutionism; it was not at all based on the metaphor of organismic growth.

> The theory of social evolution in the nineteenth century . . .
> is built upon nothing comparable to the phenomena of
> variation which Darwin described in his theory of natural
> selection. It is built upon the conception of organismic growth
> . . . such growth is *not* the model of Darwin's natural selection
> (1969:164).

Nisbet (1969:223) maintains that modern neo-evolutionary theory is based on social evolutionary assumptions, although the notion of evolutionary stages has waned. 'Whatever may have been the waning of interest in the more panoramic aspects of the theory of evolution during the first half of the century – interest in universal origins, and sequences of stages of development of mankind – there is no evidence that there was much if any waning of interest in the key concepts of evolutionary theory.' He further argues that in recent years there has even been a revival of more classic social evolutionism.

Duncan (1964) elaborates a human ecological theory of social change within a social evolutionary perspective. He is attracted to this stance, not only out of a fascination with biological evolutionary analogies, but also because he recognizes the important role that ecological factors, particularly technology, have played in evolutionary theories. Technology has been a very common basis for distinguishing stages and a central cause of change in social evolutionist theories. For Duncan, technology, in a reciprocal relationship to environment, is the main causal factor and the key characteristic distinguishing stages of social evolution. He observes that the categories of the evolutionary stage model

> are a typology of basic ecological forms. Significantly, the
> ecological differentia are systems of exploitative technology,
> rather than, say, types of environment. An ecological
> approach to social evolution does not, therefore, require the
> assumption of environmental determinism, but rather that of
> a reciprocal relationship between technology and
> environment (1964:51–2)

Technology is the key variable and is taken as the main causal

225

force of societal evolution in a highly *deterministic* sense. These factors creating an 'ecological expansion' (analogous to organismic growth) are taken by Duncan (1964:57) as the 'key to the transition from one major "level" of social evolution to the next.' Technological evolution has its own dynamic and *determines* changes in social organization through functional adaptation. 'Social institutions, which serve to maintain social continuity and to preserve social integration, do not themselves evolve, but rather adjust to new conditions, originating either from environmental change or from technological development' (Duncan, 1964:52).

This technological and environmental determinist theory of social change is formulated in classical evolutionary fashion, retaining all the basic assumptions discussed above (except perhaps immanence). It is posited in terms of a simple construction of unilinear evolutionary 'stages' that range from lower to higher forms of technological advancement. Disparate historical societies are forced into the model and made to appear to have evolved from one another. And because historical complexity fails to conform even with the use of this device, Duncan takes the further classic evolutionist step of divorcing the ecological evolutionism from history.

> The taxonomy does not purport . . . to represent the 'course' of evolution in terms of the documented or inferred history of all known societies. It is, in fact, more nearly a taxonomy of levels of 'general evolution' than of specific societies (1964:53)

The only social evolutionist assumption that Duncan explicitly rejects is the assumption of *immanence*. Because of the heavy reliance on technology as the central variable, the widespread and obvious occurrence of technological diffusion seemingly negates the assumption of immanent evolution from internal structure and developmental tendencies. yet even here, when speaking of 'general evolution' this recognition gets 'swallowed by the metaphor,' and technology is implicitly treated as a progressive unilinear and *immanent* process of organismic growth.

Duncan (1964:48–61) makes all the other evolutionist assumptions implicitly or explicitly. Change is natural. Change is directional: from lower to higher; from simple to complex, through (organismic) growth and differentiation; from small to large through 'ecological expansion.' Change is continuous in the sense that there are no discontinuities; all higher forms rest in a continuity of gradual evolution from lower to higher forms. Change is necessary – evolutionary development in the general form is assumed inevitable; it could have been no other way. Change flows from uniform causes.

Weber's approach is contrary to the basic social evolutionist assumptions.

> Weber's approach is incompatible with evolutionist theories of change. As Robert Nisbet has shown conclusively, the latter assume change to be natural, directional, immanent, continuous, necessary and proceeding from uniform causes. None of these attributes fits Weber's approach (Bendix 1970:170).

Immanence is perhaps the central key assumption of social evolutionary theory. For Weber, changes do not follow from immanent and inevitable development from the metaphorical 'seed'; rather, change occurs from the shifting balance of forces, of causal factors and groups. Such determination is fortuitous, dependent on contingency – and productive of uniqueness. Change in the social balance of forces is not an interwoven organismic development, but a constellation of mosaic elements each with its own dynamic and fortuitous internal and external causal elements.

Some social evolutionary theorists, such as Parsons, mistakenly seek to picture Weber as a social evolutionist. They mistake his use of heuristic models as evolutionary theories in the above sense. They have pointed, for instance, to Weber's concern for the development of rationalization as an evolutionary theory. For Weber, the use of particular historical stages, pertaining to particular societies, was merely a heuristic descriptive device. His concern for such developments as rationalization refers to specific historical developments, not aspects of a general evolutionary construction. This can be clearly seen in Weber's sociology of law:

> The general development of law from charismatic legal revelation by law prophets to the systematic elaboration of law and the professional administration of justice is a succession of stages superficially similar to the evolutionary models put forward in the nineteenth century. But this line of development appears only as a convenient summary towards the end of the volume. In Weber's view such schemes explain nothing (Bendix 1970:168)

Any such tracing of lines of development is done for particular institutional constellations (not general whole societies). Such schemes *must* show *actual* historical links and influences (both internal and external). They must be explained by complex actual historical factors and constellations of social action. The specification of summary heuristic stages explains nothing.

227

Weber rejects the notion of linear evolutionary stages which mistakenly simplify complex differences. 'Stages' do not explain anything and thus they cannot be the goal of scientific investigation. Weber, for instance, criticizes Hildebrand's social evolutionary theory of early development. Hildebrand's theory is essentially an ecological evolutionary scheme, almost identical to Duncan's (1964:168) model including the notion of an initial and universal nomadic stage. Hildebrand drew analogies from contemporary Bedouin nomadism, extrapolating from this case claims of a universal nomadic stage in social evolution. He assumed that since Bedouin nomads did not engage in agricultural labor, Germanic nomads must not have done so either. Weber criticizes both this particular historical interpretation and the general illegitimate use of cultural-stage evolutionary reasoning: 'This theory is one of the attempts, recently so numerous, to comprehend cultural development in the manner of biological processes as a lawful sequence of universal stages' (as cited by Roth, 1968:xxxvii).

> This procedure . . . is a good example of the manner in which the concept of 'cultural stages' should not be applied scientifically. Concepts such as 'nomadic,' 'semi-nomadic,' etc., are indispensable for descriptive purposes. For research, the continuous comparison of the developmental stages of peoples and the search for analogies are heuristic means well suited, if cautiously used, to explain the causes of distinctiveness of each individual development. But it is a serious misunderstanding of the rationale of cultural history to consider the construction of stages as *more* than such a heuristic means (ibid.:xxxviii).

Thus Weber rejects the social evolutionary use of universal, unilinear stages in general as well as the specific notion of a universal nomadic stage:

> The belief in a universal 'stage' of nomadic existence, through which all tribes passed and from which the settlement developed, can no longer be retained in view of our knowledge of the development of Asiatic peoples. . . . At any rate, this knowledge of a by no means primitive form of agriculture among the Indo-Germanic peoples goes back into the darkest past (as quoted by Roth, ibid).

The specific historical differences among Bedouin nomadic existence that rejected agriculture, Asian patterns that moved from nomadic crop-raising to intensive agriculture, and European patterns that proceeded from initial nomadic livestock raising could not be seen as a simple 'nomadic' ecological stage in social evolution (Weber, 1927:37–8; 1976:37, 68–9). It is important to note that differing environmental conditions and technological adaptations played important causal roles in creating these divergent historical social developments. This is another example of Weber's ecological analysis. However, this diversity, and the key role of ecological factors in producing this diversity, must not be artificially obscured by inaccurate social evolutionary metaphors.

The neo-evolutionists have recognized the oversimplification of universal, unilinear stages and have thus posited 'multilinear' evolution, which comes close to Weber's view. This multilinear modification, however, still rests on the organismic growth metaphor assumption which searches for analogies, parallels, and uniformities. In contrast, the object of scientific investigation, for Weber, is the detailed explanation of historical differences and diversity of unique historical constellations. Weber objected to the multilinear neo-evolutionists' search for analogies and parallels as the *purpose* of inquiry.

One final point with respect to Weber's critique of ecological evolutionism: he rejects single-factor technological determinism of social change and any form of social evolutionary theory of human ecology that posits technological and environmental determinism.

Thus, from Weber's point of view, formulations of ecological analysis in relation to social change theories of social evolution and technological determinism are open to serious questions. This does not mean that environmental and technological causal factors are irrelevant to explaining historical social structures and social change. Indeed, from Weber's point of view, they are an important aspect of historical explanation in interaction with other causal factors. In contrast to the social evolutionary approach of Duncan and others, Weber adopts a more 'historicist' approach to the ecological analysis of history and social change. Ecological factors of environment and technology are important interacting causes of specific changes in particular historical institutions and societies.

This approach to the ecological aspects of historical social development and change does not rely on the metaphor of organismic growth. Rather it focuses on the complex analysis of the relationship between unique historical social structures existing in diverse ecological contexts. The diversity of ecological habitats contributed to divergent developments in different social orders as we saw above in the contrast between Western European feudalism and almost universal patrimonialism.

Thus, Weber's approach to the ecological analysis of historical social change and development can be seen as 'evolutionary' in a radically different sense than the usual meaning of the social evolutionary perspective. These general socio-ecological causal forms constitute a set of mechanisms for the study of ecological relations in the unique 'evolution' of specific historical social structures. This approach stands much closer to *actual* Darwinian (not social-Darwinist!) evolution based on 'selective survival' in adaptation to specific habitats than the old social evolutionary theory that sought grand sweeping laws of social development based on the metaphor of organismic growth.

The role of ideas in Weber's human ecology

Cultural ideas play an important role in Weber's ecological analysis of society-environment interactions. Although this stance is axiomatic in anthropological human ecology, it is still a hard-fought point in sociological human ecology with its metaphors of morphological ecological processes analogous to the ecology of the natural world in which culture plays no role (Wallace, 1969:18; Duncan, 1964; Duncan and Schnore, 1959; Gibbs and Martin, 1959).

It is also crucial to examine the role of ideas because Weber's human ecology must be understood within the context of the polemical contrast of 'materialist' and 'idealist' social theories of his day. Rather than trying to prove the correctness of one or another stance, he sought, in characteristic fashion, to determine the proper balance and the complex interactions between them.

Weber's contributions to the understanding of the interaction of cultural and ecological factors are found primarily in his analysis of the relationship between religious and economic institutions in history. In order to understand just how Weber approached this interaction, it is important to summarize his theory of the independent role of ideas. The primary role of religious culture is not through the internalization of 'moral values', but operates as a process of ideological legitimation, and through the internalization of 'cognitive' religious ideas or 'images' that shape or refract ideal or material interests

> Not ideas, but material and ideal interests, directly govern men's conduct. Yet very frequently, the 'images' that have been created by 'ideas' have, like switchmen, determined the tracks along which action has been pushed by the dynamic of interest. 'From what' and 'for what' one wished to be redeemed, depended upon one's image of the world (Weber 1946:280.

Weber's analysis of the rise of capitalism will now be reviewed from the perspective of the interaction of cultural and ecological factors.

Cultural-ecological interactions in the origins of capitalism

Favorable conditions of trade were an essential element in the development of capitalism in Weber's view. These conditions were determined in large measure by technological changes and environmental factors. Technological advance in the transportation of goods, particularly the development of effective sailing methods in England in the sixteenth and seventeenth centuries was a key change that was important to capitalism.

Weber asserts that these favorable developments occurred in an area where geographical conditions favored trade relations and the development of capitalism. He contrasts these favorable geographic conditions with unfavorable conditions in China and India

> The external conditions for the development of capitalism are . . . first, geographical in character. In China and India, the enormous costs of transportation, connected with decisively inland commerce of the regions, necessarily formed serious obstructions for the classes who were in a position to make profits through trade and to use trading capital in the construction of a capitalistic system; while in the West the position of the Mediterranean as an inland sea, and the abundant interconnections through the rivers, favored the opposite development of international commerce (1927:354).

While stressing the importance of these environmental factors in favoring economic strata conducive to capitalism, Weber is careful to point out that these conditions did not in themselves determine capitalism.

The technological changes in industrial production were of great importance in the development of capitalism. The steam engine was important but it did not determine capitalistic factory organization. In addition to steam power, developments in the wool, paper, cotton manufacture and pottery technology in England all contributed to the initial development of capitalism.

However, none of these factors, singly or in combination, was sufficient to produce capitalism. For Weber, of course, religious ideas presented the decisive moment in the origin and initial development of the capitalistic ethos through the refraction of ideal interests. This thesis is so well known that it will not be treated in detail here.

The effect of these religious ideas, however, was decisive

231

primarily during the *origins* of the capitalistic spirit and early capitalistic organization and only in interaction with environmental, technological, and economic preconditions. The further development of this form of economic organization interacted with other ecological conditions of environment and technology that were decisive for the ultimate ascendance and development of capitalism.

Once the capitalistic ethos and economic organization had been created, its fate lay precariously in the hands of physically material changes in natural resources and productive technology. The initial industrial revolution that accompanied the creation of capitalism was fueled by wind and water, and crucially by charcoal that was used in the production of steel. Weber observes that 'Until the 18th century . . . smelting and all preparation of iron was done with charcoal.' This reliance on wood as the key energy resource in rapid capitalistic industrial expansion caused deforestation wherever the industrial revolution was based upon this resource:

> the destruction of the forest brought the industrial revolution to a standstill at a certain point . . . in contrast with the expansion of the textile industry, the English iron industry had shrunk step by step until at the beginning of the 18th century, it gave the impression of having reached its end (Weber 1927:304)

The fate of the iron industry was, for Weber, decisive for the fate of the industrial revolution and capitalism. This exploitation of envrionmental resources brought capitalism and the industrial revolution to its knees. Had it not been for the union of iron and coal, Weber (1927:304) believed that the industrial revolution 'might have stopped, and modern capitalism in its most characteristic form never appeared.'

Conclusion

Weber's implicit human ecology can be summarized in the following way:

1 Environmental factors are not all-pervasive determinants but may become causally relevant at certain key junctures in the histories of specific societies.
2 Environmental influences are non-deterministic, interactive components of complex causal models.
3 Environmental influences frequently affect complex societies through favoring the 'selective survival' of certain social strata over others.

4 These interactions are viewed in terms of a complex conflict functional model involving conflict amongst competing strata and institutions and 'selective survival' over time. However, Weber emphasizes that adaptation and selective survival must be viewed neither in a social-Darwinist nor a social evolutionist framework, but rather from a value-neutral, historicist perspective.

5 Cultural factors, and especially the role of cognitive culture in the refraction of interests, play an important interactive role in Weber's ecological causal models.

Such a perspective has direct relevance for understanding the role of ecological factors in the current and future changes in today's 'advanced' complex societies, not by drawing direct parallels or evolutionary conclusions from past societies, but rather from the careful, appropriate considerations of society-environment interactions in the manner in which Weber approached such relations in historical complex societies. We learn from the past, not that history repeats itself, but rather that the ecological conditions of human existence and organization reassert their constraints in different unique interactive ways in different spatio-temporal contexts. The narrow a-historical sociology of the present fosters the myth that we may be the first unique exception, but viewed from the vast historical scale with which Weber worked, we recognize the folly of such illusions.

Contemporary environmental, energy, and material 'crises' may not bring an immediate or total 'limit to growth'; but their constraints promise to impinge increasingly as central causal factors in emerging societal transformations in both the developed and developing world. A reorientation to a broader ecological sociology as Weber envisioned it will be crucial for understanding these societal changes and grappling with their consequences.

Notes

* The author wishes to express his appreciation to R. Stephen Warner and William R. Burch, Jr., for comments on an earlier draft of this chapter.

1 The task of this chapter is to present the substance of Weber's implied ecological perspective. It is beyond its scope to develop a comprehensive contrast and integration with the major strains of human ecology as they have developed in sociology, anthropology, and geography.

2 Technology, of course, is composed of both cognitive cultural components and physically material components. Technology as an ecological factor refers to these latter material aspects.

3 For a more complete exposition of these and other historical cases of

ecological analysis in Weber's works, see West (1975). For a discussion of ecological factors in the decline of the Roman empire see Weber (1976:307, 360ff). Note in this case that societal decline was tied not to Malthusian natural resource exhaustion and overpopulation, but rather to the more subtle factors of geographical shifts from a coastal trading society to an inland natural economy and a demographic decline in the availability of slaves for this slave-based economy.

4 For patrimonialism versus feudalism see Chapters 3, 8, and 9 and Charts 3.3 and 3.4.

5 Weber (1978:390) also is careful to note that just because the progress of 'selection,' a concept borrowed from biology, is somewhat relevant to the analysis of social institutions, this does not mean that racial biology theories of social differences are scientifically valid especially as single factor determinants. He repeatedly debunks specific racial biology notions of differential ethnic and national characteristics (1978:306; 1976:53).

Appendix

The conceptual dichotomy of feudalism versus patrimonialism has not been much noticed in historical-comparative research in spite of its enormous potentialities in sorting out the data and formulating basic propositions.

If and when some new power structures, however small, decentralized, or disorganized, emerge by breaking away from an old patrimonialist empire, they cannot and should not be indiscriminately labeled 'feudal.' Neither can the frequent periods of anarchy between two dynasties or two regimes – or to use a favorite expression of many patriotic historians, 'times of trouble' – nor the cases marginal to or transitional between feudalism and patrimonialism automatically be declared 'feudal' without examining basic attributes in each single case. In some instances, when a patrimonialist power structure for whatever reasons shows signs of weakness, there is usually an opening for a province or region with some distinctive national characteristics of its own to develop a new power structure. In all these instances Western-trained specialists are too quick to use the term 'feudalism' for any and all of these almost natural developments toward change.

From Montesquieu, who said that 'feudalism was an event which happened once in the world and which will perhaps never happen again,' to Marx and his posterity, and in spite of support for Montesquieu, feudalism as a concept became increasingly separated from the context of time and space in which it existed. Without any evidence it was made part of a rigid dogmatic system of an inevitable universal (second) stage of development. As Hall said the indiscriminate reference to 'feudal' goes 'with little concern over the theoretical problems engendered by such usage.'

The term has entered popular literature where it is applied to any of a wide variety of traits . . . feudalism has taken on a popular pejorative meaning which is applied to almost any aspect of contemporary life which seems old-fashioned . . . – a term with which children criticize their parents, or socialists label their conservative opponents (1962:19).

Weber's and Sprenkel's 'feudal' label for pre-patrimonialist China, which ended with unification by Ch'in Shih Huang Ti, 246–206 BC (see pp. 194–6), is highly questionable. Whatever the final choice of concepts and labels for that pre-patrimonialist period in Chinese history, it was not feudalism, as Sprenkel said, but an anarchy of approximately fifty-five warring kingdoms that was replaced by Ch'in's patrimonialist empire, which was indeed 'a unitary and bureaucratically administered empire, a political arrangement to which the Chinese world became habituated, and which it came to regard as a part of the natural order of things, during the four centuries of the Former and Later Han, 206 BC–AD 220' (1964:359). Equally questionable is the feudal label for the 'subsequent age of discussion which began with the collapse and disintegration of Han and [which] lasted until the Sui reunification in 589' (ibid.).

Sprenkel's label 'age of disunion' here and 'Age of Division' used elsewhere (1964:361) are much more appropriate than 'feudal.' However, Sprenkel is correct in criticizing Weber's comment on 'the appropriation of prebends' by the mandarins as hereditary quasi-feudal territorial nobility in the centuries from 960 to 1911: 'No hereditary nobility existed during these centuries, nor were there any discernible signs of a process of refeudalization' (1964:359).

Probably under the impact of powerful historical memories and the legacy of the celebrated civilization of the land of the Pharaohs Egypt repeatedly attempted to break away from the Byzantine and subsequent Islamic patrimonialist empires. Still Western-trained byzantologists and islamicists invariably interpreted these break-aways as the beginning of feudal development in the respective empires. Weber's subtype of 'prebendal feudalism', which he constructed in sharp contrast to 'fief-feudalism' (1956:148ff; 1968:255ff) and which, in his words, is to account for transitional and marginal cases in Islam and elsewhere, is not supported by current research. Islamicists liberated from the Western 'stage-categorizing' and other terminology conditioned by the Western experience agree that any appearance of 'feudal-like' phenomena are simply the result of a decline in the capacity of the central all-powerful rulership to prevent corruption of its officeholders, including mercenaries at the court and in the provinces, or to re-establish total patrimonialist control. All subsequent changes which were usually directed towards increasing political expediency, especially under Suleiman the Magnificent in the sixteenth century, were initiated and sanctioned only by imperial authority, thus once again subordinating them to imperial control and supervision.

Even those islamicists who still occasionally use the 'feudal' label emphasize that most of the characteristic features of Western feudalism were missing in most, if not all, Islamic power structures for several reasons. Above all else was the Islamic allegiance to the caliph or sultan succeeding to the authority of Muhammad.

Byzantine patrimonialism

In Byzantine and Russian studies there is clearly an ever-present reluctance to drop the totally inapplicable 'feudal' label due to the traditional political claims of both empires to the Roman imperial heritage and sole Christian orthodoxy, which they denied to the Western (Holy) empire and the Roman church. This author (1984, 1971b) has presented an analysis of Russian patrimonialism, modern and traditionalist respectively; therefore, only Byzantine patrimonialism will be accounted for here.

The landed *pronoia* (meaning providence, care, or foresight) was a Byzantine variant of the patrimonialist benefice, by which the basileus gave a portion of the state land in care of his servant notables as a temporary reward for their past and future services. At the notable's death the *pronoia* ceased to exist and reverted back to the ruler. Kantorowicz summarized the general consensus:

> The term feudalism . . . in the sense of a complex organization of feudal society, does not seem applicable to Byzantine conditions. . . . The 'daydream' of feudal structure . . . was completely absent from the Byzantine East. On the contrary, what feudal features did exist were always somewhat isolated and accidental, and they were 'deviations' from the normal pattern of state organization, the ideal of which was always a state governed centrally by the Christ-like basileus and his heliocentrically working officials (1956:152–3)

With a newly added section in the revised edition of his classic work, Vasiliev (1952:563–79) challenged this generally accepted view. To support his belief that certain traces of feudalism could be discovered if one looks very hard, he quoted two sources from the time of Justinian the Great (AD 527–65), in which Justinian accused some families in two provinces, Cappadocia and Egypt, of attempting to appropriate governmental powers including state lands. Justinian's novel no. 30 clearly describes a state of anarchy in Cappadocia. Another source accuses the Egyptian Apions of pretending to be a ruling family with all the monarchical prerequisites: their own military forces, treasury and tax collectors, police and prisons, postal services, etc. If the accusations were correct, the ruling families, whatever their motivation or origin of power, were trying to achieve independence. What appears 'private' from the point of view of the basileus' universalism might well be 'public' to the Egyptian or Cappadocian. In the monistic doctrine of the basileus' universal *imperium*, no claim to independence can be tolerated. These two isolated phenomena deviating from the constitutional pattern cannot be classified even remotely as feudal.

Vasiliev also forced another superficial analogy

> between the Western feudal lords . . . and the exarchs at the close of the sixth century, who under emperor Maurice, 582–602, stood at the head of the vast territorial organizations, the exarchates of Ravenna and of Carthage or Africa. The exarchs or the governors general, first of all military officers, gradually concentrated in their hands the administrative and judicical functions. . . . It is not surprising that from time to time the exarchs raised the banner of revolt . . . and advanced claims to the imperial throne (1952:575–6).

Both exarchs at Ravenna and Carthage, Byzantine governors in the western parts of the formerly unified Roman empire, were executives at the top. They were 'substitutes' for the emperor in the West, appointed by him and exclusively responsible to him. They held a unique office defined in the *ius publicum*. If these powerful western 'substitutes' of the basileus attempted a *coup d'état*, they were following traditionally consecrated blueprints of the Byzantine palace 'revolutions' which frequently decided the 'right' to succession. There were no traces of feudalism in this predictable patrimonialist power struggle on the top.

Vasiliev's (1952:568) analysis of Byzantine patrimonialism based on *pronoia* is about the same as that of Ostrogorsky:

> A grant of *pronoia* . . . was held by the recipient for a defined period, usually until his death, and was therefore not transferable either by alienation or by inheritance. . . . [The *pronoia*] was something which was met with in early Byzantine days, not in the golden age of imperial sovereignty during the middle Byzantine period, and when it reappeared again in the eleventh century it was a sign of the weakness of the central authority. (1957:292).

Ostrogorsky points to the 'south-slavic countries of Byzantine culture,' Bulgaria, Macedonia, Montenegro, and Serbia, in which *pronoia* was directly continued from the Byzantine origin and speaks of the similarity between *pronoia* and *pomestie* in Muscovy. He also argues in favor of the continuity of *pronoia* and Turkish *zijam* and *timar* (1969:127–8, 341–2), which apparently is not accepted or at least is still questioned by a number of specialists. In spite of his detailed discussion of the rule of the Byzantine bureaucratic (servant) nobility, based on *pronoia*, Ostrogorsky persists in lumping the Western 'feud,' *pronoia, pomestie, timar* and *zijam* together under one and the same expression (*izraz*) that pertains to a fully developed feudalism (1969:142ff, 342).

Japan: Which way?

Certain aristocratic features displayed during the pre-Tokugawa and Tokugawa periods by the daimios inspired Bloch to rekindle an old argument that feudalism was a type of general societal development rather than a specific Western development, because there were at least two feudalisms: Western and Japanese. Bloch, however, emphasized the positive correlation between the representative systems of England (Parliament), France (*états*), Germany (*Stände*), and feudalism.

> It was assuredly no accident that the representative system
> . . . originated in states which were only just emerging from
> the feudal stage and still bore its imprint. Nor was it an
> accident that in Japan, where the vassal's submission was
> much more unilateral and where, moreover, the divine power
> of the emperor remained outside the structure of vassal
> engagements, nothing of the kind emerged from a regime
> which was nevertheless in many respects closely akin to the
> feudalism in the West (1961:452).

This major distinction and some others to be discussed below are so fundamental that the respective systems are apparently not 'closely akin' at all.

Weber, who also uses the term 'Japanese feudalism,' speaks of rather stark personal and arbitrary control of the emperor over his staff officials, the daimios. Originally the emperor granted non-hereditary benefices to the daimios and the daimios in turn re-granted some of these benefices to their own soldiers, the samurai. Even in the periods of weak emperors, control of daimios remained unchallenged. A number of stringent patrimonialist conditions imposed on the daimios illustrate their extreme dependence on the emperor: the requirement that the daimio resides at the emperor's court every other year while his family resides there permanently; and short duration of the daimio's assignment of service connected with many other limitations, such as not being permitted to serve in regions where he has relatives or friends or in his region of origin; prohibition to build fortresses, enter into any alliances with other daimios or with foreign countries; and the emperor's right to penalize the daimio for misbehavior by removing him to another region or to remove him without cause for reasons of political expediency (1956:151, 613, 637ff).

In publishing the documents from pre-Tokugawa and Tokugawa shogunates, Asakawa said that there were two rival doctrines; however, both

> agreed, the first one implying and the second declaring, that the emperor was sovereign, and that the business of government should be conducted by his responsible agents. The theoretical foundation of this doctrine was the Chinese political philosophy, which taught that the ruler was sovereign, and the people were . . . the chief object of his rule; and that government should be carried on by officials to whom he delegated powers and who were responsible ultimately to him for his official acts. (1929:75)

'It was the sovereign who sanctioned the office of shogun,' Asakawa said, and enabled him to create his hierarchical organization. And 'whenever that structure was weakened it was again loyalty to the imperial authority which was invoked as justification' for any subsequent changes. He emphasized the impact of 'the abiding presence of the emperor as the sole fountain of all sovereign rights' (1957:216;1929:78). When comparing specific attributes of Western feudalism with similar phenomena in Japan, Asakawa recognized several differences, especially in the areas of the relationships between lords and vassals, including the peculiar nature and weaknesses of the contract; the absence of judicial and administrative aspects within their structure; and also the ambiguities of the public and private aspects in general. Asakawa recognized that 'the word "public" . . . is necessarily used in an elastic sense' (1929:40, 42, 54, 65–8, 74, 78, 81ff).

To Hintze, who carefully evaluated the work of Kan'ichi Asakawa, Tokuzo, Fukada, Karl Rathgen, Max Weber and others, Japanese feudalism essentially differed from Western feudalism by the specific legal characteristics of the Western feudal contract which was based on the concept of equality of rights and reciprocity. In the West the declaration of a free man to his peers in a public assembly that he will join a lord voluntarily is the foundation of the contractual relationship. It was a status-granting relationship which was not lowered, but it was frequently enhanced when the lord was a prince or a king. In contrast to it, in Japan the relationship reflected an extensive subordination of the vassal to his lord and an overwhelming patriarchal domination of the lord over his vassals. This basic relationship remained in force from the beginning and never became a relationship between two equal parties. Following the durable Japanese cultural heritage, the status relationship was that of a younger brother or son toward a powerful head of the family, the father, legitimized by the common worship of ancestors as a sacred doctrine reinforcing the total power structure. For example, it was considered a high honor for the vassal to assume the lord's family name and wear the family crest if offered by the lord (Hintze, 1962:166–8; translated and summarized by V.M.).

Finally, the impact of Confucianism, Shintoism, and Buddhism and Chinese civilization in general is not to be overlooked. Asakawa shows that the religious institutions were much older than the limited 'feudal' eras and 'had wider contacts than the feudal with national life, for the organization of the former was in part independent of the division of seigniores, and the religious acts of warriors were hardly different in motive and expression from those of other persons' and 'Confucianism was taught among the warriors for the interest of the existing social order' (1929:69, 81). Also 'the lord generally sought to buttress his political domination . . . by inculcating the teachings of Confucianism, especially that of loyalty. The feudal regime of Japan had thus fallen into the keeping of the paternalistic lord-prince and the loyal vassal-subject' (1929:76). Asakawa speaks of 'the elaborate bureaucracy of the imperial civil government' and 'the conventional impersonal dignity and the moral platitudes characteristic of the Chinese officialdom copied in Japan' (1929:77).

Asakawa's research has influenced Hintze, Hall, and others. Here are some conclusions:

> The religious doctrines and practices of Confucianism as well as Buddhism and Shintoism were instrumental in granting and safeguarding the lord's parental (patriarchal, patrimonialist) domination over his vassals. These religions lacked the rational and legal Christian heritage that the Christian church, especially the Roman, had inherited from the Roman empire, which in turn made it possible for the church to perform such an important role in the political power configuration in the West (Hintze, 1962:168–9; translated and summarized by V.M.).

'The condition of extreme political decentralization . . . lasted for a comparatively short time in Japan.' And Hall continued:

The great civil wars which engulfed Japan from the 1530's through 1590 and which culminated in the formation of a new national hegemony gave rise to conditions which served to eliminate the most typical feudal practices from many sectors of Japanese society. Ironically, when Japan was for the first time brought completely under the role of 'feudal lords', those very lords had begun to divest themselves of the most fundamentally feudal aspects of their means of governance (1962:45).

Asakawa (1929:74) said:

The stern but paternalistic policy was inspired by the exigencies of warfare and fiscal pressure. . . . Legal and philosophical principles and usages corresponding to European manners of making reciprocal agreements and to the idea of *iustitia* inculcated by the Church and accepted as a theory by secular rulers, were lacking in feudal Japan except as general, natural concepts. Instead, the lord fell back upon the Chinese doctrine of sovereignty and bureaucracy and the Chinese principles of paternalistic rule. . . . The difference has had the most significant effects upon national life.

In conclusion, feudalism developed only in some of the Western European countries, not in all of them. As Bloch said, in the West

the map of feudalism reveals some large blank spaces. . . . We find between the Loire and the Rhine, and in Burgundy . . . a heavily shaded area, which, in the eleventh century, is suddenly enlarged by the Norman conquests of England and southern Italy. All round this central nucleus there is an almost regular shading-off till, in Saxony and especially in Leon and Castile, the stippling becomes very sparse indeed. Finally the entire shaded area is surrounded by blank spaces (1961:445–6).

In some instances the specialists would disagree with some of Bloch's specific shades of intensity. For some historical approximations of feudalism see Bendix (1960:368–74).

There are some other instances not frequently discussed, e.g., the power structures in Catalonia, Aragon, Valencia and other territories, conquered in the fifteenth century by the new monarchy in the Iberian peninsula, displayed a variety of attributes from those very close to feudalism at one end of the scale to those of patrimonialism at the other end. This basically new patrimonialist empire experienced serious difficulties with the traditions of political liberty, which forced the conqueror to share the legislative powers with the *Cortes*. Soon this imperial patri-monialism was exported to America: the new conquest fell to Castile alone and not to Spain. Speaking on the consensus that 'Portugal did not fit the classic European type' of feudalism, Schwartzmann said, 'The centralized, bureaucratic, and patri-monial structure of government was transplanted in Brazil' (1973:218). On the other edge of Western Europe, in spite of an abundance of written documents from the early centuries, Barada and Kostrenčić were locked in an unsettled controversy concerning the originality or similarity of feudalism in Croatia with the rest.

All the marginal or transitional cases could be placed quite specifically between two opposing ends of the conceptual scale of patrimonialism versus feudalism by accounting for the presence or absence of a few, some, or many of their contrasting attributes.

Bibliography

ABEL, THEODORE (1948), 'The operation called verstehen,' *American Journal of Sociology*, vol. 54, pp. 211–18

ABU-LUGHOD, IBRAHIM (1966), 'Retreat from secular path: Islamic dilemmas of Arab politics,' *Review of Politics,* vol. 28, pp. 447–76.

AKHAVI, SHAHROUGH (1975), 'Egypt: Neo-patrimonial elite,' in FRANK TACHAU (ed.), *Political Elites and Political Development in the Middle East*, New York, Halsted Press, pp. 69–114.

ALGAR, HAMID (1969), *Religion and State in Iran 1785–1906: The Role of the Ulama in the Qajar Period*, Berkeley, University of California Press.

APTER, DAVID E. (1963), 'Political religion in the new nations,' in C. GEERTZ (ed.), *Old Societies and New States*, New York, The Free Press, pp. 57–104.

ARNOLD, THOMAS W. (1924), *The Caliphate*, London, Oxford University Press.

ASAKAWA, KAN'ICHI (1929), *The Documents of Iriki*, New Haven, Yale University Press.

ASAKAWA, KAN'ICHI (1957), 'Feudalism – Japan,' *Encyclopedia of the Social Sciences*, New York, Macmillan, vol. 6, pp. 214–18.

BALBUS, ISAAC D. (1971), 'The concept of interest in pluralist and Marxian analysis', *Politics and Society*, vol. 1, pp. 151–77.

BALDUS, BERND (1975), 'The study of power: Suggestions for an alternative,' *Canadian Journal of Sociology*, vol. 1, pp. 179–201.

BARADA, MIHO (1952), *Hrvatski vlasteoski feudalizam*, Zagreb.

BAUER, WOLFGANG (1976), *China and Search for Happiness*, trans. MICHAEL SHAW, New York, Seabury.

BAUMGARTEN, EDUARD (1964), *Max Weber: Werk und Person*, Tübingen, Mohr.

BECK, HANS-GEORG (1954), 'Byzanz: Der weg zu seinem geschicht-lichen verständniss,' *Saeculum*, vol. 5, pp. 87–103.

BECKER, HOWARD P. (1940), 'Constructive typology in the social sciences,' in H. E. BARNES, H. BECKER, and F. BECKER (eds), *Contemporary Social Theory*, New York, Appleton-Century, pp. 17–42.

BECKER, HOWARD P. (1945), 'Interpretive sociology and constructive typology,' in G. GURVITCH and W. E. MOORE (eds), *Twentieth Century Sociology*, New York, Philosophical Library, pp. 70–95.

BECKER, HOWARD P. (1956), *Man in Reciprocity*, New York, Praeger.

BECKER, HOWARD P., and ALVIN BOSKOFF (eds) (1957), *Modern Sociological Theory in Continuity and Change*, New York, The Dryden Press.

BEETHAM, DAVID (1974), *Max Weber and the Theory of Modern Politics*, London, Allen & Unwin.

BENDIX, REINHARD (1960), *Max Weber: Intellectual Portrait*, New York, Doubleday.

BENDIX, REINHARD (1965), 'Max Weber's sociology today,' *International Social Science, Journal*, vol. 17, pp. 9–22.

BENDIX, REINHARD, (1969), 'Review essay: Economy and society by Max Weber,' *American Sociological Review*, vol. 34, pp. 555–8.

BENDIX, REINHARD (1970), *Embattled Reason: Essays on Social Knowledge*, New York, Oxford University Press.

BENDIX, REINHARD and GUENTHER ROTH (1971), *Scholarship and Partisanship: Essays on Max Weber*, Berkeley, University of California Press.

BENN, S. I. (1959–60), ' "Interest" in politics,' *Proceedings of the Aristotelian Society*, vol. 60, pp. 123–40.

BERDYAEV, NICHOLAS (1948), *The Origin of Russian Communism*, London, Bles.

BERGER, MORROE (1962), *The Arab World Today*, New York, Anchor.

BERKES, NIYAZI (1963), 'Religious and secular institutions in comparative perspective', *Archives de Sociologie des Religions*, vol. 8, pp. 65–72.

BERKES, NIYAZI (1974), 'The two facets of the Kemalist revolution' *Muslim World*, vol. 64, pp. 292–306.

BINDER, LEONARD (1964), *The Ideological Revolution in the Middle East*, New York, Wiley.

BLOCH, MARC (1961), *Feudal Society*, University of Chicago Press: Phoenix Books.

BOSWORTH, CLIFFORD E. (1962), 'The imperial policy of the early Ghaznavids,' *Islamic Studies*, vol. 1, pp. 49–82.

BOSWORTH, CLIFFORD E. (1963), *The Ghaznavids*, Edinburgh University Press.

BRUNNER, OTTO (1956), *Neue Wege zur Sozialgeschichte*, Göttingen, Vandenhöck.

BURGER, THOMAS (1976), *Max Weber's Theory of Concept Formation: History, Laws, Ideal Types*, Durham, North Carolina, Duke University Press.

BUSSE, H. (1973), 'The revival of Persian kingship under the Buyids,' in D. S. RICHARDS (ed.), *Islamic Civilization*, Oxford, Cassirer, pp. 47–69.

CAHEN, CLAUDE (1967), 'The body politic,' in G. E. GRUNEBAUM (ed.), *Unity and Variety in Muslim Civilization*, University of Chicago Press, pp. 132–63.

CAHEN, CLAUDE (1968), *Pre-Ottoman Turkey*, New York, Taplinger.

CALVERLEY, EDWIN E. (1951), 'Islamic religion,' in T. C. YOUNG (ed.), *Near Eastern Culture and Society*, Princeton University Press, pp. 99–116.

CASEY, ROBERT PIERCE (1946), *Religion in Russia*, New York, Harper.

CHAN WING-TSIT (ed.) (1963), *A Source Book in Chinese Philosophy*, Princeton University Press.

CHEN, JEROME (1970), *Mao Papers: Anthology and Bibliography*, London, Oxford University Press.

CONNOLLY, WILLIAM E. (1972), 'On "interests" in politics,' *Politics and Society*, vol. 2, pp. 459–77.

DAHLHAUS, CARL (1972), 'Über sinn und sinnlosigkeit in der musik', in RUDOLF STEPHEN (ed.), *Die Musik der sechziger Jahre*, Mainz, Schott, pp. 90–9.

DAHRENDORF, RALF (1959), *Class and Class Conflict in Industrial Society*, Stanford University Press.

DARBY, H. C. (1956), 'The clearing of the woodland in Europe,' in W. L. THOMAS, JR. (ed.), *Man's Role in Changing the Face of the Earth*, University of Chicago Press, pp. 183–216.

DAVIS, KINGSLEY (1959), 'The myth of functional analysis as a special method in sociology and anthropology,' *American Sociological Review*, vol. 24, pp. 757–72.

DE BARY, THEODORE (ed.) (1975), *The Unfolding of Neo-Confucianism*, New York, Columbia University Press.

DEUTSCH, KARL W. (1971), 'Discussion on Max Weber and power-politics,' in O. STAMMER (ed.), *Max Weber and Sociology Today*, New York, Harper & Row, pp. 116–122.

DIVINE, ROBINSON DONNA (1977), 'Approaching the study of Egyptian society: An analysis of the language of the social sciences,' *Sociological Analysis and Theory*, vol. 7, pp. 135–63.

DJILAS, MILOVAN (1957), *The New Class*, New York, Praeger.

DJUREKOVIĆ, STJEPAN (1982), *Ja, Josip Broz-Tito*, New York, International Books-USA

DJUREKOVIĆ, STJEPAN (1983a), *Crveni Manageri*, New York, International Books-USA.

DJUREKOVIĆ, STJEPAN (1983b), *Slom Ideala*, New York, International Books-USA.

DUCHESNE-GUILLEMIN, JACQUES (1967), 'How does Islam stand?', in G. E. GRUNEBAUM (ed.), *Unity and Variety in Muslim Civilization*, University of Chicago Press, pp. 3–14.

DUMONT, LOUIS (1970), *Homo Hierarchicus*, University of Chicago Press.

DUNCAN, O. D. (1964), 'Social organization and the ecosystem,' in R. FARRIS (ed.), *Handbook of Modern Sociology*, Chicago, Rand McNally, pp. 37–82.

DUNCAN, O. D. and L. F. SCHNORE (1959), 'Cultural, behavioral, and ecological perspectives in the study of social organization,' *American Journal of Sociology*, vol. 65, pp. 132–46.

EHRLICH, EUGEN (1970), 'The study of the living law,' in RICHARD SCHWARTZ and JEROME SKOLNICK (eds), *Society and the Legal Order*, New York, Basic Books, pp. 149–54.

ENGISCH, KARL (1966), 'Max Weber als rechtsphilosoph und rechtssoziologe,' in K. ENGISCH, B. PFISTER and J. WINCKELMANN (eds), *Max Weber*, Berlin, Duncker & Humblot, pp. 67–88.

ETZKORN, K. PETER (1960), *Musical and Social Patterns of Songwriters: An Exploratory Sociological Study*, Ann Arbor, Michigan, University Microfilms.

ETZKORN, K. PETER (1973a), 'On the sphere of artistic validity in African art,' in WARREN L. D'AZEUEDO (ed.), *The Traditional Artist in African Societies*, Bloomington, Indiana University Press, pp. 343–78.

ETZKORN, K. PETER (1973b), *Music and Society: The Later Writings of Paul Honigsheim*, New York, Wiley.

ETZKORN, K. PETER (1976), 'Manufacturing music,' *Society*, vol, 14, pp. 19–23.

FAORO, RAYMUNDO (1958), *Os Donos do Poder*, Rio de Janeiro, Editora Globo.

FAROGHI, SURAIYA (1973), 'Social mobility among the Ottoman ulama in the late sixteenth century,' *International Journal of Middle East Studies*, vol. 4, pp. 204–18.

FEIGL, HERBERT (1953), 'Notes on causality,' in H. FEIGL and M. BRODBECK (eds), *Readings in the Philosophy of Science*, New York, Appleton-Century, pp. 408–18.

FINGARETTE, HERBERT (1972), *Confucius: The Secular as Sacred*, New York, Harper.

247

FISCHER, GEORGE (1968), *The Soviet System and Modern Society*, New York, Atherton.

FRANKE, HERBERT (1966), 'Max Webers soziologie der ostasiatischen religionen' in KARL ENGISH *et al.* (eds), *Max Weber*, Berlin, Duncker & Humblot, pp. 115–30.

FRANKE, OTTO, *Geschichte des chinesischen Reiches*, 5 vols, Berlin, Gruyter, vol. 1, 1930, vol. 3, 1937.

FREUND, JULIEN (1969), *The Sociology of Max Weber*, trans. M. ILFORD, New York, Vintage.

FUNG YU-LAN (1952), *A History of Chinese Philosophy*, vol. 1, Trans. DERK BODDE, Princeton University Press.

GELLAR, SHELDON (1973), 'State-building and nation-building in West Africa,' in S. N. EISENSTADT and S. ROKKAN (eds), *Building States and Nations, vol. II*, Beverly Hills, Sage Publications, pp. 384–426.

GELLNER, ERNEST (1975), 'The Kathmandu option: Patrimony and bureaucracy,' *Encounter*, vol. 45, pp. 56–68.

GIBB, HAMILTON A. R. (1962), *Studies on the Civilization of Islam*, Boston, Beacon Press.

GIBBS, J. and W. MARTIN (1959), 'Toward a theoretical system of human ecology,' *Pacific Sociological Review*, vol. 2, pp. 29–36.

GIDDENS, ANTHONY (1975), *The Class Structure of the Advanced Societies*, New York, Harper.

GOITEIN, S. D. (1957), 'The rise of the near-eastern bourgeoisie in early Islamic times,' *Cahiers d'Histoire Mondiale*, pp. 583–604.

GRIMM, CLAUS (1979), ' "Kunst," kultursoziologisch betrachtet, ein beitrag zur soziologischen geschichtsrevision,' *Kölner Zeitschrift für Soziologie und Sozialpsychologie*, vol. 31, pp. 527–58.

GRUNEBAUM, G. E. (1955), *Islam: Essays in the Nature and Growth of a Cultural Tradition*, London, Routledge & Kegan Paul.

GRUNEBAUM, G. E. (1964), *Modern Islam: The Search for Cultural Identity*, New York, Vintage.

HALL, JOHN WHITNEY (1962), 'Feudalism in Japan. A reassessment,' *Comparative Studies in Society and History*, vol. 5, pp. 15–51.

HART, H. L. A. and HONORÉ, A. M. (1973), *Causation in the Law*, London, Oxford University Press.

HEMPEL, CARL G. (1959), 'The logic of functional analysis,' in L. GROSS (ed), *Symposium on Sociological Theory*, New York, Harper, pp. 271–307.

HEUSS, THEODORE (1971), 'Max Weber in seiner Gegenwart,' in MAX WEBER, *Gesammelte Politische Schriften*, Tübingen, Mohr, pp. vii–xxxi.

HINTZE, OTTO (1962), *Staat and Verfassung*, 2nd edn, Göttingen, Vandenhöck.

HIRST, PAUL Q. (1976), *Social Evolution and Sociological Categories*, New York, Homes & Meier.

HODGSON, M. S. C. (1975), *The Venture of Islam*, 2 vols, University of Chicago Press.

HONIGSHEIM, PAUL (1963), 'Erinnerungen an Max Weber,' in R. KÖNIG and J. WINCKELMANN (eds), *Max Weber zum Gedächtnis, Kölner Zeitschrift für Soziologie und Socialpsychologie*, (special issue 7), pp. 234–49.

HONIGSHEIM, PAUL (1968), On *Max Weber*. trans. J. RYTINA, New York, The Free Press.

INALCIK, HALIL (1970), 'The rise of the Ottoman empire,' *Cambridge History of Islam*, vol. I, Cambridge University Press.

INALCIK, HALIL (1973), *The Ottoman Empire: The Classical Age 1300–1600*, London, Weidenfeld & Nicolson.

INGHAM, G. K. (1970), 'Social stratification: Individual attributes and social relationships,' *Sociology*, vol. 4, pp. 105–13.

JELLINEK, GEORG (1919), *Allgemeine Staatslehre*, 3rd edn, Berlin, Springer.

JONES, BRYAN (1975), 'Max Weber and the concept of social class,' *Sociological Review*, vol. 23, pp. 729–58.

KANT, IMMANUEL (1929), *The Critique of Pure Reason*, London, Macmillan.

KANT, IMMANUEL (1953), *Prolegomena to Any Future Metaphysics*, Manchester University Press.

KANT, IMMANUEL (1976), *The Critique of Practical Reason*, New York, Garland.

KANTOROWICZ, ERNEST H. (1956), ' "Feudalism" in the Byzantine empire,' in R. COULBORN (ed.), *Feudalism in History*, Princeton University Press, pp. 151–66.

KARTAŠEV, ANTON V. (1948), 'Pravoslavie v ego otnošenii k istoričeskomu procesu,' *Pravoslavnaja Mysl*, vol. 6, Paris.

KILLEN, LINDA (1982), 'Self-determination versus territorial integrity,' *Nationalities Papers*, vol. 10, pp. 65–78.

KOSTRENČIČ, MARKO (1953), *O radnji prof. dr. Mihe Barade, Hrvatski vlasteoski feudalism*, Zagreb.

LAMBTON, A. K. S. (1954), 'The theory of kingship in the Hasihat ul-Muluk of Ghazali,' *Islamic Quarterly*, vol. 1, pp. 47–55.

LAMBTON, A. K. S. (1956), 'Quis custodiet custodes? Some reflections on the Persian theory of government,' *Studia Islamica*, vol. 5, 125–48 and vol. 6, 125–46.

LANE, DAVID (1971), *The End of Inequality? Stratification under State Socialism*, Harmondsworth, Penguin.

LEACH, EDMUND (1964), 'Anthropological aspects of language: Animal categories and verbal abuse,' in ERIC H. LENNEBERG (ed.), *New Directions in the Study of Language*, Cambridge, Massachusetts, MIT Press, pp. 23–63.

LEGGE, JAMES (1950), 'The Doctrine of Mean,' *The Chinese Classics*, vol. 1, trans. JAMES LEGGE, Hong Kong University Press.

LEV, DANIEL (1972), *Islamic Courts in Indonesia: A Study in the Political Bases of Legal Institutions*, Berkeley, University of California Press.

LEWIS, BERNARD (1973), *Islam in History*, New York, Library Press.

LEWIS, BERNARD (1974), *Islam from the Prophet Muhammad to the Capture of Constantinople*, 2 vols, New York, Harper.

LOEWE, MICHAEL (1975), 'The vilification of Confucius: Themes in Chinese history and ideology,' *Encounter* (November), pp. 56–60.

LOEWENSTEIN, KARL (1966a), 'Personliche Erinnerungen an Max Weber,' in KARL ENGISCH, B. PFISTER and J. WINCKELMANN (eds), *Max Weber: Gedächtnisschrift . . . zur 100. Wiederkehr seines Geburtstages 1964*, Berlin, Duncker & Humblot, pp. 27–38.

LOEWENSTEIN, KARL (1966b), 'Max Webers Beitrag zur Staatslehre in der sicht unserer Zeit,' in KARL ENGISCH, B. PFISTER and J. WINCKELMANN (eds), *Max Weber: Gedächtnisschrift . . . zur 100. Wiederkehr seines Geburtstages 1964*, Berlin, Duncker & Humblot, pp. 131–46.

LORTHOLARY, ALBERT (1951), *Le Mirage russe en France au 18ᵉ siècle*, Paris, Éditions Contemporaines.

LUKES, STEVEN (1974), *Power*, London, Macmillan.

MACINNES, DONALD (ed.), (1972), *Religious Policy and Practices in Communist China,* New York, Macmillan.

MAKDISI, GEORGE (1970), 'Madrasa and university in the Middle Ages,' *Studia Islamica*, vol. 32, pp. 255–64.

MAKDISI, GEORGE (1979), 'The significance of the Sunni schools of law in Islamic religious history,' *International Journal of Middle East Studies*, vol. 10, pp. 1–8.

MAO ZEDONG (MAO TSE-TUNG), *Selected Works of Mao Tse-tung*, Peking, Foreign Languages Press, 1977, 1975 and 1967.

MAO ZEDONG (1973), *Poems of Mao Tse-tung*, trans. HUA-LING NIEH ENGLE and PAUL ENGLE, New York, Dell.

MARTINDALE, DON (1959), (Sociological theory and the ideal type,' in L. GROSS (ed.), *Symposium on Sociological Theory*, New York, Harper, pp. 57–91.

MEISNER, MAURICE (1968), 'Utopian goals and ascetic values in Chinese communist ideology,' *Journal of Asian Studies*, vol. 28, pp. 101–10.

METZGER, THOMAS (1977), *Escape from Predicament*, New York, Columbia University Press.

MILIBAND, RALPH (1977), *Marxism and Politics*, Oxford University Press.

MOLLOY, STEPHEN (1980), 'Max Weber and the religions of China: Any way out of the maze?', *British Journal of Sociology*, vol. 31, pp. 377–400.

MORRISON, KARL F., (1969), *Tradition and Authority in the Western Church 300–1140,* Princeton University Press.

MUNRO, DONALD (1969), *The Concept of Man in Early China*, Stanford University Press.

MUNRO, DONALD, (1977), *The Concept of Man in Contemporary China*, Ann Arbor, University of Michigan Press.

MURVAR, VATRO (1966), 'Some tentative modifications of Weber's typology: Occidental versus oriental city,' *Social Forces*, vol. 44, pp. 381–9, (Also reprinted in P. MEADOWS and E. H. MIZRUCHI (eds), *Urbanism, Urbanization and Change: Comparative Perspectives*, Reading, Massachusetts, Addison-Wesley, pp. 51–63, 1969.)

MURVAR, VATRO (1967), 'Max Weber's urban typology and Russia,' *Sociological Quarterly*, vol. 8, pp. 481–94.

MURVAR, VATRO (1968), 'Russian religious structures: A study in persistent church subservience,' *Journal for The Scientific Study of Religion*, vol. 7, pp. 1–22.

MURVAR, VATRO (1971a), 'Messianism in Russia: Religious and revolutionary,' *Journal for the Scientific Study of Religion*, vol. 10, pp. 277–338.

MURVAR, VATRO (1971b), 'Patrimonial-feudal dichotomy and political structure in pre-revolutionary Russia,' *Sociological Quarterly*, vol. 12 pp. 500–24.

MURVAR, VATRO (1972), 'Nontheistic systems of beliefs: an urgently needed conceptual tool,' *American Behavioral Scientist*, vol. 16, pp. 169–194.

MURVAR, VATRO (1979), 'Integrative and revolutionary capabilities of religion,' in H. M. JOHNSON (ed.), *Religious Change and Continuity: Sociological Perspectives*, San Francisco, Jossey-Bass, pp. 74–86.

MURVAR, VATRO (1983), *Max Weber Today – An Introduction to a Living Legacy: Selected Bibliography*, Brookfield, Wisconsin, Max Weber Colloquia and Symposia at the University of Wisconsin-Milwaukee.

MURVAR, VATRO (1984) 'Max Weber and the two nonrevolutionary events in Russia, 1917: Scientific achievements or prophetic failures?' in R. GLASSMAN and V. MURVAR (eds.), *Max Weber's*

Political Sociology, Westport, Connecticut, Greenwood Press, pp. 237–72.

NEEDHAM, JOSEPH (1974), 'Christian hope and social evolution,' *China Notes*, vol. 12, pp. 13–20.

NEWMAN, K. J. (1963), 'Papst, Kaisser, Kalif und Basileus,' *Politische Vierteljahresschrift*, vol. 4, pp. 18–42.

NISBET, R. A. (1969), *Social Change and History: Aspects of the Western Theory of Development*, London, Oxford University Press.

OKSENBERG, MICHEL (1977), 'The political leader,' in DICK WILSON (ed.), *Mao Tse-Tung in the Scales of History*, London, Cambridge University Press.

OSTROGORSKY, GEORGE (1957), *History of the Byzantine State*, trans. JOAN HUSSEY, New Brunswick, N.J., Rutgers University Press.

OSTROGORSKY, GEORGE (1969), *O Vizantijskom Feudalizmu*, Belgrade, Prosveta.

PARSONS, TALCOTT (1949), *The Structure of Social Action*, New York, Free Press.

PARSONS, TALCOTT (1977), 'Value-freedom and objectivity,' in F. DALLMAYR and T. MCCARTHY (eds), *Understanding and Social Inquiry*, University of Notre Dame Press, pp. 56–65.

PETERSEN, WILLIAM (1963), 'Introduction,' in W. PETERSEN (ed.), *The Realities of World Communism*, Englewood Cliffs. N. J., Prentice-Hall, pp. 11–18.

PLAMENATZ, JOHN (1954), 'Interests,' *Political Studies*, vol. 2, pp. 1–8

PLAMENATZ, JOHN (1963) *Man and Society*, vol. 2, New York, McGraw-Hill.

POLANYI, K., C. M. ARENSBERG and W. PEARSON (1957), *Trade and Market in the Early Empires*, Glencoe, Free Press.

POUND, ROSCO (1910). 'Law in books and law in action,' *American Law Review*, vol. 44, pp. 12–36.

RHEINSTEIN, MAX (1954), 'Introduction,' in *Max Weber on Law in Economy and Society*, Cambridge, Massachusetts, Harvard University Press, pp. xxv–lxxii.

ROSENTHAL, ERWIN I. J. (1958), *Political Thought in Medieval Islam*, Cambridge University Press.

ROSSIDES, DANIEL M. (1972), 'The legacy of Max Weber: A nonmetaphysical politics,' *Sociological Inquiry*, vol. 42, pp. 183–210.

ROTH, GUENTHER (1968), 'Introduction,' in G. ROTH and C. WITTICH (eds and trans.), *Max Weber, Economy and Society*, 3 vols. New York, Bedminster Press, pp. xxvii–ci.

ROTH, GUENTHER and WOLFGANG SCHLUCHTER (1979), *Max Weber's*

Vision of History: Ethics and Methods, Berkeley: University of California Press.

RUNCIMAN, WALTER GARRISON (1970), 'Class, status and power?', in W. G. RUNCIMAN (ed.), *Sociology in Its Place*, Cambridge University Press, pp. 102–40.

SAMUELS, MARVIN S. (1978), Review of *The City in Later Imperial China, Journal of Asian Studies*, vol. 37, pp. 713–23.

SCHACHT, J. (1970), 'Law and justice,' *Cambridge History of Islam*, vol. 2., Cambridge University Press.

SCHRAM, STUART R. (1967), 'Mao Tse-tung as a charismatic leader,' *Asian Survey*, vol. 7, pp. 383–8.

SCHRAM, STUART R. (1971), 'Mao Tse-tung and the theory of permanent revolution: 1958–1969,' *China Quarterly*, vol. 46, pp. 221–44.

SCHRAM, STUART R. (1977), 'The Marxist,' in DICK WILSON (ed.), *Mao Tse-tung in the Scales of History*, London, Cambridge University Press, pp. 35–69.

SCHWARTZMANN, SIMON (1973), 'Regional contrasts within a continental-scale state: Brazil,' in S. N. EISENSTADT and S. ROKKAN (eds), *Building States and Nations*, Beverly Hills, California, Sage Publications, pp. 209–31.

SCOTT, DEREK J. R. (1961), *Russian Political Institutions*, New York, Praeger University Series.

SCOTT, JOHN (1974), 'Sociological theorizing and the Althusserian ideal,' *Sociological Analysis and Theory*, vol. 4, pp. 89–113.

SHAW, STANFORD (1976), *History of the Ottoman Empire and Modern Turkey*, vol. 1, Cambridge University Press.

SHEIKHOLESLAMI, A. REZA (1978), 'The patrimonial structure of Iranian bureaucracy in the late nineteenth century,' *Iranian Studies*, vol. 11, pp. 199–257.

SILBERMANN, ALPHONS (1963), 'Max Webers musikalischer exkurs,' in RENÉ KÖNIG and J. WINCKELMANN (eds.), *Kölner Zeitschrift für Soziologie und Sozialpsychologie*, (special issue 7), pp. 448–69.

SILBERMANN, ALPHONS (1973), *Empirische Kunstsoziologie*, Stuttgart, Enke.

SILBERMANN, ALPHONS (ed.) (1979), *Klassiker der Kunstsoziologie*, Munich, Beck.

SIMEY, T. S. (1967), 'Weber's sociological theory and the modern dilemma of value in the social sciences,' in J. BROTHERS (ed.), *Readings in the Sociology of Religion*, Oxford, Pergamon Press, pp. 89–114.

SIMIRENKO, ALEX (1970), Review of George Fischer, *The Soviet System and Modern Society*, 1968, *American Sociological Review*, vol. 35, pp. 391–2.

SKINNER, G. WILLIAM (ed.) (1977), *The City in Later Imperial China*, Stanford University Press.

SMITH, HUSTON (1967), 'Transcendence in traditional China,' *Religious Studies*, vol. 2, pp. 185–96.

SPRENKEL, OTTO B. VAN DER (1964), 'Max Weber on China,' *History and Theory*, vol. 3, pp. 348–70.

SPULER, BERTOLD (1967), 'Iran: The persistent heritage', in G. E. GRUNEBAUM (ed.), *Unity and Variety in Muslim Civilization*, University of Chicago Press, pp. 167–82.

STAMMER, OTTO (ed.) (1971), *Max Weber and Sociology Today*, trans. K. MORRIS, New York, Harper & Row.

STARR, JOHN (1979), *Continuing the Revolution: The Political Thought of Mao*, Princeton University Press.

STRAYER, J. R. (1958), 'The state and religion: Greece and Rome, the west, Islam,' *Comparative Studies in Society and History*, vol. 1, pp. 38–43.

STURZO, LUIGI (1946), *Nationalism and Internationalism*, New York, Roy.

SUPEK, IVAN (1983), *Crown Witness against Hebrang*, Chicago, Markanton Press.

TEGGART, F. J. (1960), *Theory and Processes of History*, Berkeley, University of California Press.

THERBORN, GÖRAN (1976), 'What does the ruling class do when it rules?', *Insurgent Sociologist*, vol. 6, pp. 3–16.

TOPITSCH, ERNST (1971), 'Max Weber and sociology today,' in O. STAMMER (ed.), *Max Weber and Sociology Today*, trans. K. MORRIS, New York, Harper & Row, pp. 8–25.

TOPPING, AUDREY (1978), 'China's incredible find,' *National Geographic*, vol. 153, pp. 440–59.

TRUBEK, DAVID M. (1972), 'Max Weber on law and the rise of capitalism,' *Wisconsin Law Review*, vol. 3, pp. 720–53.

TUDJMAN, FRANJO (1981), *Nationalism in Contemporary Europe*, New York, Columbia University Press.

TUMARKIN, NINA (1983), *Lenin Lives!: The Lenin Cult in Soviet Russia*, Cambridge, Massachusetts, Harvard University Press.

TURNER, BRYAN S. (1974), *Weber and Islam*, London, Routledge & Kegan Paul.

TURNER, BRYAN S. (1977), 'The structuralist critique of Weber's sociology,' *British Journal of Sociology*, vol. 28, pp. 1–16.

URICOECHEA, FERNANDO (1980), *The Patrimonial Foundations of the Brazilian Bureaucratic State*, Berkeley, University of California, Press.

VASILIEV, A. A. (1952), *History of the Byzantine Empire: 324–1453*, Madison, University of Wisconsin Press.

WAKEMAN, FREDERICK (1973), *History and Will: Philosophical*

Perspectives of Mao Tse-tung's Thought, Berkeley, University of California Press

WAKEMAN, FREDERICK (1977), 'Rebellion and revolution: The study of popular movements in Chinese history,' *Journal of Asian Studies*, vol. 36, pp. 201–37.

WALLACE, W. (1969), *Sociological Theory*, Chicago, Aldine.

WARNER, WILLIAM LLOYD and PAUL S. LUNT (1941), *The Social Life of a Modern Community*, Yankee City Series, vol. I.

WATT, WILLIAM MONTGOMERY (1961), *Islam and the Integration of Society*, Evanston, Illinois, Northwestern University Press.

WATT, WILLIAM MONTGOMERY (1968), *Islamic Political Thought*, Edinburgh University Press.

WEBER, MARIANNE (1975), *Max Weber: A Biography*, trans. and ed. H. ZOHN, New York, Wiley.

WEBER, MAX (1906), 'Zur lage der bürgerlichen Demokratie in Russland,' *Archiv für Sozialwissenschaft und Sozialpolitik*, vol. 4, pp. 234–353.

WEBER, MAX (1920), *Gesammelte Aufsätze zur Religionssoziologie*, vol. I. Tübingen, Mohr.

WEBER, MAX (1927), *General Economic History*, trans. F. H. KNIGHT, New York, The Free Press.

WEBER, MAX (1930), *The Protestant Ethic and the Spirit of Capitalism*, trans. T. PARSONS, London, Allen & Unwin.

WEBER, MAX (1946), *From Max Weber: Essays in Sociology*, trans. ed. and introduction, H. H. GERTH and C. WRIGHT MILLS, London, Oxford University Press.

WEBER, MAX (1949), *The Methodology of the Social Sciences*, trans. and ed. E. SHILS and H. FINCH, New York, Free Press.

WEBER, MAX (1951), *The Religion of China: Confucianism and Taoism*, trans. and ed. H. H. GERTH, Glencoe, Illinois, New York, Free Press.

WEBER, MAX (1952), *Ancient Judaism*, trans. and ed. H. H. GERTH and D. MARTINDALE, New York, Free Press.

WEBER, MAX (1954), *Max Weber on Law in Economy and Society*, Cambridge, Massachusetts, Harvard University Press.

WEBER, MAX (1956), *Wirtschaft und Gesellschaft*, 2 vols. 4th ed, ed. J. WINCKELMAN, Tübingen, Mohr.

WEBER, MAX (1958a), *Gessamelte politische Schriften*, 2nd rev. ed, Tübingen, Mohr.

WEBER, MAX (1958b), *The Religion of India: The Sociology of Hinduism and Buddhism*, trans. and ed. H. H. GERTH and D. MARTINDALE, The Free Press.

WEBER, MAX (1958c), *The Rational and Social Foundations of Music*, trans. and ed. D. MARTINDALE *et al.*, The Free Press.

WEBER, MAX (1963), *Sociology of Religion*, Boston, Beacon Press.

WEBER, MAX (1964), *Wirtschaft und Gesellschaft,* Cologne-Berlin, Kiepenheuer & Witsch.

WEBER, MAX (1968), *Economy and Society,* 3 vols. trans. and ed. G. ROTH and C. WITTICH, New York, Bedminster Press, 1968. (Reissued as a paperback by the University of California Press.)

WEBER, MAX (1973), *Gesammelte Aufsätze zur Wissenschaftslehre,* 4th rev. ed. J. WINCKELMANN, Tübingen, Mohr.

WEBER, MAX (1975), *Roscher and Knies: The Logical Problems of Historical Economics,* trans. and ed. G. OAKES, The Free Press.

WEBER, MAX (1976), *The Agrarian Sociology of Ancient Civilizations,* trans. and ed. R. I. FRANK, London, Foundations of History Library.

WEBER, MAX (1977), Critique of Stammler, trans. and introduction G. OAKES, The Free Press.

WEBER, MAX (1978), *Weber, Selections in Translation,* W. G. RUNCIMAN (ed.) and trans. E. MATTHEWS, Cambridge University Press.

WEBER, MAX (1981), 'Some categories of interpretive sociology,' trans. ed. and introduction, EDITH GRABER, *Sociological Quarterly,* vol. 22, pp. 151–80.

WEST, PATRICK C. (1975), 'Social structure and environment: A Weberian approach to human ecological analysis,' PhD dissertation, Yale University, (published by University Microfilms, Ann Arbor, Michigan).

WHITE, D. M. (1972), 'The problem of power', *British Journal of Political Science,* vol. 2, pp. 479–90.

WHITNEY, M. (1925), *Soil and Civilisation,* New York, Van Nostrand.

WILLNER, ANN RUTH (1966), *The Neo-Traditional Accommodation to Political Independence: The Case of Indonesia,* Princeton University Center of International Studies Research Monograph 26.

YANG, CH'ING-K'UN (1959), 'Some characteristics of Chinese bureaucratic behavior,' in D. NIVISON and A. WRIGHT (eds), *Confucianism in Action,* Stanford, Stanford University Press.

YANG, CH'ING-K'UN (1967), *Religion in Chinese Society,* Berkeley, University of California Press.

YANG, CH'ING-K'UN (1968), 'Introduction,' in Max Weber, *The Religion of China: Confucianism and Taoism,* trans. and ed. H. H. GERTH, 2nd ed, New York, The Free Press.

ZIEGLER, ADOLF W. (1953), 'Die byzantinische Religionspolitik und der sog. Caesaropapismus,' pp. 81–97 in E. KOSCHMIEDER and A. SCHMAUS (eds), *Münchner Beitrage zur Slavenkunde: Festgabe für Paul Diels,* Munich, Isar Verlag.

ZINGERLE, ARNOLD (1972), *Max Weber und China,* Berlin, Duncker & Humblot.

Index

Routledge Social Science Series

Routledge & Kegan Paul
London, Boston, Melbourne and Henley

39 Store Street, London WC1E 7DD
9 Park Street, Boston, Mass 02108
296 Beaconsfield Parade, Middle Park,
Melbourne, 3206 Australia
Broadway House, Newtown Road,
Henley-on-Thames, Oxon RG9 1EN

Contents

*Authors wishing to submit manuscripts for any series
in this catalogue should send them to the Social Science Editor,
Routledge & Kegan Paul plc, 39 Store Street,
London WC1E 7DD.*
● *Books so marked are available in paperback also.*
○ *Books so marked are available in paperback only.*
*All books are in metric Demy 8vo format (216 × 138mm approx.)
unless otherwise stated.*

International Library of Sociology
General Editor John Rex

GENERAL SOCIOLOGY

Alexander, J. Theoretical Logic in Sociology.
  Volume 1: Positivism, Presuppositions and Current Controversies. *234 pp.*
  Volume 2: The Antinomies of Classical Thought: *Marx and Durkheim.*
  Volume 3: The Classical Attempt at Theoretical Synthesis: *Max Weber.*
  Volume 4: The Modern Reconstruction of Classical Thought: *Talcott Parsons.*
Barnsley, J. H. The Social Reality of Ethics. *464 pp.*
Brown, Robert. Explanation in Social Science. *208 pp.*
● Rules and Laws in Sociology. *192 pp.*
Bruford, W. H. Chekhov and His Russia. *A Sociological Study. 244 pp.*
Burton, F. and **Carlen, P.** Official Discourse. *On Discourse Analysis, Government Publications, Ideology. 160 pp.*
Cain, Maureen E. Society and the Policeman's Role. *326 pp.*
● **Fletcher, Colin.** Beneath the Surface. *An Account of Three Styles of Sociological Research. 221 pp.*
Gibson, Quentin. The Logic of Social Enquiry. *240 pp.*
Glassner, B. Essential Interactionism. *208 pp.*
Glucksmann, M. Structuralist Analysis in Contemporary Social Thought. *212 pp.*
Gurvitch, Georges. Sociology of Law. *Foreword by Roscoe Pound. 264 pp.*
Hinkle, R. Founding Theory of American Sociology 1881–1913. *376 pp.*
Homans, George C. Sentiments and Activities. *336 pp.*
Johnson, Harry M. Sociology: *A Systematic Introduction. Foreword by Robert K. Merton. 710 pp.*
● **Keat, Russell** and **Urry, John.** Social Theory as Science. *Second Edition. 278 pp.*
Mannheim, Karl. Essays on Sociology and Social Psychology. *Edited by Paul Kecskemeti. With Editorial Note by Adolph Lowe. 344 pp.*
Martindale, Don. The Nature and Types of Sociological Theory. *292 pp.*
● **Maus, Heinz.** A Short History of Sociology. *234 pp.*
Merquior, J. G. Rousseau and Weber. *A Study in the Theory of Legitimacy. 240 pp.*
Myrdal, Gunnar. Value in Social Theory: *A Collection of Essays on Methodology. Edited by Paul Streeten. 332 pp.*
Ogburn, William F. and **Nimkoff, Meyer F.** A Handbook of Sociology. *Preface by Karl Mannheim. 656 pp. 46 figures. 35 tables.*
Parsons, Talcott and **Smelser, Neil J.** Economy and Society: *A Study in the Integration of Economic and Social Theory. 362 pp.*
Payne, G., Dingwall, R., Payne, J. and **Carter, M.** Sociology and Social Research. *336 pp.*
Podgórecki, A. Practical Social Sciences. *144 pp.*
Podgórecki, A. and **Łos, M.** Multidimensional Sociology. *268 pp.*
Raffel, S. Matters of Fact. *A Sociological Inquiry. 152 pp.*
● **Rex, John.** Key Problems of Sociological Theory. *220 pp.*
  Sociology and the Demystification of the Modern World. *282 pp.*
● **Rex, John.** (Ed.) Approaches to Sociology. *Contributions by Peter Abell, Frank Bechhofer, Basil Bernstein, Ronald Fletcher, David Frisby, Miriam Glucksmann, Peter Lassman, Herminio Martins, John Rex, Roland Robertson, John Westergaard and Jock Young. 302 pp.*
Rigby, A. Alternative Realities. *352 pp.*
Roche, M. Phenomenology, Language and the Social Sciences. *374 pp.*
Sahay, A. Sociological Analysis. *220 pp.*
Strasser, Hermann. The Normative Structure of Sociology. *Conservative and Emancipatory Themes in Social Thought. 286 pp.*

Strong, P. Ceremonial Order of the Clinic. *267 pp.*
Urry, J. Reference Groups and the Theory of Revolution. *244 pp.*
Weinberg, E. Development of Sociology in the Soviet Union. *173 pp.*

FOREIGN CLASSICS OF SOCIOLOGY

● **Gerth, H. H.** and **Mills, C. Wright.** From Max Weber: *Essays in Sociology.*
502 pp.
● **Tönnies, Ferdinand.** Community and Association (*Gemeinschaft und Gesellschaft*). *Translated and Supplemented by Charles P. Loomis. Foreword by
Pitirim A. Sorokin. 334 pp.*

SOCIAL STRUCTURE

Andreski, Stanislav. Military Organization and Society. *Foreword by Professor
A. R. Radcliffe-Brown. 226 pp. 1 folder.*
Bozzoli, B. The Political Nature of a Ruling Class. *Capital and Ideology in
South Africa 1890–1939. 396 pp.*
Bauman, Z. Memories of Class. *The Prehistory and After life of Class. 240 pp.*
Broom, L., Lancaster Jones, F., McDonnell, P. and **Williams, T.** The
Inheritance of Inequality. *208 pp.*
Carlton, Eric. Ideology and Social Order. *Foreword by Professor Philip
Abrahams. 326 pp.*
Clegg, S. and **Dunkerley, D.** Organization, Class and Control. *614 pp.*
Coontz, Sydney H. Population Theories and the Economic Interpretation. *202 pp.*
Coser, Lewis. The Functions of Social Conflict. *204 pp.*
Crook, I. and **D.** The First Years of the Yangyi Commune. *304 pp., illustrated.*
Dickie-Clark, H. F. Marginal Situation: *A Sociological Study of a Coloured
Group. 240 pp. 11 tables.*
Fidler, J. The British Business Elite. *Its Attitudes to Class, Status and Power.
332 pp.*
Giner, S. and **Archer, M. S.** (Eds) Contemporary Europe: *Social Structures and
Cultural Patterns. 336 pp.*
● **Glaser, Barney** and **Strauss, Anselm L.** Status Passage: *A Formal Theory.
212 pp.*
Glass, D. V. (Ed.) Social Mobility in Britain. *Contributions by J. Berent,
T. Bottomore, R. C. Chambers, J. Floud, D. V. Glass, J. R. Hall, H. T.
Himmelweit, R. K. Kelsall, F. M. Martin, C. A. Moser, R. Mukherjee and
W. Ziegel. 420 pp.*
Kelsall, R. K. Higher Civil Servants in Britain: *From 1870 to the Present Day.
268 pp. 31 tables.*
● **Lawton, Denis.** Social Class, Language and Education. *192 pp.*
McLeish, John. The Theory of Social Change. *Four Views Considered. 128 pp.*
● **Marsh, David C.** The Changing Social Structure of England and Wales,
1871–1961. *Revised edition. 288 pp.*
Menzies, Ken. Talcott Parsons and the Social Image of Man. *206 pp.*
● **Mouzelis, Nicos.** Organization and Bureaucracy. *An Analysis of Modern
Theories. 240 pp.*
● **Ossowski, Stanislaw.** Class Structure in the Social Consciousness. *210 pp.*
● **Podgórecki, Adam.** Law and Society. *302 pp.*
Ratcliffe, P. Racism and Reaction. *A Profile of Handsworth. 388 pp.*
Renner, Karl. Institutions of Private Law and Their Social Functions. *Edited,
with an Introduction and Notes, by O. Kahn-Freud. Translated by Agnes
Schwarzschild. 316 pp.*
Rex, J. and **Tomlinson, S.** Colonial Immigrants in a British City. *A Class
Analysis. 368 pp.*
Smooha, S. Israel. *Pluralism and Conflict. 472 pp.*
Strasser, H. and **Randall, S. C.** An Introduction to Theories of Social Change.
300 pp.

4

Wesolowski, W. Class, Strata and Power. *Trans. and with Introduction by G. Kolankiewicz. 160 pp.*

Zureik, E. Palestinians in Israel. *A Study in Internal Colonialism. 264 pp.*

SOCIOLOGY AND POLITICS

Acton, T. A. Gypsy Politics and Social Change. *316 pp.*

Burton, F. Politics of Legitimacy. *Struggles in a Belfast Community. 250 pp.*

Crook, I. and D. Revolution in a Chinese Village. *Ten Mile Inn. 216 pp., illustrated.*

de Silva, S. B. D. The Political Economy of Underdevelopment. *640 pp.*

Etzioni-Halevy, E. Political Manipulation and Administrative Power. *A Comparative Study. 228 pp.*

Fielding, N. The National Front. *260 pp.*

● Hechter, Michael. Internal Colonialism. *The Celtic Fringe in British National Development, 1536–1966. 380 pp.*

Levy, N. The Foundations of the South African Cheap Labour System. *367 pp.*

Kornhauser, William. The Politics of Mass Society. *272 pp. 20 tables.*

● Korpi, W. The Working Class in Welfare Capitalism. *Work, Unions and Politics in Sweden. 472 pp.*

Kroes, R. Soldiers and Students. *A Study of Right- and Left-wing Students. 174 pp.*

Martin, Roderick. Sociology of Power. *214 pp.*

Merquior, J. G. Rousseau and Weber. *A Study in the Theory of Legitimacy. 286 pp.*

Myrdal, Gunnar. The Political Element in the Development of Economic Theory. *Translated from the German by Paul Streeten. 282 pp.*

Preston, P. W. Theories of Development. *296 pp.*

Varma, B. N. The Sociology and Politics of Development. *A Theoretical Study. 236 pp.*

Wong, S.-L. Sociology and Socialism in Contemporary China. *160 pp.*

Wootton, Graham. Workers, Unions and the State. *188 pp.*

CRIMINOLOGY

Ancel, Marc. Social Defence: *A Modern Approach to Criminal Problems. Foreword by Leon Radzinowicz. 240 pp.*

Athens, L. Violent Criminal Acts and Actors. *104 pp.*

Cain, Maureen E. Society and the Policeman's Role. *326 pp.*

Cloward, Richard A. and Ohlin, Lloyd E. Delinquency and Opportunity: *A Theory of Delinquent Gangs. 248 pp.*

Downes, David M. The Delinquent Solution. *A Study in Subcultural Theory. 296 pp.*

Friedlander, Kate. The Psycho-Analytical Approach to Juvenile Delinquency: *Theory, Case Studies, Treatment. 320 pp.*

Gleuck, Sheldon and Eleanor. Family Environment and Delinquency. *With the statistical assistance of Rose W. Kneznek. 340 pp.*

Lopez-Rey, Manuel. Crime. *An Analytical Appraisal. 288 pp.*

Mannheim, Hermann. Comparative Criminology: *A Text Book. Two volumes. 442 pp. and 380 pp.*

Morris, Terence. The Criminal Area: *A Study in Social Ecology. Foreword by Hermann Mannheim. 232 pp. 25 tables. 4 maps.*

Rock, Paul. Making People Pay. *338 pp.*

● Taylor, Ian, Walton, Paul and Young, Jock. The New Criminology. *For a Social Theory of Deviance. 325 pp.*

● Taylor, Ian, Walton, Paul and Young, Jock. (Eds) Critical Criminology. *268 pp.*

SOCIAL PSYCHOLOGY

Bagley, Christopher. The Social Psychology of the Epileptic Child. *320 pp.*
Brittan, Arthur. Meanings and Situations. *224 pp.*
Carroll, J. Break-Out from the Crystal Palace. *200 pp.*
● **Fleming, C. M.** Adolescence: Its Social Psychology. *With an Introduction to recent findings from the fields of Anthropology, Physiology, Medicine, Psychometrics and Sociometry. 288 pp.*
● The Social Psychology of Education: *An Introduction and Guide to Its Study. 136 pp.*
Linton, Ralph. The Cultural Background of Personality. *132 pp.*
● **Mayo, Elton.** The Social Problems of an Industrial Civilization. *With an Appendix on the Political Problem. 180 pp.*
Ottaway, A. K. C. Learning Through Group Experience. *176 pp.*
Plummer, Ken. Sexual Stigma. *An Interactionist Account. 254 pp.*
● **Rose, Arnold M.** (Ed.) Human Behaviour and Social Processes: *an Interactionist Approach. Contributions by Arnold M. Rose, Ralph H. Turner, Anselm Strauss, Everett C. Hughes, E. Franklin Frazier, Howard S. Becker et al. 696 pp.*
Smelser, Neil J. Theory of Collective Behaviour. *448 pp.*
Stephenson, Geoffrey M. The Development of Conscience. *128 pp.*
Young, Kimball. Handbook of Social Psychology. *658 pp. 16 figures. 10 tables.*

SOCIOLOGY OF THE FAMILY

Bell, Colin R. Middle Class Families: *Social and Geographical Mobility. 224 pp.*
Burton, Lindy. Vulnerable Children. *272 pp.*
Gavron, Hannah. The Captive Wife: *Conflicts of Household Mothers. 190 pp.*
George, Victor and **Wilding, Paul.** Motherless Families. *248 pp.*
Klein, Josephine. Samples from English Cultures.
   1. Three Preliminary Studies and Aspects of Adult Life in England. *447 pp.*
   2. Child-Rearing Practices and Index. *247 pp.*
Klein, Viola. The Feminine Character. *History of an Ideology. 244 pp.*
McWhinnie, Alexina M. Adopted Children. *How They Grow Up. 304 pp.*
● **Morgan, D. H. J.** Social Theory and the Family. *188 pp.*
● **Myrdal, Alva** and **Klein, Viola.** Women's Two Roles: *Home and Work. 238 pp. 27 tables.*
Parsons, Talcott and **Bales, Robert F.** Family: Socialization and Interaction Process. *In collaboration with James Olds, Morris Zelditch and Philip E. Slater. 456 pp. 50 figures and tables.*

SOCIAL SERVICES

Bastide, Roger. The Sociology of Mental Disorder. *Translated from the French by Jean McNeil. 260 pp.*
Carlebach, Julius. Caring for Children in Trouble. *266 pp.*
George, Victor. Foster Care. *Theory and Practice. 234 pp.*
   Social Security: *Beveridge and After. 258 pp.*
George, V. and **Wilding, P.** Motherless Families. *248 pp.*
● **Goetschius, George W.** Working with Community Groups. *256 pp.*
Goetschius, George W. and **Tash, Joan.** Working with Unattached Youth. *416 pp.*
Heywood, Jean S. Children in Care. *The Development of the Service for the Deprived Child. Third revised edition. 284 pp.*
King, Roy D., Ranes, Norma V. and **Tizard, Jack.** Patterns of Residential Care. *356 pp.*
Leigh, John. Young People and Leisure. *256 pp.*
● **Mays, John.** (Ed.) Penelope Hall's Social Services of England and Wales. *368 pp.*

6

Morris Mary. Voluntary Work and the Welfare State. *300 pp.*
Nokes. P. L. The Professional Task in Welfare Practice. *152 pp.*
Timms, Noel. Psychiatric Social Work in Great Britain (1939–1962). *280 pp.*
● Social Casework: *Principles and Practice. 256 pp.*

SOCIOLOGY OF EDUCATION

Banks, Olive. Parity and Prestige in English Secondary Education: a Study in Educational Sociology. *272 pp.*
● Blyth, W. A. L. English Primary Education. *A Sociological Description.* 2. Background. *168 pp.*
Collier, K. G. The Social Purposes of Education: *Personal and Social Values in Education. 268 pp.*
Evans, K. M. Sociometry and Education. *158 pp.*
● Ford, Julienne. Social Class and the Comprehensive School. *192 pp.*
Foster, P. J. Education and Social Change in Ghana. *336 pp. 3 maps.*
Fraser, W. R. Education and Society in Modern France. *150 pp.*
Grace, Gerald R. Role Conflict and the Teacher. *150 pp.*
Hans, Nicholas. New Trends in Education in the Eighteenth Century. *278 pp. 19 tables.*
● Comparative Education: *A Study of Educational Factors and Traditions. 360 pp.*
● Hargreaves, David. Interpersonal Relations and Education. *432 pp.*
● Social Relations in a Secondary School. *240 pp.*
School Organization and Pupil Involvement. *A Study of Secondary Schools.*
● Mannheim, Karl and Stewart, W. A. C. An Introduction to the Sociology of Education. *206 pp.*
● Musgrove, F. Youth and the Social Order. *176 pp.*
● Ottaway, A. K. C. Education and Society: An Introduction to the Sociology of Education. *With an Introduction by W. O. Lester Smith. 212 pp.*
Peers, Robert. Adult Education: *A Comparative Study. Revised edition. 398 pp.*
Stratta, Erica. The Education of Borstal Boys. *A Study of their Educational Experiences prior to, and during, Borstal Training. 256 pp.*
● Taylor, P. H., Reid, W. A. and Holley, B. J. The English Sixth Form. *A Case Study in Curriculum Research. 198 pp.*

SOCIOLOGY OF CULTURE

● Eppel, E. M. and M. Adolescents and Morality: *A Study of some Moral Values and Dilemmas of Working Adolescents in the Context of a changing Climate of Opinion. Foreword by W. J. H. Sprott. 268 pp. 39 tables.*
● Fromm, Erich. The Fear of Freedom. *286 pp.*
● The Sane Society. *400 pp.*
Johnson, L. The Cultural Critics. *From Matthew Arnold to Raymond Williams. 233 pp.*
Mannheim, Karl. Essays on the Sociology of Culture. *Edited by Ernst Mannheim in co-operation with Paul Kecskemeti. Editorial Note by Adolph Lowe. 280 pp.*
Structures of Thinking. *Edited by David Kettler, Volker Meja and Nico Stehr. 304 pp.*
Merquior, J. G. The Veil and the Mask. *Essays on Culture and Ideology. Foreword by Ernest Gellner. 140 pp.*
Zijderfeld, A. C. On Clichés. *The Supersedure of Meaning by Function in Modernity. 150 pp.*
Reality in a Looking Glass. *Rationality through an Analysis of Traditional Folly. 208 pp.*

SOCIOLOGY OF RELIGION

Argyle, Michael and **Beit-Hallahmi, Benjamin.** The Social Psychology of Religion. *256 pp.*

Glasner, Peter E. The Sociology of Secularisation. *A Critique of a Concept. 146 pp.*

Hall, J. R. The Ways Out. *Utopian Communal Groups in an Age of Babylon. 280 pp.*

Ranson, S., Hinings, B. and **Bryman, A.** Clergy, Ministers and Priests. *216 pp.*

Stark, Werner. The Sociology of Religion. *A Study of Christendom.*
Volume II. *Sectarian Religion. 368 pp.*
Volume III. *The Universal Church. 464 pp.*
Volume IV. *Types of Religious Man. 352 pp.*
Volume V. *Types of Religious Culture. 464 pp.*

Turner, B. S. Weber and Islam. *216 pp.*

Watt, W. Montgomery. Islam and the Integration of Society. 230 pp.

Pomian-Srzednicki, M. Religious Change in Contemporary Poland. *Sociology and Secularization. 280 pp.*

SOCIOLOGY OF ART AND LITERATURE

Jarvie, Ian C. Towards a Sociology of the Cinema. *A Comparative Essay on the Structure and Functioning of a Major Entertainment Industry. 405 pp.*

Rust, Frances S. Dance in Society. *An Analysis of the Relationships between the Social Dance and Society in England from the Middle Ages to the Present Day. 256 pp. 8 pp. of plates.*

Schücking, L. L. The Sociology of Literary Taste. *112 pp.*

Wolff, Janet. Hermeneutic Philosophy and the Sociology of Art. *150 pp.*

SOCIOLOGY OF KNOWLEDGE

Diesing, P. Patterns of Discovery in the Social Sciences. *262 pp.*

● **Douglas, J. D.** (Ed.) Understanding Everyday Life. *270 pp.*

● **Hamilton, P.** Knowledge and Social Structure. *174 pp.*

Jarvie, I. C. Concepts and Society. *232 pp.*

Mannheim, Karl. Essays on the Sociology of Knowledge. *Edited by Paul Kecskemeti. Editorial Note by Adolph Lowe. 353 pp.*

Remmling, Gunter W. The Sociology of Karl Mannheim. *With a Bibliographical Guide to the Sociology of Knowledge, Ideological Analysis, and Social Planning. 255 pp.*

Remmling, Gunter W. (Ed.) Towards the Sociology of Knowledge. *Origin and Development of a Sociological Thought Style. 463 pp.*

Scheler, M. Problems of a Sociology of Knowledge. *Trans. by M. S. Frings. Edited and with an Introduction by K. Stikkers. 232 pp.*

URBAN SOCIOLOGY

Aldridge, M. The British New Towns. *A Programme Without a Policy. 232 pp.*

Ashworth, William. The Genesis of Modern British Town Planning: *A Study in Economic and Social History of the Nineteenth and Twentieth Centuries. 288 pp.*

Brittan, A. The Privatised World. *196 pp.*

Cullingworth, J. B. Housing Needs and Planning Policy: *a Restatement of the Problems of Housing Need and 'Overspill' in England and Wales. 232 pp. 44 tables. 8 maps.*

Dickinson, Robert E. City and Region: *A Geographical Interpretation. 608 pp. 125 figures.*

The West European City: *A Geographical Interpretation. 600 pp. 129 maps. 29 plates.*

Humphreys, Alexander J. New Dubliners: *Urbanization and the Irish Family.*
Foreword by George C. Homans. 304 pp.
Jackson, Brian. Working Class Community: *Some General Notions raised by a*
Series of Studies in Northern England. 192 pp.
● Mann, P. H. An Approach to Urban Sociology. *240 pp.*
Mellor, J. R. Urban Sociology in an Urbanized Society. *326 pp.*
Morris, R. N. and Mogey, J. The Sociology of Housing. *Studies at Berinsfield.*
232 pp. 4 pp. plates.
Mullan, R. Stevenage Ltd. *438 pp.*
Rex, J. and Tomlinson, S. Colonial Immigrants in a British City. *A Class*
Analysis. 368 pp.
Rosser, C. and Harris, C. The Family and Social Change. *A Study of Family*
and Kinship in a South Wales Town. 352 pp. 8 maps.
● Stacey, Margaret, Batsone, Eric, Bell, Colin and Thurcott, Anne. Power,
Persistence and Change. *A Second Study of Banbury. 196 pp.*

RURAL SOCIOLOGY

● Mayer, Adrian C. Peasants in the Pacific. *A Study of Fiji Indian Rural Society.*
248 pp. 20 plates.
Williams, W. M. The Sociology of an English Village: *Gosforth. 272 pp.*
12 figures. 13 tables.

SOCIOLOGY OF INDUSTRY AND DISTRIBUTION

Dunkerley, David. The Foreman. *Aspects of Task and Structure. 192 pp.*
Eldridge, J. E. T. *Industrial Disputes. Essays in the Sociology of Industrial*
Relations. 288 pp.
Hollowell, Peter G. The Lorry Driver. *272 pp.*
● Oxaal, I., Barnett, T. and Booth, D. (Eds) Beyond the Sociology of
Development. *Economy and Society in Latin America and Africa. 295 pp.*
Smelser, Neil J. Social Change in the Industrial Revolution: *An Application of*
Theory to the Lancashire Cotton Industry, 1770–1840. 468 pp. 12 figures.
14 tables.
Watson, T. J. The Personnel Managers. *A Study in the Sociology of Work and*
Employment, 262 pp.

ANTHROPOLOGY

Brandel-Syrier, Mia. Reeftown Elite. *A Study of Social Mobility in a Modern*
African Community on the Reef. 376 pp.
Dickie-Clark, H. F. The Marginal Situation. *A Sociological Study of a Coloured*
Group. 236 pp.
Dube, S. C. Indian Village. *Foreword by Morris Edward Opler. 276 pp.*
4 plates.
India's Changing Villages: *Human Factors in Community Development.*
260 pp. 8 plates. 1 map.
Fei, H.-T. Peasant Life in China. *A Field Study of Country Life in the Yangtze*
Valley. With a foreword by Bronislaw Malinowski. 328 pp. 16 pp. plates.
Firth, Raymond. Malay Fishermen. *Their Peasant Economy. 420 pp. 17 pp.*
plates.
Gulliver, P. H. Social Control in an African Society: a Study of the Arusha,
Agricultural Masai of Northern Tanganykia. *320 pp. 8 plates. 10 figures.*
Family Herds. *288 pp.*
Jarvie, Ian C. The Revolution in Anthropology. *268 pp.*
Little, Kenneth L. Mende of Sierra Leone. *308 pp. and folder.*
Negroes in Britain. *With a New Introduction and Contemporary Study by*
Leonard Bloom. 320 pp.

Tambs-Lyche, H. London Patidars. *168 pp.*

Madan, G. R. Western Sociologists on Indian Society. *Marx, Spencer, Weber, Durkheim, Pareto. 384 pp.*

Mayer, A. C. Peasants in the Pacific. *A Study of Fiji Indian Rural Society. 248 pp.*

Meer, Fatima. Race and Suicide in South Africa. *325 pp.*

Smith, Raymond T. The Negro Family in British Guiana: *Family Structure and Social Status in the Villages. With a Foreword by Meyer Fortes. 314 pp. 8 plates. 1 figure. 4 maps.*

SOCIOLOGY AND PHILOSOPHY

● **Adriaansens, H.** Talcott Parsons and the Conceptual Dilemma. *200 pp.*

Barnsley, John H. The Social Reality of Ethics. *A Comparative Analysis of Moral Codes. 448 pp.*

Diesing, Paul. Patterns of Discovery in the Social Sciences. *362 pp.*

● **Douglas, Jack D.** (Ed.) Understanding Everyday Life. *Toward the Reconstruction of Sociological Knowledge. Contributions by Alan F. Blum, Aaron W. Cicourel, Norman K. Denzin, Jack D. Douglas, John Heeren, Peter McHugh, Peter K. Manning, Melvin Power, Matthew Speier, Roy Turner, D. Lawrence Wieder, Thomas P. Wilson and Don H. Zimmerman. 370 pp.*

Gorman, Robert A. The Dual Vision. *Alfred Schutz and the Myth of Phenomenological Social Science. 240 pp.*

Jarvie, Ian C. Concepts and Society. *216 pp.*

Kilminster, R. Praxis and Method. *A Sociological Dialogue with Lukács, Gramsci and the Early Frankfurt School. 334 pp.*

Outhwaite, W. Concept Formation in Social Science. *255 pp.*

● **Pelz, Werner.** The Scope of Understanding in Sociology. *Towards a More Radical Reorientation in the Social Humanistic Sciences. 283 pp.*

Roche, Maurice, Phenomenology, Language and the Social Sciences. *371 pp.*

Sahay, Arun. Sociological Analysis. *212 pp.*

● **Slater, P.** Origin and Significance of the Frankfurt School. *A Marxist Perspective. 185 pp.*

Spurling, L. Phenomenology and the Social World. *The Philosophy of Merleau-Ponty and its Relation to the Social Sciences. 222 pp.*

Wilson, H. T. The American Ideology. *Science, Technology and Organization as Modes of Rationality. 368 pp.*

International Library of Anthropology
General Editor   Adam Kuper

● **Ahmed, A. S.** Millennium and Charisma Among Pathans. *A Critical Essay in Social Anthropology. 192 pp.*
Pukhtun Economy and Society. *Traditional Structure and Economic Development. 422 pp.*

Barth, F. Selected Essays. *Volume 1. 256 pp.* Selected Essays. *Volume II. 200 pp.*

Brown, Paula. The Chimbu. *A Study of Change in the New Guinea Highlands. 151 pp.*

Duller, H. J. Development Technology. *192 pp.*

Foner, N. Jamaica Farewell. *200 pp.*

Gudeman, Stephen. Relationships, Residence and the Individual. *A Rural Panamanian Community. 288 pp. 11 plates, 5 figures, 2 maps, 10 tables.*
The Demise of a Rural Economy. *From Subsistence to Capitalism in a Latin American Village. 160 pp.*

Hamnett, Ian. Chieftainship and Legitimacy. *An Anthropological Study of Executive Law in Lesotho. 163 pp.*

Hanson, F. Allan. Meaning in Culture. *127 pp.*

Hazan, H. The Limbo People. *A Study of the Constitution of the Time Universe Among the Aged. 208 pp.*

Humphreys, S. C. Anthropology and the Greeks. *288 pp.*

Karp, I. Fields of Change Among the Iteso of Kenya. *140 pp.*

Kuper, A. Wives for Cattle. *Bridewealth in Southern Africa. 224 pp.*

Lloyd, P. C. Power and Independence. *Urban Africans' Perception of Social Inequality. 264 pp.*

Malinowski, B. and **de la Fuente, J.** Malinowski in Mexico. *The Economics of a Mexican Market System. Edited and Introduced by Susan Drucker-Brown. About 240 pp.*

Parry, J. P. Caste and Kinship in Kangra. *352 pp. Illustrated.*

Pettigrew, Joyce. Robber Noblemen. *A Study of the Political System of the Sikh Jats. 284 pp.*

Street, Brian V. The Savage in Literature. *Representations of 'Primitive' Society in English Fiction, 1858–1920. 207 pp.*

Van Den Berghe, Pierre L. Power and Privilege at an African University. *278 pp.*

International Library of Phenomenology and Moral Sciences
General Editor   John O'Neill

Adorno, T. W. Aesthetic Theory. Translated by C. Lenhardt.

Apel, K.-O. Towards a Transformation of Philosophy. *308 pp.*

Bologh, R. W. Dialectical Phenomenology. *Marx's Method. 287 pp.*

Fekete, J. The Critical Twilight. *Explorations in the Ideology of Anglo-American Literary Theory from Eliot to McLuhan. 300 pp.*

Green, B. S. Knowing the Poor. *A Case Study in Textual Reality Construction. 200 pp.*

McHoul, A. W. How Texts Talk. *Essays on Reading and Ethnomethodology. 163 pp.*

Medina, A. Reflection, Time and the Novel. *Towards a Communicative Theory of Literature. 143 pp.*

O'Neill, J. Essaying Montaigne. *A Study of the Renaissance Institution of Writing and Reading. 244 pp.*

Schutz. A. Life Forms and Meaning Structure. *Translated, Introduced and Annotated by Helmut Wagner. 207 pp.*

International Library of Social Policy
General Editor   Kathleen Jones

Bayley, M. Mental Handicap and Community Care. *426 pp.*

Bottoms, A. E. and **McClean, J. D.** Defendants in the Criminal Process. *284 pp.*

Bradshaw, J. The Family Fund. *An Initiative in Social Policy. 248 pp.*

Butler, J. R. Family Doctors and Public Policy. *208 pp.*

Davies, Martin. Prisoners of Society. *Attitudes and Aftercare. 204 pp.*

Gittus, Elizabeth. Flats, Families and the Under-Fives. *285 pp.*

Holman, Robert. Trading in Children. *A Study of Private Fostering. 355 pp.*

Jeffs, A. Young People and the Youth Service. *160 pp.*

Jones, Howard and **Cornes, Paul.** Open Prisons. *288 pp.*

Jones, Kathleen. History of the Mental Health Service. *428 pp.*

Jones, Kathleen with **Brown, John, Cunningham, W. J., Roberts, Julian** and **Williams, Peter.** Opening the Door. *A Study of New Policies for the Mentally Handicapped. 278 pp.*

Karn, Valerie. Retiring to the Seaside. *400 pp. 2 maps. Numerous tables.*

King, R. D. and **Elliot, K. W.** Albany: Birth of a Prison—End of an Era. *294 pp.*

Thomas, J. E. The English Prison Officer since 1850. *258 pp.*

Walton, R. G. Women in Social Work. *303 pp.*

● **Woodward, J.** To Do the Sick No Harm. *A Study of the British Voluntary Hospital System to 1875. 234 pp.*

International Library of Welfare and Philosophy
General Editors   Noel Timms and David Watson

○ **Campbell, J.** The Left and Rights. *A Conceptual Analysis of the Idea of Socialist Rights. About 296 pp.*

● **McDermott, F. E.** (Ed.) Self-Determination in Social Work. *A Collection of Essays on Self-determination and Related Concepts by Philosophers and Social Work Theorists. Contributors: F. P. Biestek, S. Bernstein, A. Keith-Lucas, D. Sayer, H. H. Perelman, C. Whittington, R. F. Stalley, F. E. McDermott, I. Berlin, H. J. McCloskey, H. L. A. Hart, J. Wilson, A. I. Melden, S. I. Benn. 254 pp.*

● **Plant, Raymond.** Community and Ideology. *104 pp.*

● **Plant, Raymond, Lesser, Harry** and **Taylor-Gooby, Peter.** Political Philosophy and Social Welfare. *Essays on the Normative Basis of Welfare Provision. 276 pp.*

Ragg, N. M. People Not Cases. *A Philosophical Approach to Social Work. 168 pp.*

Timms, Noel (Ed.) Social Welfare. *Why and How? 316 pp. 7 figures.*

● **Timms, Noel** and **Watson, David** (Eds) Talking About Welfare. *Readings in Philosophy and Social Policy. Contributors: T. H. Marshall, R. B. Brandt, G. H. von Wright, K. Nielsen, M. Cranston, R. M. Titmuss, R. S. Downie, E. Telfer, D. Donnison, J. Benson, P. Leonard. A. Keith-Lucas, D. Walsh, I. T. Ramsey. 230 pp.*

● Philosophy in Social Work. *250 pp.*

● **Weale, A.** Equality and Social Policy. *164 pp.*

Library of Social Work
General Editor   Noel Timms

● **Baldock, Peter.** Community Work and Social Work. *140 pp.*

○ **Beedell, Christopher.** Residential Life with Children. *210 pp. Crown 8vo.*

● **Berry, Juliet.** Daily Experience in Residential Life. *A Study of Children and their Care-givers. 202 pp.*

○ Social Work with Children. *190 pp. Crown 8vo.*

● **Brearley, C. Paul.** Residential Work with the Elderly. *116 pp.*

● Social Work, Ageing and Society. *126 pp.*

● **Cheetham, Juliet.** Social Work with Immigrants. *240 pp. Crown 8vo.*

● **Cross, Crispin P.** (Ed.) Interviewing and Communication in Social Work. *Contributions by C. P. Cross, D. Laurenson, B. Strutt, S. Raven. 192 pp. Crown 8vo.*

● **Curnock, Kathleen** and **Hardiker, Pauline.** Towards Practice Theory. *Skills and Methods in Social Assessments. 208 pp.*

● **Davies, Bernard.** The Use of Groups in Social Work Practice. *158 pp.*

Davies, Bleddyn and **Knapp, M.** Old People's Homes and the Production of Welfare. *264 pp.*

● **Davies, Martin.** Support Systems in Social Work. *144 pp.*

○ **Ellis, June.** (Ed.) West African Families in Britain. *A Meeting of Two Cultures. Contributions by Pat Stapleton, Vivien Biggs. 150 pp. 1 map.*

○ **Ford, J.** Human Behaviour. *Towards a Practical Understanding. About 160 pp.*

● **Hart, John.** Social Work and Sexual Conduct. *230 pp.*

Heraud, Brian. Training for Uncertainty. *A Sociological Approach to Social Work Education. 138 pp.*

Holder, D. and **Wardle, M.** Teamwork and the Development of a Unitary Approach. *212 pp.*

● **Hutten, Joan M.** Short-Term Contracts in Social Work. *Contributions by Stella M. Hall, Elsie Osborne, Mannie Sher, Eva Sternberg, Elizabeth Tuters. 134 pp.*

Jackson, Michael P. and **Valencia, B. Michael.** Financial Aid Through Social Work. *140 pp.*

● **Jones, Howard.** The Residential Community. *A Setting for Social Work. 150 pp.*

● (Ed.) Towards a New Social Work. *Contributions by Howard Jones, D. A. Fowler, J. R. Cypher, R. G. Walton, Geoffrey Mungham, Philip Priestley, Ian Shaw, M. Bartley, R. Deacon, Irwin Epstein, Geoffrey Pearson. 184 pp.*

Jones, Ray and **Pritchard, Colin.** (Eds) Social Work With Adolescents. *Contributions by Ray Jones, Colin Pritchard, Jack Dunham, Florence Rossetti, Andrew Kerslake, John Burns, William Gregory, Graham Templeman, Kenneth E. Reid, Audrey Taylor.*

○ **Jordon, William.** The Social Worker in Family Situations. *160 pp. Crown 8vo.*

● **Laycock, A. L.** Adolescents and Social Work. *128 pp. Crown 8vo.*

● **Lees, Ray.** Politics and Social Work. *128 pp. Crown 8vo.*

● Research Strategies for Social Welfare. *112 pp. Tables.*

○ **McCullough, M. K.** and **Ely, Peter J.** Social Work with Groups. *127 pp. Crown 8vo.*

● **Moffett, Jonathan.** Concepts in Casework Treatment. *128 pp. Crown 8vo.*

Parsloe, Phyllida. Juvenile Justice in Britain and the United States. *The Balance of Needs and Rights. 336 pp.*

● **Plant, Raymond.** Social and Moral Theory in Casework. *112 pp. Crown 8vo.*

Priestley, Philip, Fears, Denise and **Fuller, Roger.** Justice for Juveniles. *The 1969 Children and Young Persons Act: A Case for Reform? 128 pp.*

● **Pritchard, Colin** and **Taylor, Richard.** Social Work: Reform or Revolution? *170 pp.*

○ **Pugh, Elisabeth.** Social Work in Child Care. *128 pp. Crown 8vo.*

● **Robinson, Margaret.** Schools and Social Work. *282 pp.*

○ **Ruddock, Ralph.** Roles and Relationships. *128 pp. Crown 8vo.*

● **Sainsbury, Eric.** Social Diagnosis in Casework. *118 pp. Crown 8vo.*

● **Sainsbury, Eric, Phillips, David** and **Nixon, Stephen.** Social Work in Focus. *Clients' and Social Workers' Perceptions in Long-Term Social Work. 220 pp.*

● Social Work with Families. *Perceptions of Social Casework among Clients of a Family Service. 188pp.*

Seed, Philip. The Expansion of Social Work in Britain. *128 pp. Crown 8vo.*

● **Shaw, John.** The Self in Social Work. *124 pp.*

Smale, Gerald G. Prophecy, Behaviour and Change. *An Examination of Self-fulfilling Prophecies in Helping Relationships. 116 pp. Crown 8vo.*

Smith, Gilbert. Social Need. *Policy, Practice and Research. 155 pp.*

● Social Work and the Sociology of Organisations. *124 pp. Revised edition.*

● **Sutton, Carole.** Psychology for Social Workers and Counsellors. *An Introduction. 248 pp.*

● **Timms, Noel.** Language of Social Casework. *122 pp. Crown 8vo.*

● Recording in Social Work. *124 pp. Crown 8vo.*
● **Todd, F. Joan.** Social Work with the Mentally Subnormal. *96 pp. Crown 8vo.*
● **Walrond-Skinner, Sue.** Family Therapy. *The Treatment of Natural Systems. 172 pp.*
● **Warham, Joyce.** An Introduction to Administration for Social Workers. *Revised edition. 112 pp.*
● An Open Case. *The Organisational Context of Social Work. 172 pp.*
○ **Wittenberg, Isca Salzberger.** Psycho-Analytic Insight and Relationships. *A Kleinian Approach. 196 pp. Crown 8vo.*

Primary Socialization, Language and Education
General Editor   Basil Bernstein

Adlam, Diana S., *with the assistance of Geoffrey Turner and Lesley Lineker.* Code in Context. *272 pp.*
Bernstein, Basil. Class, Codes and Control. *3 volumes.*
●   1. *Theoretical Studies Towards a Sociology of Language. 254 pp.*
   2. *Applied Studies Towards a Sociology of Language. 377 pp.*
●   3. *Towards a Theory of Educational Transmission. 167 pp.*
Brandis, Walter and **Henderson, Dorothy.** Social Class, Language and Communication. *288 pp.*
Cook-Gumperz, Jenny. Social Control and Socialization. *A Study of Class Differences in the Language of Maternal Control. 290 pp.*
● **Gahagan, D. M.** and **G. A.** Talk Reform. *Exploration in Language for Infant School Children. 160 pp.*
Hawkins, P. R. Social Class, the Nominal Group and Verbal Strategies. *About 220 pp.*
Robinson, W. P. and **Rakstraw, Susan D. A.** A Question of Answers. *2 volumes. 192 pp. and 180 pp.*
Turner, Geoffrey J. and **Mohan, Bernard A.** A Linguistic Description and Computer Programme for Children's Speech. *208 pp.*

Reports of the Institute of Community Studies

Baker, J. The Neighbourhood Advice Centre. A Community Project in Camden. *320 pp.*
● **Cartwright, Ann.** Patients and their Doctors. *A Study of General Practice. 304 pp.*
Dench, Geoff. Maltese in London. *A Case-study in the Erosion of Ethnic Consciousness. 302 pp.*
Jackson, Brian and **Marsden, Dennis.** Education and the Working Class: *Some General Themes Raised by a Study of 88 Working-class Children in a Northern Industrial City. 268 pp. 2 folders.*
Madge, C. and **Willmott, P.** Inner City Poverty in Paris and London. *144 pp.*
Marris, Peter. The Experience of Higher Education. *232 pp. 27 tables.*
● Loss and Change. *192 pp.*
Marris, Peter and **Rein, Martin.** Dilemmas of Social Reform. *Poverty and Community Action in the United States. 256 pp.*
Marris, Peter and **Somerset, Anthony.** African Businessmen. *A Study of Entrepreneurship and Development in Kenya. 256 pp.*
Mills, Richard. Young Outsiders: *a Study in Alternative Communities. 216 pp.*
Runciman, W. G. Relative Deprivation and Social Justice. *A Study of Attitudes to Social Inequality in Twentieth-Century England. 352 pp.*

Willmott, Peter. Adolescent Boys in East London. *230 pp.*

Willmott, Peter and **Young, Michael.** Family and Class in a London Suburb.
202 pp. 47 tables.

Young, Michael and **McGeeney, Patrick.** Learning Begins at Home. *A Study of
a Junior School and its Parents. 128 pp.*

Young, Michael and **Willmott, Peter.** Family and Kinship in East London.
Foreword by Richard M. Titmuss. 252 pp. 39 tables.
The Symmetrical Family. *410 pp.*

Reports of the Institute for Social Studies in Medical Care

Cartwright, Ann, Hockey, Lisbeth and **Anderson, John J.** Life Before Death.
310 pp.

Dunnell, Karen and **Cartwright, Ann.** Medicine Takers, Prescribers and
Hoarders. *190 pp.*

Farrell, C. My Mother Said. . . *A Study of the Way Young People Learned
About Sex and Birth Control. 288 pp.*

Medicine, Illness and Society
General Editor W. M. Williams

Hall, David J. Social Relations & Innovation. *Changing the State of Play in
Hospitals. 232 pp.*

Hall, David J. and **Stacey M.** (Eds) Beyond Separation. *234 pp.*

Robinson, David. The Process of Becoming Ill. *142 pp.*

Stacey, Margaret *et al.* Hospitals, Children and Their Families. *The Report of a
Pilot Study. 202 pp.*

Stimson, G. V. and **Webb, B.** Going to See the Doctor. *The Consultation
Process in General Practice. 155 pp.*

Monographs in Social Theory
General Editor Arthur Brittan

● **Barnes, B.** Scientific Knowledge and Sociological Theory. *192 pp.*
Bauman, Zygmunt. Culture as Praxis. *204 pp.*

● **Dixon, Keith.** Sociological Theory. *Pretence and Possibility. 142 pp.*
The Sociology of Belief. *Fallacy and Foundation. 144 pp.*

Goff, T. W. Marx and Mead. *Contributions to a Sociology of Knowledge.
176 pp.*

Meltzer, B. N., Petras, J. W. and **Reynolds, L. T.** Symbolic Interactionism.
Genesis, Varieties and Criticisms. 144 pp.

● **Smith, Anthony D.** The Concept of Social Change. *A Critique of the
Functionalist Theory of Social Change. 208 pp.*

● **Tudor, Andrew.** Beyond Empiricism. *Philosophy of Science in Sociology.
224 pp.*

Routledge Social Science Journals

The British Journal of Sociology. *Editor – Angus Stewart; Associate Editor –
Leslie Sklair. Vol. 1, No. 1 – March 1950 and Quarterly. Roy. 8vo. All
back issues available. An international journal publishing original papers in
the field of sociology and related areas.*

Community Work. *Edited by David Jones and Majorie Mayo. 1973. Published annually.*

Economy and Society. *Vol. 1, No. 1. February 1972 and Quarterly. Metric Roy. 8vo. A journal for all social scientists covering sociology, philosophy, anthropology, economics and history. All back numbers available.*

Ethnic and Racial Studies. *Editor – John Stone. Vol. 1 – 1978. Published quarterly.*

Religion. Journal of Religion and Religions. *Chairman of Editorial Board, Ninian Smart. Vol. 1, No. 1, Spring 1971. A journal with an interdisciplinary approach to the study of the phenomena of religion. All back numbers available.*

Sociological Review. *Chairman of Editorial Board, S. J. Eggleston. New Series. August 1982, Vol. 30, No. 1. Published quarterly.*

Sociology of Health and Illness. *A Journal of Medical Sociology. Editor – Alan Davies; Associate Editor – Ray Jobling. Vol. 1, Spring 1979. Published 3 times per annum.*

Year Book of Social Policy in Britain. *Edited by Kathleen Jones. 1971. Published annually.*

Social and Psychological Aspects of Medical Practice
Editor Trevor Silverstone

Lader, Malcolm. Psychophysiology of Mental Illness. *280 pp.*

● **Silverstone, Trevor** and **Turner, Paul.** Drug Treatment in Psychiatry. *Third edition. 256 pp.*

Whiteley, J. S. and **Gordon, J.** Group Approaches in Psychiatry. *240 pp.*